DIVINE ENERGY

DIVINE ENERGY:

OR THE
EFFICACIOUS OPERATIONS
OF THE
SPIRIT OF GOD UPON THE SOUL OF MAN,
IN HIS
EFFECTUAL CALLING AND CONVERSION,
STATED, PROVED, AND VINDICATED.

Wherein the real Weakness and Insufficiency of Moral Suasion, without the Superaddition of the exceeding Greatness of God's Power, for Faith and Conversion to God, are fully evinced.

BEING

AN ANTIDOTE AGAINST THE PELAGIAN ERROR.

By *JOHN SKEPP,*
LATE MINISTER OF THE GOSPEL.

With a Recommendatory Preface
BY THE LATE JOHN GILL, D.D.

The Third Edition.
REVISED BY JAMES UPTON.

For I am not ashamed of the gospel of Christ; for it is the power of God unto salvation, to every one that believeth.   Rom. i. 16.

"That these things are now despised and laughed to scorn, is no part of the happiness of the present times; as the event will manifest."   *Dr. Owen on the Spirit.*

LONDON:
Printed for, and sold by the Editor
1815.

he Baptist Standard Bearer, Inc.
NUMBER ONE IRON OAKS DRIVE • PARIS, ARKANSAS 72855

Thou hast given a *standard* to them that fear thee;
that it may be displayed because of the truth.
– *Psalm 60:4*

Reprinted 2006

by

THE BAPTIST STANDARD BEARER, INC.
No. 1 Iron Oaks Drive
Paris, Arkansas 72855
(479) 963-3831

THE WALDENSIAN EMBLEM
lux lucet in tenebris
"The Light Shineth in the Darkness"

ISBN# 1579788068

PREFACE.

The Editor of the present Edition of Skepp's Divine Energy, thinks that it is quite unnecessary to trouble the Reader with a long Preface.

Were any reasons necessary to countenance his own decided opinion of the excellence of the Work, and for his publishing a new Edition, the earnest solicitations of his brethren, deacons of the church, which he has the happiness to serve, might justly be assigned as a sufficient motive; while the kindness and respect with which they are expressed in a letter, from which he begs leave to introduce the following extracts, call for his affectionate acknowledgements.

"Dear Sir,

"To the honor of the British Nation, persons who confederate to devise systems of Christian exertion, having for their object the benefit of mankind, rather than the mere advancement of a denomination, need only exhibit the possibility of success to ensure prompt and sufficient support. This strong and peculiar benevolence, which now characterizes our favoured country, and presents her a worthy example to surrounding kingdoms, is that, Sir, to which your life is devoted; so much so, that whoever points out a way of conferring new benefits on the Church of God, may be confident of your assistance and thanks. We, your brethren, enjoy this confidence, and expect a manifestation of your approbation by compliance with a request having for its object the diffusion of evangelical principles.

" Far be it from us to depreciate the productions of modern Christian writers: without intending the slightest reflection on their talents, we think some pieces written by their predecessors might be reprinted with the hope of advantage. Such is the treatise written by Mr. SKEPP, on *Divine Energy.* This work we now respectfully solicit you to republish. The importance of the subject we might urge in support of our application; for if the word " important" can ever be used with propriety and energy, it may be so employed here. Take the work of the Spirit from the gospel system, and every other part becomes weak and useless. The mere letter of scripture, aided by the Christian ministry, though the apostles were the preachers, can effect no more than a barren change of opinion, or the suppression of a few open vices, leaving the heart and character under the dominion of sin. Further, we think the worthy author happy in the management of his subject. In common with all sober-minded persons, Mr. Skepp felt his subject to be surrounded with difficulties, owing, in part, to its sublime and unfathomable nature. In the general we consider him judicious in his terms, distinctions, and arrangements of thought. On the whole we think this small work the best of the kind we have yet read, and worthy of being better known.

"Arguments for the republication of this work on you, Sir, would be thrown away; you are thoroughly convinced of its intrinsic worth, beyond our ability to represent; we therefore only add, that, in our opinion, no subject could be more seasonable. Whence those mighty efforts to subjugate the world to the Son of God? We ascribe them to the energy of the Holy Spirit. And we are ready to conclude that the man who is most under the Spirit's supernatural and sanctifying influence, will be the readiest to learn his obligations, and the most prompt in confessing them to the glory of God.

"Not only is Mr. Skepp's treatise adapted to strip us of glorying in the flesh, when contemplating our exertions, but to hold us absolutely dependant on the gracious influences of the Spirit for their success. That Paul planted, Apollos watered, but God gave the increase, are confessions which the inspired apostles were continually making, and that with the design that the faith and hope of their hearers might be in God; and no truly gracious soul will be hindered from working out his own salvation, when told that it is God who worketh in him, to will and to do of his good pleasure. Paul knew that the tendency of the principle was to promote zeal and diligence, and with this belief we shall be pleased to hear that our respectful request has not been made in vain.

" We have the happiness to be, Dear Sir,
" Your affectionate brethren in Christ,

WM. SPENCER.   CHARLES BROAD.
JAMES BUTTERS.   RUSSELL PONTIFEX.
THOMAS KING.   GEORGE FARR."

London, June, 1815.

The work of the Holy Spirit, is certainly essential to the existence of vital Christianity. It is He who quickens, enlightens, sanctifies, comforts and seals the children of God unto the day of redemption; and he is to them the earnest of their eternal inheritance. It is also under his sacred influence that sinners are " turned from darkness to light, and from the power of Satan unto God," through the preaching of the everlasting gospel. The holy scriptures abound with precious promises, and delightful declarations with reference to his Divine operations: " I will pour water upon him that is thirsty, and floods upon the dry ground: I will pour my Spirit upon thy seed, and my blessing upon thy offspring.—Thy people shall be willing in the day of thy power.—I will pour upon the house of David, and upon the inhabitants of Jerusalem, the Spirit of grace and of supplications, and they shall look on me whom they have pierced.—When he, the Spirit of truth, is come, *he* will guide you into all truth; for *he* shall not speak of *himself*; but whatsoever *he* shall hear that shall *he* speak; and *he* will shew you things to come. HE shall glorify me, for *he* shall receive of mine, and shall shew it unto you." These and similar promises have greatly encouraged the heart of the Editor in preaching the gospel of Christ, and in endeavouring to enlarge his spiritual kingdom; and he earnestly recommends it to all his brethren, to endeavour to accompany all their affectionate and faithful addresses to the consciences of their hearers with a spirit of devotion, agreeably to that admirable specimen delivered by Paul to King Agrippa, "I would to God, that not only thou, but also all that hear me this day, were both almost, and altogether such as I am, except these bonds!" May the Holy Spirit succeed with his divine blessing all the labours of the ministers of Jesus Christ, of every denomination, until the whole earth be filled with his glory! Amen and amen.

THE EDITOR.

September 9, 1815.

TO THE

Church of Christ, over whom, by Divine Providence and Designation, the Dedicator, *though unworthy, is placed as Overseer, greeting.*

Dearly Beloved,

My present care, and, who I hope will be, my future crown in the day of the Lord Jesus. I persuade myself, that that which was so acceptable, being made useful for comfort and stability to your souls from the pulpit, will not be unwelcome to you from the press.

That which first led my thoughts to study and treat of this subject, were the hearing and reading of so much slight and contempt, thrown upon the doctrine and preaching of the Spirit's work and office in the church, and with the gospel-ministry, as the great efficient of all our spiritual abilities, as to principles and performances; as though there were no need now of the Holy Spirit to accompany the word, when read or preached; in order to make it powerful and successful, for illumination, conviction, and conversion, as well as carrying on the work of faith with power.

A sad day indeed it is! when men, to make themselves popular, take upon them to hector, and run down the Spirit's work in regeneration and conversion: as if all experimental religion, and divine efficiency, were not only to be denied, and the vindicators thereof, though dead, railed on; but must just now, by a set of pretended rationalists, be hissed out of the churches and Christian world. A set of men, who, some of them, make as bold with the bible, as to the gospel part thereof, as one of the senate-houses sometimes do with a bill sent them from the other, i. e. spy faults and make amendments, only to clog the same, and render it obscure and intricate, that so it may sink it at last.

And, indeed, when men bring in another gospel, they had need have another sort of bible, or strangely metamorphose and curtail this, that is now in our hands. Now, the consideration of these things, and not knowing where, through the Divine permission, they might end; and remembering that the church of God is styled the basis and pillar of truth, and on which it stands engraved, as in capitals, to be known and read of all men; I thought it my duty, yea, my honour to hold forth this doctrine ministerially amongst you. Not so much for your information as for your encouragement, consolation and stablity; and for the public advantage of others. I say, not so much for your information; for the nature and power of the Divine Energy you have already known and believed, having known and received the grace of God in truth. Nor have I, through grace, as yet found you wavering or unsettled, nor that you needed to have the foundation laid again, as though the first was faulty, or you gone off from it. I both hope and pray, that none will ever be permitted, by God, or you, nor your survivors, so much as to attempt to lay among you any other foundation than that which is already laid, which is Jesus Christ: nor to be left to build wood, hay, and stubble, upon such a bottom.

Your foundation, as to gospel-order, was skilfully and successfully laid, in the very beginning of the troublesome time, by the indefatigable pains and care of that eminent servant and sufferer for Christ, Mr. Hanserd Knollis: and your walls were not only reared but beautified, by the labours and success of that evangelic son of consolation, Mr. Robert Steed. These two were the chief master-builders, by whose blessed ministry you were built, and continued, upon the foundation of the prophets and apostles, Jesus Christ himself being the chief corner-stone.

And now, seeing Christ and you have done me the honour to call and fix me in the pastoral charge, I look upon it my duty to take heed what I build; that it is agreeable to, though full short, through my weakness and insufficiency of what you once sat under.

Now, that I may be kept faithful, serviceable, and acceptable in my ministry, and successful in my labours amongst you, in Christ's gospel, is what I most earnestly desire; and hope I shall always labour after: and that I may attain the same and an everlasting crown of glory with you, and your aforesaid pastors, with Christ above, brethren and sisters, strive with me in your prayers for me at the throne of grace.

"Now to him that is able to keep you and I from falling, and to present us faultless before the presence of his glory, with exceeding great joy; to the only wise God our Saviour, be glory and majesty, dominion and power, both now and ever. *Amen.*"

Thus concludes, dear souls,
 Your unworthy pastor,
  Loving brother, and
   Humble servant,
    JOHN SKEPP.

The first Edition of this work appears to have been published in the year 1722; the second in 1751, by the late venerable Doctor GILL, *with the following*

RECOMMENDATORY PREFACE.

THE worthy author of the ensuing treatise being personally and intimately known by me, and his memory precious to me, as it is to many Christians now living, have induced me, upon this edition of it, to write a short preface in its recommendation; though it is sufficient to speak for itself, and needs no letters of commendation to those who knew the writer of it, or have read the work.

Mr. JOHN SKEPP was a man of singular talents and abilities; of very quick, strong, natural parts; of great diligence and industry in acquiring useful knowledge; a warm and lively preacher of the gospel; a zealous defender of the special and peculiar doctrines of it; whose ministry was blessed to many souls, for the conversion of some, and for the edification of others.

The subject-matter of this treatise, which is the only one he ever published, is of the greatest moment and importance, viz. the Conversion of Man;

without which he must be miserable, and which he cannot effect of himself, and must be done only by the invincible power and efficacious grace of God; as is clearly held forth in the Scriptures, and fully proved in the following discourses. Nothing is more common than to mistake in this great affair, and nothing more fatal; the *mistakes* about conversion and faith are plainly pointed out herein, and the true nature of them in their principles and actings declared; by which it may be known by men whether they are partakers of them or no. The insufficiency of *moral suasion* to produce these things is most clearly proved; the nature, use, reach, and compass of it are truly stated; and by undeniable arguments and instances it is shewn that there are such lets and hinderances in the way of a sinner's conversion to God and faith in Christ, as that it is impossible and impracticable for moral suasion ever to remove them; and which only can be done by the power and efficacy of Divine Grace. And though this work is effected by Divine Omnipotence, yet without forcing the will, and destroying its natural liberty; but instead of that, restoring its moral freedom, and making it truly free by the grace of God; where this worthy author rightly distinguishes between the *natural* and *moral* liberty of the will; and gives such an account of the human soul and spirit, and of their several faculties, and the various operations of them, as is very entertaining and instructive; as well as shews by what means sin seized and overspread them, and in what manner efficacious grace gains upon them, particularly the will, and proves victorious, without infringing its liberty. And whereas this work of conversion and faith is the work of the Spirit of God, as the active efficient cause of it, and not the creature; it is most clearly demonstrated that Man is passive in the reception of the Spirit as a spirit of conviction and saving grace, in regeneration, as effected by him, in a soul's vital union to Christ, and in the first beginnings of spiritual motions of grace, and even in some parts of the Spirit's work after effectual calling and conversion; as also the necessity of almighty power and invincible and efficacious grace being exerted in the conversion of a sinner is abundantly proved from scripture-metaphors and scripture-instances; and the whole is closed with an account of the peculiar work of the Spirit of God under the New Testament, and who has therefore peculiar epithets given unto him.

I have nothing more to add, only that I have divided these discourses into chapters, to facilitate the reading of them; and have summed up the contents of each chapter, which may help the understanding, and refresh the memory. And now I heartily recommend this work to the perusal of every serious Christian that is desirous of knowing the nature of true conversion, and of answering to himself that important question, *Am I born again?* or, *Am I a converted person?* And I doubt not, with the blessing of God, but he will find the reading of it pleasant and profitable to him.

JOHN GILL."

CONTENTS.

CHAP. I.
The Connection of the Words with the preceding; the Explication of them; the Doctrine from them, and Method of treating it. page 1.

CHAP. II.
Shewing the Mistakes about true Conversion and saving Faith; and wherein they both consist. p. 14.

CHAP. III
Shewing the Insufficiency of Moral Suasion to effect true Conversion to God, and Faith in Christ. p. 56.

CHAP. IV.
Proving that the Will of Man in true Conversion, and Faith, is not forced, nor its natural Liberty in the least infringed, but is by the Grace of God made truly free. p. 158.

CHAP. V.
Shewing the Passiveness of Men in several Parts of the Spirit's Work upon their Hearts, both in and after Conversion. p. 206

CHAP. VI.
Shewing the absolute Necessity of the exertion of Almighty Power, and invincible and efficacious Grace in the Conversion of a Sinner. p. 256.

CHAP. VII.
Shewing the peculiar Work of the Spirit, and the peculiar Epithets he bears with respect to Conversion under the New Testament, with the Use and Application of the whole. p. 278.

DIVINE ENERGY.

AND WHAT IS THE EXCEEDING GREATNESS OF HIS POWER TO US-WARD WHO BELIEVE.
Ephesians i. 19.

CHAP. I.

The Connection of the Words with the preceding; the Explication of them; the Doctrine from them, and Method of treating of it.

These words in their coherence are a part of the apostle's prayer and repeated request at the throne of grace, on the behalf of these believing Ephesians; as you will easily perceive by casting your eye upon the three preceding verses. In the first of which he tells them, that he not only gave thanks daily to the Father on their behalf, for what he had already graciously bestowed upon, and wrought in them; but being truly desirous of their spiritual growth and proficiency in grace, knowledge, expedience, and solid judgment, he was their constant remembrancer at the throne of grace; imploring for them the further aids and assistances of the Holy Spirit, as "the spirit of wisdom and revelation." By which he doth not mean the extraordinary gifts of the holy and blessed Spirit, but a receiving of him as the "spirit of truth," John xvi. 13; and as the "unction from the Holy One," 1 John ii. 20, whose peculiar office it is to guide believers into the mystery of gospel-truth, both doctrinal and practical, so far as is necessary and conducive to their stability and consolation in faith and holiness. And now, this wisdom and knowledge of Him, *i. e.* the Father, not exclusive of Christ, as revealed and communicated by the Holy Spirit himself, under gospel means, is not to be understood of the first gospel-knowledge necessary to conversion, and true saving faith, for this they had already received, it being part of that for which he gave thanks; but is intended of a further degree of experimental knowledge and acquaintance with God and Christ. It is to know more and more of this God and our Saviour, by way of daily communion and fellowship, so as to enjoy more of the fruits and effects of eternal love and grace in their excellency, and efficiency upon the heart. It is to know those truths more certainly, clearly, distinctly, and exactly, than they had yet attained. And furthermore, it is a knowing to such a degree and capacity, as to be able to acknowledge the mystery, and be ready to " render a reason," 1.Pet. iii. 15, of their gospel-faith and hope, and so to explain and vindicate the blessed doctrines of grace and mysteries of Christianity, as that themselves and others might be profited thereby. And this is further manifest in the 18th verse, where he suggests the benefit of receiving the Spirit under the character of the Spirit of Wisdom and Revelation; and that was, that the eyes of their understandings or minds being thereby enlightened, they might discern more clearly, and understand more distinctly, the things belonging to so great salvation. Eyes indeed they had, and the seeing eye too, but as yet they were in some measure weak and dark, and needed the further application of the true " eye-salve," Rev. iii. 18, to clear and strengthen them. It is to be noted, that the apostle, here and in other places, attributes eyes to the understanding, as if that noble faculty, which is the mental eye itself, had eyes placed in it, as distinct from it; but this, as I take it, is but a Hebraism common to the New Testament : and so the eyes of the mind are no more, but the mind or soul of man, as endowed with the powers of understanding and reason; and thus the mind or soul hath eyes; but more especially the regenerate; for together with the intellect or reason, such have the eye of faith, which is superior to reason as to its present use and importance, both as it discerns spiritual things, and also as its office is to help, guide, and regulate reason, by subjecting it to revelation. And therefore I will venture to say, the spiritual and enlightened Christian hath *two eyes*, whereas all the world besides hath but *one*, and that not clear. And now to have both these eyes, i. e. faith and reason, more enlightened and cleared by the further work of the Holy Spirit through the word upon their minds, is what the apostle chiefly aims at, in this his prayer, for a greater measure of the Spirit, as the spirit of wisdom and revelation to be given to them; that being thus privileged and capacitated, they might experimentally discern and judge of these spiritual mysteries; as,

First, " What is the hope of his calling;" and, secondly, " what are the riches of the glory of his inheritance in the saints;" and, thirdly, as in the words of my text, " what is the exceeding greatness of his power to us-ward who believe." Now as to the first, by *hope* here, is not meant hope as a grace, or gracious act; nor Christ as hope's object; nor, as I take it, the things otherwise hoped for; but hope's ground, i. e. the free promise of grace and eternal life, as revealed and published in the Gospel, both to Jew and Gentile; who, as he says, " are called in the hope of their calling;" Ephes. iv. 4. that is, they are both called and saved upon the same common bottom of covenant-love and free grace, as given to the elect part " in Christ, before the world began," 2 Tim. i. 9 : But for as much as the Gentiles knew nothing of this " mystery, kept secret from the beginning of the world," until it was " now made manifest, and preached for the obedience of faith, Rom. xvi. 25, 26; and Ephes. iii. 6—9; therefore they, till then, were said to have been without Christ, as " being aliens from the commonwealth of Israel, and strangers from the covenants of promise, having no *hope*, and without *God* in the world," Ephes. ii. 12. But if any will have it that by hope, here, are intended the things hoped for, and which they were to enjoy in this and the other world, I will not contend, but proceed.

The second thing then that he here prayed for, as the benefit of receiving the Spirit, as above said, to illuminate their minds, is, that they might also know, " what are the riches of the glory of his inheritance in the saints." The main difficulty of which text is, whether this inheritance is intended of persons or things; that is, whether it is the saints themselves that are here called "his inheritance," as being " the Lord's portion," Deut. xxxii. 9, and the Mediator's heritage; or whether their present Christian privileges; or rather, as most, I think, interpret it to be, that " inheritance" in heaven to which in the eleventh verse they are said to be predestinated; and to which inheritance, as reserved for them in heaven, they are kept by the power of God through faith unto salvation. But if, with some of good note, we understand the " inheritance" here, to be meant of the saints themselves; then the riches of the glory of this inheritance are to be interpreted of those vast and immense treasures of grace, life, wisdom, knowledge, and all sorts of spiritual gifts and gracious largesses, as Dr. Owen calls them, bestowed upon the elect here, together with the ineffable donations, and everlasting confluences of glory, with God and Christ above, which the apostle styles, " the unsearchable riches of Christ," Ephes. iii. 8; which here enrich, and shall hereafter fill, satiate, and surround the saints for ever. But if, on the other hand, we take the inheritance here, as intended of that part of the saints' portion which is to be for ever enjoyed above, as I am rather inclined, then the riches of the glory of God's inheritance as settled upon the saints in a Mediator, by a covenant transaction betwixt God and Christ, in a promise of life, and that " before the world began," Tit. i. 1, consist of that ineffable variety, and fulness of all spiritual good, bliss, and joy, which shall be shared out among the saints, and enjoyed by those glorified ones

DIVINE ENERGY. 7

to all eternity: and so it is justly styled riches; for as riches are a plenty, as well as variety of the good things of this life, laid up for many years' spending, so riches of glory here, are glory itself, in all communicable *good,* as suited to a glorified state; and that in all its vastness and variety for ever to be enjoyed.

And now to know in this life, what these riches of glory are, must be by the help and teaching of the Spirit himself; for none but the Spirit of God, who hath eternally known his mind, is able to search out, and teach the same to the saints by way of revelation: by which the spiritual, and they only, are able to discern so as to make a true judgment of the nature, excellency, and immenseness of these divine riches; which by reason of their vastness and abundance, as to communication and enjoyment, the apostle elsewhere, putting them all together, most excellently calls " an exceeding and eternal weight* of glory," 2 Cor. iv. 17. And this judgment of theirs is to be made by their receiving as

---

* Βάρ☉ δόξης. A weight or load of glory; this Hebraism is accompanied with the figure Paronomasia, in which is an allusion to the root in Hebrew, from whence כבוד cabhodh, glory, is derived, i. e. כבד Cabhadh, he was heavy or weighty; as if he had said, the saints who are now loaded down with sorrow, misery, and suffering for Christ, shall by him ere long receive a much heavier and eternal weight of glory, in the crown that he will give unto, and put upon them.

by the Lord the Spirit, some considerable foretaste, as the first-fruits and earnest of the whole.

The third thing by him prayed for, as only attainable by their first receiving the Holy Spirit as the spirit of wisdom and knowledge is, that thereby they might experimentally know, judiciously discern, and make a right judgment of that greatness of power and divine energy which is exerted and continued upon them, in their calling, conversion, faith, and perseverance: and thus in connection the words must be understood; I cease not to pray continually, that you might receive the Holy Spirit, as the spirit of wisdom and revelation, to that degree, that the eyes of your minds being more clearly enlightened, ye may know what is the exceeding greatness of his power, εἰς ἡμᾶς in us who believe: which exceeding greatness of his power in and upon us believers, adds he by the way of illustration, is the same as to its identity, and equal as to its greatness, efficiency, and success with that act of his omnipotence, or working of his mighty power which he wrought in Christ when he raised him from the dead, and set him at his own right hand in the heavenlies; far above all principalities, and powers, and dominion, and every name that is named, not in this world only, but also in that which is to come. Thus then he prayed, that they might discern more of the greatness of his power and divine energy, as exerting and shewing itself by its powerful effects upon their souls, in calling, quickening, renewing, converting, and bringing them to a true and living faith in Christ Jesus; even as it had manifestly shewed itself in raising Christ their head, and exalting him from his once humbled and debased state in our nature, and fixing that nature for ever in the dignity of the highest glory, next to that which is divine. And there is good reason, and an absolute necessity that this power and degree of operation, both on the head and members, should be the same; for as much of the state of the elect before conversion beareth a great analogy and resemblance with that of a dead body in the grave; in that they are not only said, as will be declared in its place, to be "dead in trespasses and sins," Ephes. ii. 1—5, before conversion; but this their quickening and raising from so great a death, is by our Lord set forth metaphorically by a resurrection, as it is written; "the hour cometh, and now is, when the dead shall hear the voice of the Son of God, and they that hear shall live," John v. 25; which is by him intended as declarative of the methods of grace, and the power of God, which are manifested in the quickening and converting a sinner; and thus "The Gospel is the power of God unto salvation, to every one who believeth," Rom. i. 16.

There be some indeed that "pervert the Gospel of Christ, and corrupt the word of truth," Gal. i. 7; who will needs insinuate, that this exceeding greatness of God's power to us-ward who believe, is only intended of that Almighty power put forth upon Christ upon our account, or for the common benefit of mankind, when the Father raised his dead body from the grave, &c. But that this is a sophism and mere evasion, and a manifest "handling the word of God deceitfully," 2 Cor. iv. 2, even the most weak in Christ's school may easily perceive; for nothing can, or needs be more plain than that in the 19th and 20th verses, there are two things compared and illustrated the one by the other, thus; "the exceeding greatness of God's Power in quickening and converting them who believe is, says he, like, or according to the energy or inward working of his mighty power which he wrought in Christ when he raised him from the dead, &c. So that it is manifest, that whoever he be that will interpret the text in such a manner as to confound these two acts so distinct as to make them but one individual thing, must first do violence to his own reason, before he can dare so confidently to prejudice the argument by such Pelagian shifts.

But not to take up your time in a further defence, I shall confirm and close this explication and vindication with the words of the learned Dr. Hammond in his paraphase upon the text; a man, who, as it is well known, was no friend to the doctrine of DIVINE ENERGY; no more than to the doctrines of election, and justification by a Surety's righteousness, as the matter of a sinner's justification before God, nor the rest of the quinquarticular points: his words are these; That ye might know the 'infiniteness of his power that hath been engaged in this work towards us believers, in subduing our enemies, sin, and death the punishment of sin, and raising us sinners, first to a new, and then to an eternal life; which was a work of the same Omnipotence with that which he first evidenced in that miraculous raising of Christ from the grave, and exalting him to the highest degree of glory, next to himself in heaven. An emblem and essay of the methods he hath now used towards us, by the preaching of the gospel to raise us from the grave of sin, to a new Christian life, and from thence to a glorious eternity.'

Thus much for the explication, and confirmation of my text, as being full and expressive of the exceeding greatness of power, which on God's part is put forth in and upon them that believe; as that without which no soul was ever brought into a state of true conversion and saving faith in the Lord Jesus: and it being only of this part of the DIVINE

Energy I intend chiefly to treat, I shall give you the sum of the words of this doctrinal proposition, viz.

Doct. That true conversion to God, and saving faith in our Lord Jesus Christ, are the effects of an exceeding greatness of God's mighty power, working in, and upon the soul; and are not to be effected by moral suasion, or any ability in the creature.

And the better to open, confirm, and vindicate this sacred truth, i. e. the necessity of the internal operation of the Divine power upon the heart in effectual calling and conversion; thereby to discover and lay open man's real impotency and inability, and the insufficiency of moral suasion to effect so great a change; I shall proceed in this method following, as

I. I shall shew you wherein conversion and true faith do consist.
II. Lay open, and demonstrate the real weakness and insufficiency of moral suasion to effect so great a change, as that of true conversion to God, and saving faith in the Lord Jesus Christ, from any remaining power or ability in fallen man.
III. I shall make it evident, that in true conversion, and saving faith, as they are the effects of the Divine power, and Omnipotence, working effectually and invincibly upon the heart by the

word, the will of man is not forced, nor its natural liberty in the least infringed; but, on the other hand, that noble faculty is, by renewing grace, made truly and spiritually free.

IV. I will in several instances manifest, that a person, in a true and proper sense, may be said to be passive, in some part of the Holy Spirit's work upon the heart, both in, and after conversion.

V. I shall demonstrate from the doctrine and evidence of the Holy Scriptures, that there is an absolute necessity for the exceeding greatness of God's almighty power to be invincibly and efficaciously put forth upon the heart and soul of man, to effect his conversion, and bring him to a saving faith in Christ.

VI. I will shew you out of the Holy Scriptures, that the Spirit of God has a peculiar work and office under the New Testament administration, as he is given of the Father, and sent forth by Christ, to accompany the word of the Gospel in its public ministration in the world; and also, that in respect of the church of Christ, and its particular members, he hath divers peculiar epithets given him, and much work to do upon their souls, in beginning, carrying on, and completing the whole "work of faith with power;"

thereby bringing them into a state of grace, and fitting them for glory.

VII. And lastly, I shall close the whole with some inferences, practical uses, and directions.

CHAP. II.

Shewing the Mistakes about true Conversion and saving Faith; and wherein they both consist.

I. I AM to shew you wherein true conversion and saving faith do consist; and this shall be done both negatively and positively: 1st, By endeavouring to remove some mistakes about a converted state and faith; and 2dly, by shewing wherein they do indeed consist. Now as to the mistakes about conversion, though doubtless they are many, yet I shall only instance in five, as being comprehensive, I think, of all.

The first mistake about a converted and safe state, as to another world, is when an improvement of the light and dictates of a natural conscience (where revelation, or gospel-light, and knowledge, are wanting) are thought sufficient to render men acceptable to God, and capable of enjoying him above in the regions of light and eternal happiness; as though there were no real necessity for Gospel-light and grace; but that such may be in a happy state above, who never so much as heard either of the law, or the gospel-promise of life through the woman's seed; as though the performance of a few moral duties, or smaller matters contained in the law, were sufficient for justification and acceptance; notwithstanding God hath positively declared, " That by the deeds of the law no flesh shall be justified," Rom. iii. 20; for there is no salvation in any other than in Christ, and by faith in him; there being no other name given under heaven, by which men might be saved. Acts iv. 12.

And as touching the attainments of the best heathens, notwithstanding the great noise and fine shew they made in the world at that time of day, as teachers of ethics or moral philosophy, God himself hath assured us, " That the world by wisdom knew him not," 1 Cor. i. 21, i. e. in a Mediator; without which knowledge and faith in him, it always was, and still is, impossible so to please God as to be saved by him. It is true, indeed, that from the visible creation, the being, eternal power, and necessary existence of the one true God, were deducible and easy to be collected; but then we are told, that " when they" thus " knew God, they glorified him not as God, but became vain in their imaginations,* their foolish heart being darkened; professing themselves wise they became fools, and changed the truth of God into a lie; and worshipped and served the creature more than the

* Διαλογισμοῖς; i. e. reasonings, debates, and philosophic disquisitions, about the nature of the Godhead; they multiplying the objects of divine adoration and worship, according to their vain and imperfect notions of things handed down by tradition; by which means their theology degenerated into an empty fabulous mythology, composed of poetic fictions, which the apostle styles " vain deceit," Colossians ii. 8. Hence they are charged with changing the truth of or concerning God into a lie, Rom. i. 25. That is, (as to one particular instance) what they, by travel, reading, or tradition, had picked up out of Moses, or from those who had read him; as also from the ancient Rabbies (in their cabbalistic interpretations of three numbers, degrees, or intellectual minds, in the One Jehovah Elohim) they changed and corrupted the same, by bringing in the doctrine of a triad of deities, or three gods; one most high, and independent, whom they stiled ὁ πατὴρ, and Jupiter, i. e. the father of the gods; and τὸ αὐτὸν, self existent. The second deity, whom they thought to be inferior and subordinate, they styled ὁ λογοσ, the word, and γέννημα, begotten and ὁ δημιυργὸς, the architect or framer of all things. And the third inferior and subordinate deity they styled ἡ ψυχὴ τῦ κόσμυ, the soul, or spirit of the universe; of which see more at large in St. Austin's City of God, lib. viii. cap. xi. and in Theophilus Gale's Court of the Gentiles, part 3, lib. i. cap. 3. From which error and impiety of Platonic tritheism, sprang the old Origenian and Eusebian heresy of inferiority and subordination in the blessed Trinity, lately revived and propagated by Dr. Clark in his book, falsely called the Scripture Doctrine of the Trinity; whereas, in truth, it is only the old Platonic doctrine of tritheism, revived and propagated under a scriptural and Christian name.

Creator." Rom. i. 21, 22; for that they paid worship to a plurality of gods, and that under the names and images of divers sorts of creatures; even from the sun, moon, and stars, to beasts and creeping insects, and the very herbs in the garden. And now this being the error and practice of the best of them, and of the whole Gentile world, as it then lay in idolatry, hear the just sentence of the Almighty concerning them: " The Lord looked down from heaven upon the children of men, to see if there were any that did understand, and that did seek God : but, (saith the divine oracle) there is none that understandeth, there is none that seeketh after God; they are all gone out of the way, they are altogether become unprofitable; there is none that doeth good, no not one. Destruction and misery are in their ways, and the way of peace they have not known," Psalm xiv. and Psalm liii; and Rom. iii. 10, &c. Thus " every mouth will be stopped, and the whole world will be found guilty before God," Rom. iii. 19, notwithstanding their pretensions to, and attainments of wisdom and moral virtue. And as to that light and knowledge they had attained, they were so far from living up thereto, and improving it to the grand design, that they became so much the more vain and empty; and grew still more dark and blind, through the just judgment of God upon them; as it is written,

"For this cause God gave them up to vile affections; and, as they did not like to retain God in their knowledge, God gave them over to a reprobate mind, to do those things which are not convenient," Rom. i. 26—28. This then being the case of the whole Gentile world, none of them could attain to a state of justification and life in their way; for as much as their best doings were but natural and sinful; and had they been more and better, yet we know, that in the fallen state of man, it is impossible that any, either Jew or Gentile, should be justified by the deeds of any law, except the law of faith, i. e. the Gospel. In vain then do such who call themselves Christians plead for a general charity to be extended to all, who heretofore did, or now do, live and die in a state of ignorance and error; these may be esteemed good, honest, harmless, well-meaning persons, who go out of the world as quiet as lambs, as the common people speak, which, according to the scripture, is, they die like beasts: for " man that is in honour, and understandeth not, as being without the true knowledge of God in a Mediator, is like the beast that perisheth," Psalm xlix. 20—14: not that he perishes like the beast, but acts the beast's part, and is like him as to ignorance, insensibility, and unconcernedness about a future state; and " so, like sheep," or " beasts, they are laid in the grave;" and though with the pomp and ceremony of a Christian burial, yet it alters not the case one jot: " For seeing it is a people of no understanding, they dying without knowledge, therefore he that made them (declares he) will not save them, and he that formed them will shew them no favour," Isaiah xxvii. 11. This then is the first mistake about conversion, and that none of the least, i. e. when nature, dressed up with a little negative righteousness, good-humour, and moral honesty, (though attended with gross ignorance as to God, and how he is to be worshipped aright, as was the case of the best heathens and of many who called themselves Christians,) is taken for conversion, or a safe state as to another world. The

Second mistake is, when a sober religious Christian life, as opposed to gross hypocrisy and dissimulation in religion, or open profaneness in conversation, is taken for a good and secure state; though such a person knows nothing of the nature and importance of a saving change, wrought in the soul by the work, and " washing of regeneration, and the renewing of the Holy Spirit," Tit. iii. 5. Now here I do not deny, but that wherever conversion and saving faith are, there also these things will, in some good measure, be found, as the genuine fruits and effects of the Spirit's work upon the soul; but to think that these are always a sure sign of internal grace, and a change of heart, is a great mistake; and, I fear, this Old Adam's religion, and shew of piety and holiness, hath deceived many; whereas nothing is more plain from the holy scriptures, and common observation, than that there may be a great shew of morality, religion, and zeal for good, (as men think it to be,) where the heart was never renewed, but still stands at the greatest enmity and opposition to the doctrines of free grace, and the Spirit's work upon the soul; of which you may take a taste, by an instance or two out of the Holy Scriptures, as,

First, Saul, the pharisee, and many of his own countrymen, as himself testifies, lived a life of morality, and strict observance of religious duties, being " exceeding zealous," and using much austerity to their own flesh; as that they were in their own, and the common people's eyes, the only men for holiness and religion; being in their way in good-earnest for heaven and eternal life; yet, nevertheless they were " far from righteousness," (Isaiah xlvi. 12, compared with Rom. ix. 31, 32,) and so must for ever have remained, while they, by all this, only endeavoured to establish their own, in a way of opposition to that justifying righteousness, which is only the " gift of God," Rom. v. 17. Now it is well known these men were as exceeding fierce against the doctrines of the Gospel, as they were zealous for ceremonies and traditions; and thus it fares with many in our day, who, as to religion, are strict in the way they profess, and, as to morals and works of charity, exceed many; who, like their brethren the pharisees, will sooner part with the greatest doctrinal article of their religion, than with a ceremony or tradition received from their fathers; and, by the spirit of persecution and enmity to the Gospel, manifest themselves to be of " that wicked one," 1 John iii. 12, as was Cain, who slew his brother upon a quarrel about religious worship. Again, we have a

Second instance, and that is the young man in the Gospel, who came to our Lord with a question of the greatest importance: " Good master, says he, what good thing shall I do to inherit eternal life?" Matt. xix. 16—20. And being examined about his obedience to the several duties required in the law, he came off well, in his own opinion, saying, " All these things have I observed from my youth: what lack I yet?" Now here were sobriety, religion, and practice; and these, in a young man and ruler, looked very lovely, and greatly affected Christ as man. Hence we read, " that Jesus beholding him, loved him; and said, One thing thou lackest." Mark x. 21. And what was this? The Spirit's work of renovation to sanctify his heart, and to empty and lay him low, and bring him to part with all, in order to follow Christ, and become a disciple of the cross : and now the lack of submission to this rendered all the rest, though otherwise good, altogether insignificant and lost, as to point of acceptance with God. Thus I think it appears plain from scripture evidence, that a strict, sober, moral life, accompanied with a religious zeal, may be found, where both heart and tongue are at the greatest enmity and contrariety to God's way of saving sinners.

The third mistake about a converted state, is, when such as once were professed enemies and opposers of the doctrines of free grace, and the invincible work of the Spirit upon the heart in effectual calling, are not only of a sudden changed, as to their former principles and dispositions; but, of opposers, become preachers, and zealous defenders of these truths; and, from thence, are esteemed sound converts and true believers. Converts indeed they may be, as to doctrines and particular opinions; but real Christianity, though it is not without this, is something distinct from all these things; forasmuch as many have a sound doctrinal faith, and clear notions, who never received the Gospel, as the power of God, renewing and sanctifying their hearts; their state being only that of the stony-ground hearers in the parable, who " received the word," Matt. xiii. 20, 21. i. e. the Gospel-doctrines, and truths of Christianity and free-grace, " with joy, which immediately sprang up" into a free open profession before men; " but they had no root in them;" that is, the doctrines they professed never powerfully reached their hearts, by the Spirit's work of renovation, and implantation into Christ, as a living and fruitful root of all spiritual fulness and influence; and therefore these, in the time of temptation, are liable to fall away, either by deserting religion, as many of the Jews, who once fell in with Christianity, did; or else, by turning the doctrines of grace into wantonness, as did the Christians called Gnosticks, and many others of the first converts to Christianity, who were not savingly wrought upon by the Lord the Spirit: these quite laid aside the right use of the royal law, as the rule of a Christian's conduct in a Mediator's hand, and gave themselves up to commit iniquity with greediness; making use of religion, in the free-grace part thereof, as a cloak and excuse for sin. And others of these stony-ground hearers fell away from their own steadfastness, by apostatizing into grievous damnable heresies and errors, making shipwreck of this their doctrinal faith and a good conscience. And concerning all such as went off, and fell away into one or another error, in point of judgment and practice, the apostle John, by the direction and guidance of the unerring Spirit, testifies, saying, " They went out from us, but they were not of us : for if they had been of us, they would no doubt have continued with us : but they went out, that they might be made manifest, that they were not all of us." 1 John ii. 19.

Thus then it appears, from the sentence of the Holy Spirit, that conversion to God doth not consist only in a coming off from error, and embracing sound doctrine ; for as much as it is manifest from scripture, and common observation, that there may be a change of principles, and religion in the name, where there is no real and thorough change of heart; and this, I think, is sufficiently evident, in that many of these relapse into error, or a loose and vain conversation, as has already been instanced, in the apostatizing Jews and Gnosticks, in the first ages of the church. But if they should not backslide, yet, it is in true Christianity, as St. Paul says of the spiritual Jew, " He is not a Jew, who is one outwardly ; neither is that circumcision, which is outward in the flesh : But he is a Jew, who is one inwardly, and circumcision is that of the heart, in the spirit, and not in the letter ; whose praise is not of men, but of God." Rom. ii. 28, 29. So neither is he a Christian, or true convert, who has only changed his religion, but is a stranger to a new heart. There is also a

Fourth mistake, as to conversion, and that is, when a sudden change or reformation in the life, or outward conversation from loose, sinful, wicked practices to a strictness in religion, is taken for conversion, or a sure sign thereof. It is true indeed, that wherever there is a thorough, saving conversion, and gracious change; there also is a reformation and visible turning from sin and Satan unto God; but yet, reformation and conversion are two distinct things.

Thus, although in all true conversion "the wicked forsakes his way, and the unrighteous man his thoughts," Isai. lv. 7; yet, this is a distinct thing from that which is further added, "and let him return unto the Lord, and he will have mercy upon him, and to our God, for he will abundantly pardon." From whence, it is plain, that turning from sin, and returning to the Lord, are distinct things: and though true conversion is never without reformation, yet reformation may be without a saving change: and then it is called "washing the outside of the cup and platter," Matt. xiii. 25, &c. while the inside remains filthy and unclean. And thus not having the "root of the matter" in them, like the stony-ground hearers, as was before instanced, these often relapse: and of such, St. Peter says, "It is happened to them according to the old proverb, the dog is returned to his own vomit again; and the sow that was washed, to her wallowing in the mire," 2 Pet. ii. 22.

The Fifth, and last mistake about a converted state is, when such persons are esteemed sound converts, who were born within the pale of the church, as some express it, and initiated into the Christian name and privilege; and receiving from their childhood a religious education, they thereby become sober, and piously inclined. When these, I say, from this fine appearance are taken for sound converts, and in a safe state, though they never experienced a heart-change, from the work of the Spirit upon their souls, under the ministry of the word.

I will with all readiness grant, that sobriety, sound principles, and a competency of scripture-knowledge, attended with a good disposition and inclination to wait constantly at Wisdom's door, are lovely, and to be commended in young ones, and ought to be encouraged in all; yet too too oft, we see, this goodness of theirs proves but " like the morning cloud, and early dew, it quickly passeth away," Hos. vi. 4. Not but that there are, God be praised for it! divers instances, where this good beginning of sobriety and religion has terminated in a true and sound conversion, the Spirit's work upon the heart. And now, that more of this morning-goodness, as to sobriety and religion, might appear in young ones, I would here, by the way, recommend and exhort the people of God to be careful and zealous in keeping up family duties;

such as reading, praying, and catechizing of the children and servants under their charge. This is what Solomon calls " training up a child (or youth) in the way he should go," Prov. xxii. 6. And the Holy Spirit by St. Paul speaks to you, Christian parents, after this manner, " And ye fathers, provoke not your children to wrath; but bring them up in the nurture, and admonition of the Lord," Ephes. vi. 4. In the former text there is a pointing at the very method; for to train up, is to instruct in a catechetic manner, by constant exercise, and repeating it over and over again unto them; and in both texts the earliness of this is suggested, as being to be performed towards them in their early days, when newly weaned from the breasts; as the prophet hints to us, where he says " Whom shall he teach knowledge? And whom shall he make to understand doctrine? (to which he himself replies) Them that are weaned from the milk, and drawn from the breast," Isai. xxviii. 9. This being the most proper time for parents to begin to feed their children with the sincere milk of the word, that so they may be " nourished up in the words of faith, and good doctrine," 1 Tim. iv. 6. And, to the commendation both of Timothy, and his parents, Paul reminds him of the advantage he had of an early and pious education, where he thus exhorts; " But continue thou in the things which thou hast learned, and hast been assured of, knowing of whom thou hast learned them. And that from a child thou hast known the holy scriptures, which are able to make thee wise unto salvation, through faith which is in Christ Jesus," 2 Tim. iii. 14, 15. But now to take this good disposition, and forwardness in knowledge, and the duties of Christianity, for real true conversion, or a sufficient sign of grace and a heart-change is, give me leave to say, the way to deceive both ourselves and them. And though I would by no means discourage these hopeful youths, and good beginnings, yet I must take liberty to suggest, that one thing is, or may possibly still be, lacking; as it was in that lovely youth before-mentioned: such indeed are not far from the kingdom of God, and yet, like him, they may go off and never come there. And therefore to take these into the church or visible kingdom, while this one thing is wanting, is, I fear, going a little too far in our charity; forasmuch as the temple or church of Christ, is a spiritual house, and ought to be built with none but living stones, as being first quickened, hewed and squared, and so made meet for the spiritual building, by the workmanship of God the Spirit,* in a gracious change of heart; by giving them a thorough conviction of their lost miserable

* 1 Cor. iii. 10,—12,—14 and 1 Pet. ii. 4, 5. and Ephes. ii. 20, 21, 22.

state by nature, and the necessity of a new birth, and a better righteousness for justification and acceptance with God, than their own; and also of the necessity of faith in Christ, as it brings the soul to deal with the Lord Jesus, for the true riches of grace, wisdom, righteousness, sanctification and redemption; and so to glory only in the Lord, as being brought quite off from a dependance upon any thing they have attained or performed, more than others. And where this is not to be found, the state of such lovely creatures is, at present, but like that of the foolish virgins. Lamps it is true they have, but there wants the Spirit's work of saving grace: and therefore when the Bridegroom comes, these, so continuing, will have the true oil to seek, when the wise virgins will only have their lamps to trim. This then is the fifth mistake.

And thus having endeavoured to lay before you the most material mistakes about conversion, I should now have proceeded immediately to shew you what are the most important mistakes about true faith; but before I come to the consideration of these, I think it may not be amiss to take notice of and endeavour the removing some objections that may possibly be thrown in our way, in relation to what has been already laid down; as,

First of all, some perhaps will here object, and say, that by this means the gate and way which leads to life is made much straiter and narrower than it needs to be; but especially the way into church-relation and communion at the Lord's table, seeing man cannot judge the heart: and therefore " Whosoever believeth that Jesus is the Christ, is born of God," 1 John v. 1, and ought to be received into communion, if of a good conversation, whatever may be their private sentiments, as to those things which are matter of controversy, and disputable. To which I answer,

1st. These objectors give an occasion of suspicion, that they are either strangers to the internal change and new birth; or else that they have no just idea of the proper materials of a true gospel church, as it is to be composed only of living, spiritual stones, as has been already hinted. But more particularly as to the scripture objected, I answer, that although a verbal confession, or owning Jesus to be the true Messias, was once sufficient to ground a judgment of charity upon, with respect of the new birth, as to a Jew; and the coming off from idolatry, and a public owning the Christian religion by an open profession of faith in Christ Jesus, attended with a willingness to submit to baptism, were once thought a sufficient test, as to church-membership; yet this will prove but a very imperfect way of trying who they are, that are true believers, and sound converts in this our day; in which all sorts of heretics, and men of rotten principles, yea, and the loosest livers will, with one consent say, 'They believe that Jesus is the true Messias.' And as to such as are for receiving every one into communion, that owns Jesus to be Christ, if not of a bad character as to their conversation, I shall not be ashamed to say, these men give too great a ground of suspicion they themselves are not only strangers to the new birth, as it is a saving work of God upon the soul; but also that they are, as to principles, not very sound, and therefore want, and plead for, a general charity for themselves and friends, as an act of grace and indemnity, to save them from a just censure at Christ's bar in Sion. This making the church a sort of Noah's Ark, or rather a Babel of confusion, is what they have no warrant for. However, as the Apostle saith in a lesser case, "We have no such *custom*, neither the churches of Christ," 1 Cor. xi. 16. But on the other hand are commanded " To be perfectly joined together in the same mind, and in the same judgment," 1. Cor. i. 10. or sentiment, as to doctrine and practice; that so church-members may all speak the same thing, and be free from divisions, and falling into sects and parties among themselves. But then,

2dly. I further answer, If all persons of unspotted morals, being religiously disposed and inclined, are to be accounted good Christians, and sound converts, and such as ought not to have their supposed Christianity called into question, nor to stand excluded, or debarred from communion at the Lord's table, whatever their notions or different sentiments may be, and though never so heterodox and heretical: then let a man be a Deist, Tritheist, Arian, Pelagian, or Socinian, &c. or one who disbelieves, nay blasphemes the doctrines of the blessed Trinity in Unity, and the true and proper divinity of the Word, and Holy Spirit; or let him be the vilest scoffer or calumniator of the doctrines of free-grace, and of justification by the righteousness of Christ our surety, as imputed to, and received by faith alone. If the same be a sober, honest, and good-natured man, he ought, according to this new scheme, to be esteemed a Christian, and allowed a common place in our affections. Thus neither Hymeneus, nor Philetus, whom St. Paul, by his apostolic authority in the churches of Christ, did excommunicate, and deliver over to Satan, under the severest curse for heresy and blasphemy; nor Cerinthus, nor Ebion; no, nor none of those false apostles, and deceitful workers and seducers, who transformed themselves into the ministers of Christ, 2 Cor. xi. 13,—15, though in truth they were Satan's ministers, and devouring wolves, in the sheep's habit; even these, I say, according to some men's superabundant charity, falsely so called, ought not to have been so tartly treated, nor yet turned out of the Christian churches; because they differed in their sentiments of religion from those of the common and more illiterate sort of Christians; who, as some say, exalt faith above reason, seeing they believed in one God, as supreme over all; and that " Jesus of Nazareth" was the true Messiah and common Saviour.

But, Secondly, there are some others, that perhaps will say, though we ought not to esteem such as these for true Christians, and sound converts, so as to retain them in Christian churches, and communion at the Lord's table; yet we ought to esteem all men who profess the Christian faith to be good Christians, and in a safe state, unless they manifest the contrary, by falling off, into dangerous and destructive errors, or into an open scandalous life. To which I reply,

That men and women are not born gracious, nor true Christians; nor are they made spiritually alive, and sound converts by baptism; but by a special sanctifying and saving work of the Spirit, through the Divine effiacy of the word upon the heart; and this is what we ought to look for, and, in some good measure, discern, as to its fruits and effects, before we form a scripture-judgment of the saving faith and conversion of such persons; notwithstanding their open profession of Christianity, as accompanied with a sober moral life: for the foolish virgins, and the man without the wedding-garment, are sufficient proofs that all are not Christians who appear so. But then,

Thirdly, some perhaps will still object, and say, how shall we judge of a person's grace and sincerity, but from these fine appearances of religion and sobriety? Doth not our blessed Saviour tell us, "The tree is known by its fruits?" Luke vi. 44. I answer: it is true enough, and a most certain rule, that the tree is known, and distinguished by its fruit; and it is as true also, that wherever grace is, there it will evidence itself by proper fruits, as effects of the Spirit's work, in a supernatural change; from whence a judgment of charity is to be formed: but then pray mind it, as the fruit partakes of the nature of the tree it springs from, and grows upon, so it sufficiently informs the judicious of what sort or kind the tree is. Thus the olive tree is distinguished from the vine, and the fig tree from both, by their different sorts of fruit; since every tree yields fruit according to its nature and kind, except it is altered by grafture or inoculation; so that " The fig tree cannot bear olive berries, nor the vine figs," James iii. 12. Nor do men gather grapes of the bramble bush, nor figs of thistles. Matt. vii. 16. Thus nature cannot yield grace, nor produce the fruits and effects thereof: though, if it be well cultivated and improved, it may bear that which hath a near resemblance to the spiritual fruits, and produce of saving grace; for all such things as these, i. e. sobriety, justice, mercy, truth and charity, &c. do always, more or less, discover themselves in the person where grace is; not as its natural produce, but as constant concomitants; for these are fruits that spring from moral principles improved by grace, but are not saving-grace itself; they being oft, as I have said, to be found where persons never knew, nor experienced the power and grace of God in truth. It is not fruit then, but good fruit, that proves the tree to be so. The wild olive, and the crab tree, or wilding, growing in the common hedge-row, by the highway-side, are oftentimes found to be very fruitful, and to bear more fruit, and fairer to look at, than those grafted and enclosed, on whom much cost and labour have been bestowed: but still the fruit of the wild tree is, like the tree itself, wild, sour, and in a manner unprofitable. But this is not all; for the meaning of our Lord in these words, is chiefly to teach, how to discover men of unsound principles, who are false teachers, heretical and deceitful workers, Satan's ministers, though coming in Christ's name, and in sheep's clothing for a disguise; and these are to be known by their doctrines; as he saith, "By their fruits ye may know them;" so that fruits here are intended of the doctrines men teach; and you are to welcome and receive, or reject and shun them, according to the doctrines they bring, and not according to the mask they wear, nor the fair speech and good-nature they make use of, to deceive and beguile the simple. Hence, says the apostle Paul, "Though we, or an angel from heaven, preach any other gospel unto you, than that which we have preached unto you, and that ye have received, let him be accursed:* I say let him be accursed." Gal. i. 8, 9. And saith the beloved disciple John, "If there come any unto you, and bring not this doctrine, receive him not into your house, neither bid him God speed," (i. e. do not so much as salute him;) "for he that biddeth him God speed, is partaker of his evil deeds," 2 John 10, 11.

Thus then I think it is proved very plain, that as

* 'Aνάθεμα, is the sentence of excommunication; and answers to the Hebrew חרם kherem; which was the second sort of censure used by the Jews; by which sentence the person was separated from the congregation, and not allowed to join with them in their public worship; nor were they permitted to have friendly society and communion with him in eating or drinking, at their mixtures and banquets: and of this sort of excommunication is that mentioned 1 *Cor.* v. 5. and hence agreeably you read, ver. 11, "with such an one keep no company, no not to eat."—And this sort of excommunication Paul wishes upon himself, for his brethren's sake, *Rom.* ix. 3.

corrupt, or unsound doctrines, are the fruits by which false teachers and wolves to Christ's flock may be easily discovered and detected; and sound doctrine that which discovers the man to be a minister of Christ's gospel: so fruits of morality and zeal, and strictness in religion, only prove a man to be sober, and, in some measure, to live up to what he professes; which is commendable, and worthy the imitation of all; but it proves not a man to have grace: for it is only those fruits, which are the genuine offspring of gracious principles, and the Spirit's work upon the heart, that can demonstrate and evidence the truth of grace, and soundness of conversion; which they certainly are strangers and enemies to, who laugh at, and deride these things in others.

Thus having removed the mistakes about conversion, and answered the objections which some have made, or are ready to throw in our way, I shall now proceed to remove the mistakes about the nature and properties of true saving faith; and they are chiefly these two; as,

First, When a professed assent to, and approbation of this, or the other proposition of divine truth, is judged a sufficient sign of grace, and taken for that faith that gives a right to gospel-ordinances and privileges. Hence some have taught, as has been already hinted, that this one article of faith professed and owned, is enough to entitle any man to the name and benefits of a Christian; viz. the belief of one supreme God, and of Jesus of Nazareth's being the true Messias, and the Saviour of the world. Others propose the believing and maintaining 'the six principles,' Heb. vi. 2. as they call them, accompanied with a strict and religious abstinence from 'four things prohibited to the first Gentile converts,' Acts xv. 20. And others, perhaps, think it necessary, that all they admit shall own, and it may be, subscribe their private or public confessions, or articles of faith: but if they make any of these things a test of inward Christianity, or a certain sign of true saving faith, they may soon be deceived; and it is this only I would guard against, i. e. a mistake about the nature and properties of that faith, which is saving, and not take upon me here to inquire into the nature, necessity, or general usefulness of open confessions of faith, either to be taught publicly or privately in a catechetic manner; or as articles of the Christian faith, to be openly owned and professed by all; but especially those who undertake the teaching and government of others. But forasmuch as all doctrinal truths may be owned, heartily believed, and publicly confessed by persons who never as yet passed under the Spirit's work, therefore I conclude, and I think very justly, that an assent to, and a belief and open profession of all doctrinal truths, necessary to be known, believed, and put in practice, is not that very faith by which a man believeth to the saving of his soul. The foolish virgins, as has already been intimated, had this doctrinal faith, (which is only an assent to this, or the other truth, as a proposition to be believed, publicly owned, and professed before men,) and yet were rejected. But there is also another mistake about the nature and properties of true justifying and saving faith; and that is,

Secondly, When assurance itself, or a positiveness of being interested in the covenant of grace, is taken for the only act of faith, as saving, or the certain sign thereof: as if that faith, through which we are said to be justified and saved, or by which a soul comes to Christ, and believes on him, was no more, nor nothing less, than a person's being fully sure and positive, that he or she is elected, redeemed, adopted, and justified; and that they shall certainly and infallibly be saved. Now though I deny not, but affirm, faith to be a persuasion and an act of appropriation, and that there is such a thing as assurance; which according to its nature and degree, is called either "A full assurance of hope," Heb. vi. 11, or "A full assurance of faith," Heb. x. 22, and "A full assurance of understanding," Col. ii. 2; yet, true justifying faith is something distinct from assurance itself; especially from that vain confidence and positiveness, with which some are puffed up, and boast; notwithstanding they live a loose life, to the stumbling and offending the weak, and to the great scandal of the gospel: and this I hope will more plainly be evidenced when I come to shew what are the nature and distinct acts of this true faith. Thus having removed the most material mistakes about conversion and saving faith, I shall proceed to the

Second branch of this head, and shew positively what true conversion is, and wherein it doth consist; and then lay open to you the true nature and peculiar actings of true saving faith.

First of all, then, as to conversion itself: this may be considered in two parts; 1st. In the principle from whence it flows, and by which it is continued and maintained: and, 2dly. In the genuine actings of the soul, as the result of such a gracious work wrought, previous to this its evangelic return. Now as to the principle from whence true conversion flows: it is that new nature, new heart, and new spirit, which is received, or rather wrought in the soul at the time of effectual calling; which is also called the new birth, and the new creature: and this gracious principle contains in it not only spiritual life and activity, but also a disposition and love to inward and practical holiness; by which means the whole soul is set right God-ward, with a propensity to hate and eschew sin, and to love and labour after that purity of heart and life, " without which no man shall see the Lord," Heb. xii. 14; and this is the nature or instinct, give me leave to say, of the new creature; which, accordcording to the image of him who created it, is renewed in knowledge, and created in righteousness and true holiness, Col. iii. 10, and Eph. iv. 24. And this heart-change is what Ephraim prayed so earnestly for, saying, "Turn thou me, and I shall be turned. Surely, after I was turned, I repented; and after that I was instructed, I smote upon my thigh," Jer. xxxi. 18, 19. This is what the Scripture calls " circumcising the heart to love and fear the Lord," Deut. xxx. 6, " taking away the heart of stone, and giving a heart of flesh," Ezek. xxxvi. 27, *compared with* Psalm li. 7. and writing the gospel-laws, i. e. of faith, love, and evangelical obedience, in the heart, and putting his fear therein, so as to secure his people's obedience, and perseverance in his ways; which, also, in the New Testament, is styled a " being born again," John iii. 3, Tit. iii. 5; and that from above; a being renewed by the Holy Spirit; and also created in Christ Jesus unto good works, and the like, Eph. ii. 10. And now this foundation of grace and santification being, by the work of the Holy

Spirit, first laid in the soul, whereby it is savingly wrought upon and turned to the Lord; then in the second place, the active part of conversion follows, and is next to be considered, as manifesting itself both to God and man. And that,

First, In the converted soul's abhorrence of sin, and debasement of itself for it, as the greatest evil committed against the chiefest good; being that which defaces God's image in man's soul, and tramples upon his authority, and eclipses his manifestative glory in the world, which is dearer to him than all things. And by this means the soul is brought to a becoming humility in God's presence; and to a lying low before him, glorifying of his righteousness and justice; admiring his patience, forbearance, and long-suffering: thus the soul always justifies God, and judges and condemns itself. Upon which follows, in the

Second place, Godly sorrow, or mourning for sin; which arises from a heart truly broken and contrite before God; which issues in a repentance unto life, wherein the soul looking upon, and steadfastly beholding Christ, as once made sin, "mourns, and is in bitterness, as a man that mourneth for his first-born," Zech. xii. 10, and how this godly sorrow affects the soul, and hath influence upon the present and after conduct, I cannot better set forth than in those words of the apostle to the godly Corinthians; "Now I rejoice, not that ye were made sorry, but that ye sorrowed to repentance; for ye were made sorry after a godly manner: for godly sorrow worketh repentance to salvation, not to be repented of; but the sorrow of the world worketh death: for behold this self-same thing, that ye sorrowed after a godly sort, what carefulness it wrought in you, yea, what clearing of yourselves, yea, what indignation, yea, what fear, yea, what vehement desire, yea, what zeal, yea, what revenge!" 2 Cor. vii. 9—11. All this is the genuine effect of grace in the heart, whereby a soul comes to be truly broken, and humbled for sin. Upon which, as next in order, will follow, in the

Third place, a hating and forsaking sin. Forsaking sin, and returning to the Lord, are indeed two distinct acts; and the first may be without the latter; yet, as has already been hinted to you, the latter is never without the former: for wherever the soul returns to God, by a repentance unto life, and faith unfeigned, there always follows a hating and forsaking sin; as having this glorious encouragement set before it in the word and ministry, "Let the wicked forsake his ways, and the unrighteous man his thoughts: and let him return unto the Lord, and he will have mercy upon him; and to our God, for he will abundantly pardon," Isa. lv. 7. Thus "he that confesseth and forsaketh his sins," Prov. xxviii. 13, has the promise of finding mercy and pardon, when the same is accompanied with the soul's return to the Lord: which manifests itself to be sincere and true, in that it is attended in the last place, with a full pursuit after all that is morally and spiritually good, with "full purpose of heart to cleave unto the Lord," Acts xi. 23, so as to follow him fully; desiring and labouring after "Glorifying of God with the body and the spirit, which are the Lord's," 1 Cor. vi. 20; and its inquiry is, "Lord, what wilt thou have me to do?" Acts ix. 6; for now the soul begins to love, and delight itself in the law of the Lord, after the inward man, and to meditate therein both day and night; esteeming the words of God's mouth more than his necessary food; yea, it is more to him than thousands of gold and silver; holiness of heart and life being as much his desire and pursuit, as eternal happiness itself. Thus much as to the nature and gracious actings of the soul under the Spirit's work in conversion. There is indeed one ingredient more, essential to true evangelic conversion; and that is faith in the promise of mercy, life, and salvation by Christ, as the soul is then helped, and enabled to look to, and deal with the blood of sprinkling; but this falls more directly under our consideration in the second branch of this first general head; and that is to shew, what are the nature and peculiar acts of true saving faith, as it specifically differs from all other sorts, which are common both to devils, and *almost Christians*. 1st, Then, as to the nature of this grace, it is truly spiritual, and from above; it being one of the principal graces of the new creature, arising from the Spirit's work, as the Spirit of grace, and renovation in the heart; and is peculiar only to God's elect, as called, and regenerated. Hence it is said to be the " gift of God," Jam. i. 17; and is not in any sense our own; it being one of those spiritual gifts which comes from above, from the Father of lights; and is to be received only out of Christ's fulness; who is also called its author and finisher, as he is the great undertaker for all those the Father has given to him. And furthermore, if this faith be considered as to the instrumental means, it comes by hearing of the gospel preached, as it is a message of peace, grace, and life eternal, coming to us through a Redeemer; which calls for credit and affiance: and so it is also a firm persuasion, and dependance on the word of promise, for the benefits contained therein. Thus it is more than a bare assent, or credit given to the word, which is all that is in the other sorts of faith; for that they are seated only in the understanding and judgment, but this principally in the heart and will. And here let it be noted, as a fundamental principle, that this faith is peculiar only to God's elect, and is his gift to, and work in the soul; and is to be found in them only, as regenerated and born of God: and so it is more than a moral act of the rational creature, I say more than moral, and more than rational, it being spiritual, and evangelical: there is indeed a moral rational faith, which is our reasonable duty, and arises only out of the force that truth, as coming from God, has upon our natural intellect; and is what cannot be avoided, because of the strength of the evidence. Thus, if I believe there is a God, I cannot help believing he is good, holy, just, and true: but then this is common to men as men, and also to devils as intellectual beings: hence they are said " to believe and tremble," James ii. 19. But now as to this supernatural grace of faith, as wrought in the hearts of God's elect, though it is a very reasonable duty to believe, and the most rational act that the soul is capable of; yet it is not the act of mere reason, or of man, as natural, but only as he is created anew in Christ Jesus. It is, I say, the act only of the new creature, or of man as he is renewed by grace, and made spiritual, by partaking of the spirit of life from Christ, and of his nature and image, as he is our second Adam, our spiritual and everlasting Father. And furthermore, let it be settled as a preliminary, that this faith, whereof I am now treating, is not so seated in any one faculty of the soul as to be shut out, or wholly excluded the other: for, as the soul, though supposed to be principally seated in some one part, or rather in all the more principal parts of the body, in which she in a peculiar manner performs and discharges her various distinct functions, is not excluded from any other part, no not the least; though she discovers more of her noble nature, and excellent manner of operation in the head, than in the little fingers or toes; even so, although faith may be said to be more principally seated in the heart, as it is the seat of affiance and trust, as well as of love and affection, yet so as that it is present in all the other more noble faculties, and discovers itself in a different way of operation, according to the nature and use of the several powers of man's soul : and a due attention to, and consideration of this, will help us to take in a just and agreeable idea of the different scripture-phrases, relating to the acts and office of true saving faith. I know looking to, or seeing the Son, coming to, and believing on him, &c. are looked upon, and interpreted by many as synonymous, i. e. words of the same signification and import; and, in a sense, it is true ; yet, nevertheless, though these are all the acts of true faith, they are, notwithstanding, distinct acts, and, as it were, so many several ways of faith's dealing with

Christ, or as so many steps and degrees towards the grand act of trust and reliance; not that one is before the other in order of time, but only in order of nature, and accordingly are, and ought to be opened and distinguished.

First of all, then, we will consider this grace of faith as seated in the understanding, and so it is of a twofold use; 1st. as a spiritual visive power, which we may call the new creature's eye, as it is a grace peculiarly created for, and suited to the spiritual use of the new creature; and as such, is appointed to a distinct work and office in the soul, by which it looks out towards, and fixes itself fast, with an intenseness of mind, upon Christ, as crucified, and bearing our sins, answerable to these words; " Look unto me, and be ye saved, all the ends of the earth; for I am God, and there is none else; and besides me there is no Saviour," Isai. xlv. 22. Thus, as the natural organ, or eye of the body, in a stung Israelite, was appointed to exercise itself, by looking, in order to obtain a bodily cure, from the typical serpent lifted up; even so this eye of the new creature is suited, and commanded as such, to be in act and exercise, by looking upon its proper and peculiar object Christ, as he was once made *sin* and a *curse*; and agreeably our Lord applies the type, and expounds the mystery as figurative, of believing in himself as crucified, saying, " For as Moses lifted up the serpent in the wilderness, even so must the Son of man be lifted up, (i. e. crucified,) that whosoever believeth on him should not perish, but have eternal life," John iii. 14, 15. This believing on him, as it is a firm trust and affiance, is the last part of faith's act, which began with " seeing the Son," chap. vi. 40, as thus exhibited in the gospel, not with the eye of the body, but that of faith; and as this seeing eye of faith, which is from the Lord, is suited and ordained to look to Christ, as now crucified; so it was suited to look forwards, so as to discern the promise of his incarnation at a distance, and all that depended thereon, in the times of the Old Testament. This was that eye, by which all the ante and post-diluvian fathers " saw the promises afar off," Heb. xi. 13; and this is that eye, by which the " things not seen, are evidenced," (Ibid. v. 1,) and realized to us, and by which we discern and converse with invisible realities and glories, though still at a distance. This then is one of the peculiar acts of that faith, which is to be found only in God's elect, and that only as they come under the exceeding greatness of his power, and omnipotence. There is indeed a second use of this faith, as seated and working in the understanding; and that is an assent to the truth and divine testimony of the word; but this being an act common to the other sorts of faith, which are but natural, and is to be found, as has been hinted, even among the devils, though in the true believer it is of a better and more noble nature, I shall not now stand to enlarge thereon, but pass to another distinct act of faith, which follows that of looking to, yea, through, the promise, so as to see the Son, who is exhibited therein, as faith's peculiar object and Lord.

Secondly, then, faith is to be considered, as it is seated and operates in the noble faculty of reason or judgment, from whence arises one of its great and essential properties and acts; and that is persuasion: this persuasion is the result of reason, as enlightened and subjected to Divine Revelation, as the way of life and salvation is declared and held forth in the new covenant, by a promise of life given in Christ; whereby the soul, like Sarah of old, "judges him faithful that has thus promised, as knowing that what he promised he is able to perform," Heb. xi. 11. Hence we read, that those who saw the promises, though at so great a distance, yet knowing and considering who it was that made them, and engaged for their performance, "they were persuaded of them," verse 13; that is, of the truth, reality, and accomplishment of the things promised, and "confirmed by an oath," Heb. vi. 17, 18. Thus Abraham's faith got the start of sense and carnal reason; and, by the art of divine reasoning, he argued, and "believed in hope against hope," Rom. iv. 18, 19, 20, 21; wherein he did not draw any unbelieving conclusions from his own imbecility, neither from the barrenness of Sarah's womb; but he drew just conclusions from the faithfulness and power of God, who made the promise; as being fully persuaded, that what he had promised he would certainly perform. Thus the soul, under the efficacious work of this exceeding great and mighty power of God, not only hears the promise, in its publication; but, looking to the object of soul-health and cure, is fully persuaded of the truth and certainty of life, to be had only in Christ Jesus. And, upon this so reasonable a persuasion begat in the heart, a

Third step, or further degree of the acting of true faith, comes now in order to be performed, and next to be considered; and that is, the soul's spiritual motion towards its proper object, and alone Saviour; this in scripture is called coming to Christ; and thus it may be considered as an act of the affections; these being the legs or feet of the soul, and the hands to receive and embrace the promise, and object of faith: and so faith is called in scripture a coming to Christ, i. e. as the alone Saviour, for life and salvation, through his mediation and satisfaction given, and righteousness wrought out, and carried in unto the Father, for our justification and acceptance with God. Hence you have such encouraging words as these, "Come unto me, all ye that labour and are heavy laden, and I will give you rest," Mat. xi. 28. And again, "All that the Father giveth me shall come to me; and him that cometh to me I will in no wise cast out," John vi. 37. And again, " He that cometh to me shall never hunger, and he that believeth on me shall never thirst," &c. verse 35. Thus faith, by the affections, carries the soul forth to Christ. But, besides this, it has a

Fourth act, and that is to receive Christ, according to that text, " To as many as received him, to them he gave power to become the sons of God, even to them that believe on his name: which were born not of blood, nor of the will of the flesh, nor of the will of man, but of God," John i. 12, 13. And again, " As ye have received Christ Jesus the Lord, so walk in him," Coloss. ii. 6. Thus those who of old saw the promises afar off, so as to be persuaded of their reality and certainty; even these were said " to embrace the promises," Heb. xi. 13, as by the arms of faith, in the outgoings of their souls, thereby meeting them at so great a distance. Thus Abraham not only "saw Christ's day" (John viii. 56, and Heb. xi. 19.) in the promise, but he, after a sort, embraced him as in the flesh, in the promised Son; especially when, after an unexpected manner, he in a figure received Isaac as from the dead. And now next to this coming to, and embracing of the promised Saviour, and all saving benefits in and by him, in the

Fifth place, faith has another distinct act peculiar to it, as justifying and saving; and that is, believing on him, by trusting in, and relying on him; called also leaning, staying, and committing the soul to him by the way of dependance: as giving itself wholly up to him, both as King and Saviour; and so it is an act of the heart, soul, or whole man; yet principally it is here an act of the will: and this may be called the perfecting and completing act; forasmuch as now, and not before, the act of faith, as it deals with Christ for life, and ventures on him for salvation, is completed and perfected: and this is that act which is properly the uniting act of faith, whereby the soul, giving itself up with full consent, is now united to Christ in the conjugal tie, or marriage-union; because now the soul, as the damsel in marriage, gives itself up to, and joins heart and spirit with the Lord: and as in marriage, a new union and relation commences, whereby two are made one flesh: so in this act of faith, the soul joins itself to the Lord, so as to be "one spirit," 1 Cor. vi. 17. And here we are to distinguish between a spiritual vital union, which is the Spirit's act upon the soul; and this conjugal union which is effected only by faith. And so likewise, as to a new covenant-interest, the first part of the title arises out of that grace, that was settled upon all the elect, by way of covenant, as " Grace was given us in Christ before the world began," 2 Tim. i. 9; and the purchased title, which Christ, by his death, procured for all his; these also are distinct and prior to this marriage, interest, and title: but as a jointure, though promised, agreed to, and sealed before marriage, yet takes not place in due form of law, until the couple are actually married, even so the believing soul's manifestative and declared right and interest in these covenant-blessings and privileges, are now justly said to commence and take place, as in due form of law: even as our Lord has declared, "that he who believeth is passed from death to life," John v. 24; for now it is, that, as in marriage, the condition or state is actually changed, and all conjugal relation and interest begin: and the soul, who is thus joined to the Lord, has a just and undoubted open right and claim to all the blessings of the new covenant. Thus I have endeavoured to lay open to you the nature and distinct acts of true conversion, and of justifying and saving faith, as proposed to be handled under this first head; proper uses wherewith to close this, may be inferences and examination. And,

First, if there are so many great mistakes about conversion and saving faith, then we may hence infer, that few persons, comparatively, among the professors of Christianity ever attain to it: and here, if ever, we may justly apply those words of our Lord ; " Strait is the gate, and narrow is the way, that leadeth to life, and few there be that find it," Mat. vii. 14. Again,

Secondly, from this description of conversion and faith, as being agreeable to the word and experiences of God's people in all ages, we may next infer, that many proud, carnal, conceited professors and preachers will one day meet with a sad disappointment ; when, instead of hearing Christ bid them welcome, with "Come, ye blessed of my Father," (Mat. xxv. 34,) they shall meet with that surprising repulse, " I never knew you : depart from me, ye cursed, into everlasting fire, prepared for the devil and his angels," Mat. vii. 22, 23 ; and chap. xxv. 41. And seeing it will be so with many, suffer me to propose to you a word or two, by way of examination. As,

First of all, ask thy soul seriously how thou camest to be a Christian, or church-member? Say thus with thyself: is the gate strait, and the way narrow that leadeth to life, and are there few that find it? How then came it to pass, that I found it, so as to enter thereat? Am I got in aright?

Did I not climb up some other way? Am I not the man, or woman, that among the guests, has none of the wedding garment, or marriage token, to shew, when the royal Bridegroom comes? And now, in order to resolve the first question aright, ask thy soul a

Second, saying; if this is the nature of true and sound conversion to God, and if these be the genuine acts of true saving faith, what of this exceeding greatness of Almighty power have I felt and undergone in my own soul? What of these genuine actings of the new creature have I experienced between God and my own heart? Thus having finished the first general head, I shall proceed to the next.

CHAP. III.

Shewing the Insufficiency of Moral Suasion to effect true Conversion to God, and Faith in Christ.

II. I SHALL lay open and demonstrate the weakness and insufficiency of moral suasion to effect so great a change, as that of true conversion to God, and saving faith in the Lord Jesus, from any remaining power or ability in fallen man. And this shall be managed in the following order: as 1st, I shall shew you what moral suasion is, and what possibly it may produce. 2dly, That though God doth in his word, and by the daily ministration thereof, make use of arguments and reasonings; and points and enforces these with promises and threatenings, suited to the capacity and duty of a reasonable creature; yet, where he has a design of making them effectual to the salvation of this or the other particular person whom he has loved, chosen, and predestinated to life eternal, he always adds to these the efficacious power of his Spirit and grace, to quicken and renew their souls; thereby working in them both to will and to do of his own good pleasure. 3dly, I shall shew, that, as to the rest, God affords them only the means, but doth not with this exert his Almighty power upon their hearts, as in those, whom according to his eternal purpose, he effectually calls and saves. 4thly, I shall make it appear, that, upon a neglect, or rejection of the outward means and admonitions, God very justly upbraids and condemns these non-improvers and despisers of gospel-light and grace. 5thly, I shall under this head shew you, That there are such lets and hinderances in the way of a sinner's conversion, both from within and without, as render it utterly impracticable and impossible, without the concurrence of his efficacious grace and omnipotence.

First of all, moral suasion, so far as it relates to the teacher, is an endeavour, by proper methods and arguments, to persuade a man, in a natural unrenewed state, not only to break off and forsake his evil courses of sin and folly, but also closely to adhere unto the practice of moral and religious duties; or to put forth his power, and use his utmost endeavour to convert himself, and become a new man, and to live according to the strict rules of the gospel; which require repentance towards God, and faith in our Lord Jesus, with a constant perseverance therein: and this is to be set home, and pressed, after the best manner, by exhortations and arguments, drawn either from the Divine Being himself, as to his nature; or from his right and propriety in us, and authority and dominion over us; or from his promises and displayed bounty, mercy, goodness, patience, long-suffering, and forbearance towards his sinful creatures; or, on the other hand, by arguments taken from his justice, threatenings, and utmost severity, when provoked by the incorrigible and impenitent: which method of playing the orator, and using the art of persuasion to the best advantage in preaching, is what some think to be the most proper means, and sufficient to effect, with the concurrence and utmost endeavour of the creature, all that is required by God in the gospel, as necessary to salvation: but if we do but strictly attend to the holy scriptures, and from thence inform ourselves thoroughly concerning the present state and condition of a fallen, miserable, and helpless sinner, and the ancient way of evangelizing, we shall easily perceive this method not only deficient but culpable, and founded altogether upon an old mistake, i. e. that God, in the gospel, requires no more of man than he is able, if he will but put forth himself in an earnest and sincere manner, to perform: the contrary of which will, I trust, be sufficiently manifest throughout this work. But besides the grand mistake and error already mentioned in this method proposed to convert a sinner, as some manage it, it is still more criminal; and that is, when it is advanced against, and managed in a direct opposition to, and with reproaching of God's sovereign efficacious grace, and the invincible efficacy of his Spirit and power: and where it is not attended with such an evil design and tendency, it still is really weak and ineffectual, as to the grand attempt of converting a sinner, and persuading him into a living and justifying faith; forasmuch as it makes no provision, on man's part, to overcome the difficulties, nor to remove the obstructions which lie in the sinner's way; nor will it allow of an Almighty or invincible power, on God's part, to quicken and raise those that are spiritually dead, or effectually to cure the blind, deaf, and impotent. It indeed sets dead, impotent, and blind men to work, but removes none of those obstructions and hinderances which will certainly and effectually let, until, by a superior power, they are taken out of the way; as shall be declared in its place. The most then that the art of moral suasion, as used in the ministry, can effect, is only to reform the life, and adorn it with the outward appearances of virtue and religion; which our blessed Lord styles " washing the outside of the cup and platter," (Mat. xxiii. 25, 26, 27; and Luke xi. 39, 40) whilst the inside remains polluted and unclean. Thus Herod, upon hearing the doctrine of repentance and reformation preached up, and pressed home upon the auditory, by John the Baptist, " he observed him, and when he heard him, he did many things, and heard him gladly," Mark vi. 20. But all this, and much more of the same kind, falls exceeding short of conversion and saving faith: nor is it possible, for reasons hereafter to be assigned, that of itself it should, without the superaddition of the exceeding greatness of the Divine power: but notwithstanding this its real weakness in itself, I shall proceed to shew you, in the

Second place, that God doth, for the most part, make use of arguments and reasonings in the word and ministry; and oft points out and enforces the same, with promises of rewards, and threatenings of present and future punishments to " the neglecters of so great salvation," Heb. ii. 3; yet so, as that he always superadds the efficacious power of his Spirit and grace, to quicken and renew those souls, for whom he has had an eternal purpose of love and grace; by which power he effectually works in them both to will and do. And hence it is, that in the gospel part of the Old and New Testament, we so frequently meet with exhortations, invitations, expostulations, and arguments used with the chiefest of sinners, and these backed with suitable promises and encouragements: and also, on the other hand, there is an use made of counsel, admonition, and threatenings; yea, and of the sharpest reproofs, to such as are obstinate and rebellious. I do not say the gospel itself, strictly considered in its own nature, is compounded of these; no, it is nothing but the blessed news, and glad tidings of a salvation that is all of grace: these, then, are a sort of adjuncts, or necessary concomitants attending the ministry of the word, as it relates to some part of man's duty, who is always to be treated with as a reasonable creature, and not as a brute beast, or senseless machine. And therefore this way of reasoning, either with saints or sinners, is not to be discarded out of the ministry, nor slighted or turned to another meaning; though, if I might be allowed freedom of speech, I think few handle these so usefully and distinctly, as to keep themselves and others clear from Arminianism, in its notion of the creature's power and liberty of will to do all that is required of a sinner by the gospel-ministry; and though they may not design this, yet the ignorant and unskilful part of their auditory perceive no difference betwixt Calvinists and Arminians, when upon awakening and practical subjects. And I well remember, that when I was young, having learned the Assembly's Catechism, and read some Confessions of Faith, and the doctrinal Articles of the reformed Churches, with their arguments against Papists and Arminians, I used to be stumbled at Arminian discourses, from such who were accounted strict Calvinists. I call them Arminian Discourses; for it is not the throwing in a few words, by way of a parenthesis, that will mend the matter, nor sufficiently atone for an hour's practical discourse in the Arminian dialect, where the Spirit's work, both as to previous renovation, or continued influences and assistance, is not so much as mentioned, till just at last; and then only with this Arminian or Semi-pelagian close—' I know you cannot do these things of yourselves, unless God enable you; and therefore you must rely upon him, and earnestly beg the Divine assistance.' This then is what I say, that exhortations to duty, moral or religious, either to saints or sinners, enforced by proper arguments and reasonings are not to be discarded, but carefully and distinctly used; whilst still we, agreeably to scripture, maintain and defend the necessity of the DIVINE ENERGY, or the Holy Spirit's work of renovation, and efficacious grace: these things being not at all repugnant, but agreeable and consistent, as appears in these words of the apostle, "work out your own salvation with fear and trembling: for it is God which worketh in you both to will and to do of his good pleasure," Philip. ii. 12, 13. Agreeably to which, good St. Austin frequently prayed, "Lord, give what thou commandest, and command what thou wilt." And whoever will with diligence, and without prejudice, consider the scriptures, one with another, will find, that although there are exhortations, commands, and arguments, used to excite to this or the other duty; yet, besides these, there is a provision made, by way of covenant, for some; else what mean such promises on God's part as these? "The Lord thy God will circumcise thy heart, and the heart of thy seed, to love the Lord with all thy heart, and with all thy soul, that thou mayest live," Deut. xxx. 6. And again, "Then will I sprinkle clean water upon you, and ye shall be clean: from all your filthiness, and from all your idols will I cleanse you. A new heart also, and a new spirit will I give you, and I will take away the stony heart out of your flesh, and give you a heart of flesh. And I will put my spirit within you, and cause you to walk in my statutes, and ye shall keep my judgments and do them," Ezek. xxxvi. 25, 26, 27. And again, " This is the covenant that I will make with the house of Israel, after those days, saith the Lord ; I will put my law in their inward parts, and write it in their hearts, and I will be their God, and they shall be my people," Jer. xxxi. 33, and Heb. viii. 10. And again, " I will give them one heart, and one way, that they may fear me for ever. And I will make an everlasting covenant with them, that I will not turn away from them to do them good ; but I will put my fear in their hearts, that they shall not depart from me," Jer xxxii. 39, 40. These are some of those exceeding great and precious promises, by which we are made partakers of the Divine nature, 2 Pet. i. 4, as being absolute and free, and not clogged with any conditions, required of fallen, helpless creatures. Thus it appears plain from the word, that, together with exhortations and rational arguments, used in the ministry, God puts forth an exceeding greatness of his mighty power, in and upon the souls of his elect, in their effectual calling and conversion : but as to others, as I shall now shew, in the

Third place, God only affords them the external means and ministry, with many pressing arguments and exhortations; but not putting forth his exceeding great and efficacious power upon their hearts, to enlighten, renew, and turn them to himself, they still remain in the gall of bitterness, and bands of their own iniquities; and so they eternally perish. Therefore you hear him only reasoning with such, and exhorting them to duty, while, as to their parts, they wholly neglect and disregard the same. Thus, however, he calls; "Circumcise therefore the foreskin of your heart, and be no more stiff-necked: for the Lord your God is God of gods, and Lord of lords; a great God, a mighty, and a terrible, who respects not persons, nor taketh rewards," Deut. x. 16, 17: and yet the necessity of this heart-circumcision appears from what the apostles and prophets jointly teach; for, says Paul, "He is not a Jew who is one outwardly; neither is that circumcision, which is outward in the flesh: but he is a Jew, who is one inwardly; and circumcision is that of the heart, in the spirit, and not in the letter, whose praise is not of men, but of God," Rom. ii. 28, 29. Hence the Lord calls out by the prophet; "Thus saith the Lord to the men of Judah and Jerusalem, break up your fallow ground, and sow not among thorns: circumcise yourselves to the Lord, and take away the fore-skins of your hearts, ye men of Judah, and inhabitants of Jerusalem: lest my fury come forth like fire, and burn that none can quench it, because of the evil of your doings," Jer. iv. 3, 4. But these exhortations and reasonings being disregarded by them, and being also weak and ineffectual of themselves, they remained still in a state of uncircumcision and alienation; upon which he threatens them severely by the same prophet, saying; "Behold the days come, saith the Lord, that I will punish the circumcised with the uncircumcised; Egypt, Judah, Edom, and the children of Ammon, and Moab, and all that are in the utmost corners, that dwell in the wilderness; for all these nations are uncircumcised, and all the house of Israel are uncircumcised in the heart," Jer. ix. 25, 26. So again by another prophet he calls upon them; "Repent and turn yourselves from all your transgressions, so iniquity shall not be your ruin. Cast away from you all your transgressions whereby ye have transgressed, and make you a new heart and a new spirit; for why will ye die, O house of Israel? For I have no pleasure in the death of him that dieth, saith the Lord God: wherefore turn yourselves, and ye shall live," Ezek. xviii. 30, 31, 32. But forasmuch as by this ministry of the prophets, he only argued with them, and did not at the same time put forth the exceeding greatness of his power in and upon their hearts and wills, to sanctify, renew, and bow them effectually, they remained uncircumcised and rebellious, and so pined away in their iniquities. And that God doth not effectually work upon all, so as to cure their blindness and unbelief, while he affords them the outward means of conviction and faith, is manifest; for Moses declares to their faces, saying; "Ye have beheld all that the Lord did before your eyes in the land of Egypt—the great temptations which thine eyes have seen, the signs and those great miracles. Yet the Lord hath not given you an heart to perceive, and eyes to see, and ears to hear unto this day," Deut. xxix. 2, 3, 4. And now for lack of this omnipotent and efficacious power being put forth upon the heart, on God's part, all arguments and miracles prove ineffectual, and prevail nothing, as it is written, "But though he had done so many miracles before them, yet they believed not on him; that the saying of Esaias the prophet might be fulfilled, which he spake, Lord, who hath believed our report? And to whom hath the arm of the Lord been revealed? Therefore they could not believe, because that Esaias said again, he hath blinded their eyes, and hardened their heart; that they should not see with their eyes, nor understand with their heart, and be converted, and I should heal them. These things said Esaias, when he saw HIS glory and spake of HIM,"

John xii. 37, 38, 39, 40, 41. Thus then, although he calls out by the prophet, saying, "O Jerusalem, wash thine heart from wickedness, that thou mayest be saved: how long shall thy vain thoughts lodge within thee?" Jer. iv. 14; yet they remained filthy and unclean; and so will every soul, unless God perform upon them this new covenant promise, "I will sprinkle clean water upon you, and ye shall be clean; from all your idols and filthiness will I cleanse you: a new heart also will I give unto you, and a new spirit will I put within you, &c." Ezek. xxxvi. 25, 26. With much more of the like nature and importance, as I have already quoted at large under the second branch of this head. And to close this, I think it may be worth your notice to read and consider, what that good man Elihu, though young, has remarked to us upon this head, as to the different manner of God's procedure with persons laid under conviction by the means he then afforded them: and this to me makes the distinction the more remarkable, in that the story of Job is, by the most judicious, thought to be very antient, being, as some think, transacted and penned about the latter end of Israel's cruel bondage in Egypt; but be that as it will, Elihu, in his defence for God, describes the usual methods of Providence, in laying sinners under common convictions, in order to their being reclaimed and reformed from their wonted follies, saying; "and if they be bound in fetters, and holden fast in the cords of affliction: then he sheweth them their work, and their transgressions that they have exceeded. He openeth also their ear to discipline, and commandeth that they return from iniquity. If they obey and serve him, they shall spend their days in prosperity, and their years in pleasures; but if they obey not, they shall perish by the sword, and die without knowledge," Job xxxvi. 3, 9, 10. Thus in these he only awakens, jogs, and excites their natural conscience to perform its office, to which, if they hearken so as to obey, they shall reap a present benefit and advantage: as it is written, "If ye be willing and obedient, ye shall eat the good of the land: but if ye refuse and rebel, ye shall die by the sword," Iai. i. 19, 20: and after this old covenant method, did God long ago deal with Cain; "If thou doest well, shalt thou not be accepted? but if thou dost not well, sin lieth at the door," Gen. iv. 7; i. e. it is thine own fault, Cain, and thou must take what follows. But now, that this is not the only method that God takes with all, appears plainly by his new covenant-engagements to some, as has been already remarked; and also by another way, in which God not only awakens and commands, but also works efficaciously on their hearts, as Elihu suggests; " God speaks once, yea, twice, but man perceives it not," Job. xxxiii. 14, &c. That is, they do not so observe it further as to take the hint or watch-word, which is once and again given unto their natural and drowsy consciences; and yet God proceeded, having an eternal purpose of grace towards them, to open their ears, and to seal instruction to them, that so he may withdraw man from his purpose, and hide pride from him. He keepeth back his soul from the pit, and his life from perishing by the sword. And now if there be a messenger with him, an interpeter, one of a thousand, to shew unto man his uprightness; then he is gracious unto him, and saith, Deliver him from going down to the pit, I have found a ransom, &c. From whence, I think, it plainly appears, that God always did, and still doth something more than use arguments in the effectual conversion of an elect sinner. For surely to open the ear, and then to seal instruction, and to send a messenger, one of a thousand, thus to instruct him, is more than only to open the ear in a way of common awakenings and convictions, and nothing but command the man to return; and so leave the success wholly to depend upon a corrupt, depraved and evil-disposed will, as in the other instances given: even as it is more to circumcise the heart of a man, by taking away the stony heart, and giving a heart of flesh, than only to command him to do it, and let it rest upon the creature's hand. But leaving this to be more fully demonstrated under another head, I shall pass on to the

Fourth branch of this second head; and that is to shew, that God, upon man's neglect of duty, or contempt of gospel-grace and means, justly reproves, upbraids, and condemns the sinner for the same. Thus we find the Mediator and great Prophet raised up by God, under the character of Wisdom, calling and inviting a people to come under his gospel-ministry, and upon their neglect and disobedience, upbraiding and threatening them with the saddest calamities; "How long, ye simple ones, will ye love folly? and the scorners delight in their scornings, and fools hate knowledge? Turn ye at my reproof: behold I will pour out my Spirit unto you, I will make known my words unto you.—Because I have called and ye refused, I have stretched out my hand, and no man regarded; but ye have set at nought all my counsel, and would none of my reproof; I also will laugh at your calamity, and mock when your fear cometh: when your fear cometh as desolation, and your destruction as a whirlwind; when distress and anguish cometh upon you. Then they shall call upon me, but I will not answer; they shall seek me early, but they shall not find me: for that they hated knowledge, and did not chuse the fear of the Lord. They would none of my counsel; they despised all my reproof: therefore they shall eat of the fruit of their own way, and be filled with their own devices," Prov. i. 22, to the 31st. These things were indeed prophetic of the body of the Jewish nation's rejecting the true Messias, for which they were judicially given up to destruction and ruin: and though when besieged with the Roman armies, and almost perished through famine, they sacrificed, and called aloud for mercy; buoying themselves up with false hopes under a pious pretence of dying for the sanctuary, yet the Holy One never regarded them, but was deaf to their misery and distress: and upon them was fulfilled the prophecy of Esaias, as it is written; " To you it is given to know the mysteries of the kingdom of heaven, but to them it is not given : therefore spake I to them in parables; because they seeing, see not : and hearing, they hear not; neither do they understand: but in them is fulfilled the prophecy of Esaias, who saith, By hearing ye shall hear, and shall not understand, and seeing ye shall see, and shall not perceive: for this people's heart is waxed gross, and their ears are dull of hearing, and their eyes they have closed; lest at any time they should see with their eyes, and hear with their ears, and understand with their hearts, and be converted, and I should heal them," Matt. xiii. 11, 12, 13, 14, 15. Thus man's impotency, wilfulness, and impenitency appear; and though it is declared by Christ, that "none can come to him except it is given him from the Father," John vi. 44—65; and that some believed not, because they were none of his sheep, chap. x. 26; which were to be brought to the knowledge and owning of him, as the true Messias, and Son of God, their Saviour; yet he justly upbraids their neglect and unbelief, " Ye will not come to me, that ye might have life," chap. v. 40: and although " this stone, Christ, was set for the fall, and for the rising again of many in Israel," Luke xi. 34; forasmuch as himself declares, that "for judgment he was come into this world, that they that see not, might see, and that those who see, might be made blind," John ix. 39; yet he justly upbraids those cities in which most of his mighty works were done, because they believed not: "Wo unto thee, Chorazin! Wo unto thee, Bethsaida! for if the mighty works which were done in you, had been done in Tyre and Sidon, they would have repented long ago in sackcloth and ashes. And thou, Capernaum, which art, (as to privilege,) exalted unto heaven, shalt be brought down to hell: for if the mighty works done in thee, had been done in Sodom, it would have remained until this day," Matt. xi. 20, &c. And now, how it came to pass, that the one had no such warning, nor exalted privilege; and that among these who had, so many were left to themselves, having only the word ministered to them, but not attended with the exceeding greatness of the Divine power, to make it effectual and saving in the event, himself plainly declares, and confesses to the Father's glory; " I thank thee, O Father, Lord of heaven and earth, because thou hast hid these things from the wise and prudent, and hast revealed them unto babes. Even so, Father, for so it seemed good in thy sight. All things are delivered unto me of my Father: and no man knoweth the Son but the Father: neither knoweth any man the Father, save the Son, and he to whomsoever the Son will reveal him," Matt. xi. 25, 26. Thus from these and the like testimonies, it is plain, that the same ministry is made powerful and efficacious unto some; whereby it becomes " a savour of life unto life," 2 Cor. ii. 16; i.e. first of grace and then of glory; whereas to others it comes in word only, and not in power. Nor are we to imagine, that when God promises to give his people a clean and new heart, that he intends it only of his concurrence and assistance in their making it new and clean, according to the letter of his command. It is somewhat odd to think, that when David prayed to God, to 'create a clean heart, and to renew a right spirit within him;' he only desired God to assist him in the doing of it himself: but much more odd would it be to say, he prayed to God to do that for him, which he might, and must do of himself, without the concurrence of his Divine efficacy; who, in the prophet's language and confession, is thus addressed, "Lord, thou wilt ordain peace for us: for thou hast wrought all our works in us," Isai. xxvi. 12. And surely, when Ephraim, supplicating at the throne of grace, is brought in praying after this manner, " Turn thou me, and I shall be turned," Jer. xxxi. 18, he meant something more than this; Lord, thou hast bid me turn, and convert myself, and accordingly I will now, in sincerity and good-earnest, set about it. It seems to me, as if some professors and preachers had never sincerely, and in good-earnest, prayed for converting grace, or a new heart, either for themselves or others; or else they have a peculiar way of expressing their sincere desires, That God would, of his mere grace and by his Spirit, work that in them which they verily believe and affirm they can, and must do for themselves; either wholly, and exclusive of the exceeding greatness of his Almighty power, or else only through some common assistances: and let us take it either way, it is still the man himself that doth it; for whatsoever I do, though it be by the assistance of the Spirit and grace of God, yet it is

I that do it : as for instance, it is man who believes, repents, and obeys, God commanding; and so it is man that prays, and preaches, &c. and not God, nor the Spirit, that helps him : and yet all this, if real and spiritual, is done from, and by the aids and assistances of the Spirit and grace of God; who works in us both the will and ability to perform; even as he also assists in the performance itself. And yet, though it is proper speech, and sound divinity, to say, that David prayed and repented, it would sound harsh to a good Christian, and I fear offensive to the Divine Being, that any should say David circumcised his own heart, or that he renewed a right spirit within himself; for " who can say (in the presence of God and not lie) I have made my heart clean ?" Prov. xx. 9. And yet, if I mistake not, according to some men's divinity and teaching, it is man, as I said, either with or without God's assistance, that softens his own heart; and by taking away the heart of stone, makes himself a new heart and a right spirit : for if God only helps our sincere endeavours in conversion and faith, and in making ourselves a clean and new heart and right spirit, much after the same manner that he assists and blesses the " diligent hand," Prov. x. 4, to make its owner rich: or if so be he teaches man to perform all sorts of duties required in his word, only as he teaches the husbandman how to plough and sow, and by what proper instruments to thresh out his grain; then it is man that doth them, and not God. And which way these men take to exclude boasting, I cannot tell; unless it be that of the proud Pharisee; "I thank God I am not like other men, extortioners, unjust, adulterers, or even as this publican," Luke xviii. 11. Thus, indeed, many an old covetous miser has been heard to thank God, that though his friends did not leave him a groat to begin the world with, yet, through hard labour, good husbandry and industry, he had got aforehand; and then he, with modesty, adds, others might have had as much, and lived as well, who were now indigent, and relieved by friends, if they would have been as laborious and frugal as himself; and all this may indeed be true as to the instrumental, but not as to the SUPREME CAUSE of riches and poverty among some. But though these thank God for the present difference betwixt them and others; yet, it is no more than a common and customary compliment; for it was not God so much as man, that made both these to differ.

But this may suffice as to the nature of moral suasion and the utmost it can effect; as also that in conversion, God doth more than barely use arguments; for he puts forth power with the word, and works in us what he, as to the internal part, requires of us; yet so as that he leaves all those wholly without just excuse, who have either wilfully despised or neglected the gospel-means. That which now remains upon this head, is to shew you, in the

Fifth place, that there are such lets and hinderances, both within and without, that stand in the way of a sinner's conversion to God, as render it wholly impracticable and impossible, without the concurrence of his efficacious grace and omnipotence. And these may be considered under four general heads; 1st. Impotency, through a spiritual death, that has seized all mankind in the fall. 2ndly, Inbred enmity and rebellion, as seated in the heart and will. 3dly, The present reigning power, prevalency, and dominion of sin. 4thly, The fast hold, and firm possession that Satan has of every natural unregenerate man; together with his present reigning power in, and influence over the heart.

First of all, then, the scripture teaches us, that the state and condition of all mankind, as lying in the ruins of the fall of the first man Adam, is such, that they are not only guilty and vile before a just and holy God, both as to their persons, nature, and best performances, but also helpless and altogether unable to will and perform that which is good, until prevented, renewed, and enabled by the efficacy of the exceeding greatness of his Almighty power. And therefore this impotency and inability of fallen man is set forth in scripture by divers metaphors, which bear a very great resemblance and analogy thereunto; and hence more generally, we are said " To be weak and without strength, when Christ died for us," Rom. v. 5. Which weakness is intended of our inability to perform what the exact holy law of God, though broken, yet requires of all mankind, and of which it will make no abatements, notwithstanding man, as fallen, is become bankrupt and a poor helpless creature. Satisfaction in a way to justice for past offences, and an internal conformity, as well as perfect obedience to all its precepts, it must and will have, either from the sinner or his surety, or he is undone for ever. Hence, says the apostle, " What the law could not do in that it was weak through the flesh, God sending his own Son in the likeness of sinful flesh, and for sin condemned sin in the flesh," Rom. viii. 3. And though the first thing that the apostle here had in his eye was, that we were weak and without strength, as to duty, in keeping the whole law perfectly and constantly to our lives end; yet this is not all; but we are insufficient as to the performance of any part thereof; forasmuch as speaking of himself he saith, " I know that in me, that is in my flesh, (or unregenerate part,) there dwells no good thing," chap. vii. 18; and he further adds, "That we are not sufficient as of ourselves to think a good thought, but our sufficiency is of God," 2 Cor. iii. 5. There is therefore a great mistake, as to the point now in hand, among professors: most men imagine, and some in plain words affirm, that man's case considered as now under the gospel, is but like a man in prison or slavery, who might be set at liberty if he would; and as for the rigorous exactions of a perfect obedience demanded by the law, as a first covenant of works, these, say they, are entirely put to an end by Christ, for all those who will come up to the terms or conditions of the gospel, or new law; requiring repentance, faith, love, perseverance in holiness, and new obedience; as if these were such easy things to be performed by man in his lapsed, disabled state, before regeneration and spiritual union with Christ, as a living head and root; whereas in truth, though man, while in a natural state, is in some respects like a slave, or man in close confinement, yet it is with this difference, the slave in chains, and the man confined in prison, would gladly get out if they could, and had but opportunity; but as for fallen degenerate man, he wants both will and strength. He hath no heart, nor inclination to this true and spiritual liberty; but on the other hand, an aversion and backwardness to all good prevails; keeping him in the love and service of sin, and under its dominion and power. And as for these supposed milder terms of the new law, he has neither will nor power, in a dead, unregenerate state, to perform any. It is not with man as with the traveller who hath lost his way, or is benighted, who only stands in need of light and direction, or a skilful guide; nor is his case like that of a strong, lusty, healthful servant, who hath a capacity, both as to strength and ingenuity, but is slothful, and will not exert himself according to his ability, by a strict and industrious application to his master's business: but on the other hand, scripture and experience witness, that the state and condition of a sinner, till quickened and renewed by grace, is like that of the man in the parable, " that fell among thieves, who robbed, stript, and wounded him; and departed, leaving him half dead upon the road," Luke x. 30; where he had most certainly perished, if he had not received mercy and beneficence from another hand. Just so must the poor and miserable sinner be prevented by a special act of grace and mercy from the Lord Jesus, as the physician of souls; for as for ability and will, he has none; and moral suasion is but of little use to such a dead or disabled soul; since all it can say and do amounts to no more than a dead and helpless exhortation: as if one coming to a person in the aforesaid condition, should say to him, ' Come, man, why dost lie thus? endeavour to get up, and go about your immediate work and business: do not lie here to be starved with cold and hunger; rise up, do your best, and God will assist you.' This is the import and genuine language of moral suasion, and as far as it can go; and yet this is the helpless, lifeless way of preaching and reasoning now in vogue with our high and mighty rationalists, and doctors of free-will: and I heartily wish it were not to be found among some others, who profess to know better, and to have experienced something more than those who set themselves to oppose the Spirit's efficacious and invincible work upon the soul in regeneration; without which, their lifeless motives and spiritless exhortations and offers are as ineffectual as the prophet's staff in Gehazi's hand: for spiritual gospel-duties, and moral duties too, require more ability and skill than most men seem to be aware of: forasmuch as all mankind sustained such a loss in the fall of Adam, and received such a deadly blow and mortal wound, in a moral and Scripture sense, as can never be made up to them but by the gift of grace and righteousness through Christ Jesus; together with the Spirit of life and strength, communicated from him, as the second Adam, and new covenant-head, in such a manner as to quicken their souls and renew their hearts; thereby working in them a principle to will, and also an ability suited for the performance of all sorts of duties, whether moral or evangelical. Thus man must first have a soul physician to heal his wounds, and recover his lost strength, before he is fit for Gospel-service. 'He, like the bed-ridden servant,' as * Mr. Walter Marshal well expresses it, ' must first know how he may be enabled to go about his master's business: for, as he adds, men shew themselves strangely forgetful, or hypocritical, in professing original sin, in their prayers, catechisms, and confessions of faith, while they urge upon themselves and others the practice of the law, without the consideration of any strengthening and enabling means; as if there was no want of ability, but only of activity. And thus, adds he, the inquiry of most, when they begin to have a sense of religion is, ' What good thing shall I do, that I may inherit eternal life?' Not, how shall I be enabled to do any thing that is good? Yea, many that are accounted powerful preachers, spend all their zeal in the earnest pressing the immediate practice of the law, without any discovery of the effectual means of performance.'

And now, if the performance of moral duties re-

* Gospel-mystery of Sanctification, pages 6, 7.

quire an ability beyond what is to be found in a fallen creature, before he is quickened and regenerate, much more do the spiritual gospel duties of faith, love, mortification, and new obedience, require a superior power and skill to perform them, in a right and acceptable manner. And sure I am, that moral suasion may much sooner and easier cure all the lunatics or distempered heads in Bedlam, than it can quicken and convert one dead sinner. Hence it is, that in scripture, the recovery of a fallen creature into a state of grace and spiritual life, is set forth by a new birth, a resurrection, and new creation; all and every of which, are as far out of the power of moral suasion, as the heavens are above the earth. And sooner might a well-composed piece of oratory have raised the dry bones in Ezekiel's vision, than arguments, without the the super-addition of the exceeding greatness of the Divine Power, can quicken and convert a company of helpless, listless, dead sinners.

The state of every elect sinner, when God first begins in a gracious manner to work upon him, and manifest himself to him, may very well be resembled to that of the new-born infant lying in the open field, as you may read and consider at your leisure, in the 16th of Ezekiel; it being the true state and real condition of the New Testament church, as well as of the Old: and had he who was said to pass by that way, only said 'live,' by way of moral suasion or argument, and not in a way of gracious efficacy and power, they had perished every soul of them; even as the infant in the parable had certainly died upon the spot, if he who made, and brought the provision near, had not also applied it to that helpless and almost expiring object with his own hand: the bringing it water, food, and raiment, had nothing availed, without one to perform the necessary offices and assistances requisite to make them effectual. And let proud man boast never so much of his pretended natural ability and free-will, he stands in as much need of the gracious, powerful, and efficacious work of the Holy Spirit, as he did of a Saviour to die for him; till which time, of making him willing in the day of Christ's power, all his pretended power and freedom of will, will only be employed in opposing and resisting the only effectual means: for till then, every unregenerate and unconverted man wants both will and power to do any thing truly and spiritually good, either as the law or gospel requires: and sure we are, both from scripture and experience, that in the flesh-part, or unregenerate state, there dwelleth nothing good; that is, there is nothing truly so in God's account; nor yet in the account of the truly spiritual and experienced. But besides this moral impotence and spiritual death that have seized the souls of all mankind, and are such effectual lets and hinderances as moral suasion can never conquer nor remove, there is a

Second and far greater obstacle in the way of a sinner's true and saving conversion.; and that is, an inbred enmity and principle of rebellion, seated in the will; by which he is carried forth with a propensity to evil, and hatred to good : nay, this principle of enmity so far prevails as to carry the unregenerate in a headstrong manner, into acts of open rebellion ; so that *by* their actions, if not in words, they say, " we are lords, we will come no more unto thee," Jer. ii. 31. Or like the Jews concerning Jesus of Nazareth, " We will not have this man to reign over us," Luke xix. 14. And now, that I may set this in a full light, I will first shew you from scripture evidence, that there is such an inbred enmity and contrariety seated in the hearts and wills of all mankind, considered as descendants of the first Adam, and under the influence and prevalency of the fall. And 2dly, that this inbred and prevailing enmity, which is the sin that dwelleth in us, is too potent and prevalent to be mastered and removed by moral arguments, though accompanied with the greatest resolutions and utmost endeavours of a fallen creature: for it is not subject to the law of God; neither indeed can be. The

1st, Scripture-arguments and evidence that I shall produce upon this head shall be that of the apostle. "But the natural man receiveth not the things of the Spirit of God: for they are foolishness unto him; neither can he know them, because they are spiritually discerned," 1 Cor. ii. 14. In which words of the Holy Spirit, there appear to be two manifest lets and hinderances, in every natural man's way, which obstruct and hinder him from discerning and receiving the things of the Spirit of God: the first is incapacity; he cannot know them, because they are spiritually discerned; whereas he, while in a natural state, wants a suitable organ, i. e. the spiritual eye, or enlightened understanding and judgment, whereby he might perceive and make a right judgment concerning their spiritual excellency and use. 2dly, They are foolishness unto him, i. e. in his account and esteem of them: therefore he will not receive them: for that he looks upon them, however they stand recommended by some, to be weak, foolish, and absurd; nay, so far is he from approving and receiving them, that he rejects and explodes them with the utmost scorn and contempt, as unintelligible, inexplicable, and repugnant to reason. They are unsavoury to his palate; for so much the word imports; and hence it is, that the things of the Spirit of God (i. e. the mysteries, provisions and doctrines of free grace, together with the necessary efficacious operations of grace in the Spirit's hand, to make all this new covenant-provision effectual to God's elect) are esteemed by the natural man as strange things; and this way of evangelizing is accounted foolish and weak: and nothing offends him more than to tell him that the foolishness of God is wiser than men; and the weakness of God is stronger than men: and that God hath chosen the foolish things of the world to confound the wise; and the weak things of the world to confound the things which are mighty; and the base things of the world, and things which are despised, hath God chosen, yea, and things which are not, to bring to nought things that are: that no flesh should glory in his presence, 1 Cor. i. 27, 28, 29. From whence it appears plain, that God has made natural men's wisdom to be foolishness: so that they are as much out in their theology, as those were in their morals and politics, of whom the prophet speaks, "Wo unto them that call evil good, and good evil; that put bitter for sweet, and sweet for bitter. Wo unto them that are wise in their own eyes, and prudent in their own sight." Isai. v. 20, 21.

But now, the great question upon this text is,

Who this natural man is, and how he may be known? In order therefore to set him in a proper light, I will first shew you how he may be known and easily discerned by a spiritual man. Secondly, I shall give you his character and description, in the words of some of the learned and judicious.

First of all, then, we are to remark from the context, that the natural man here stands distinguished and opposed to the spiritual, as in the following verse: "But he that is spiritual judgeth all things, yet he himself is judged of no man;" that is, none but the truly spiritual, who are enlightened by the Spirit, can discern and make a true judgment of the things that are spiritual; nor is the spiritual man himself any more known, nor discernible by the natural man, than the things of God are; they being both of a divine and heavenly extract or original; as it is written, "Therefore the world knows us not, because it knew not him," 1 John iii. 1. This spiritual man is one who is born of God: born from above. All things are become new to him, and in him, chap. iii. 9. He is one "who is born, not of blood, nor of the will of the flesh, nor of the will of man, but of God," John i. 13. And as the spiritual man is one who is regenerated, and renewed by the workmanship of the Holy Spirit, so he is also possessed of the Spirit as his teacher and guide: that is, he is not only one who hath an understanding given to him, that he may know him that is true, but he is possessed of the Holy Spirit, in such a manner as the world can neither know nor receive him; as it is written, "Now we have received, not the Spirit, which is of the world, but the Spirit which is of God; that we might know the things that are freely given to us of God. Which things also we speak, not in the words which man's wisdom teacheth, but which the Holy Spirit teacheth; comparing spiritual things with spiritual," 1 Cor. ii. 12, 13. And this is agreeable to that glorious promise of our blessed Lord to all his, as the fruit and benefit of his death, resurrection, ascension and intercession. "And I will pray the Father, and he shall give you another Comforter, that he may abide with you for ever; even the Spirit of Truth, whom the world cannot receive, because it seeth him not, neither knoweth him: but ye know him, for he dwelleth with you, and shall be in you," John xiv. 16, 17. Thus the elect at conversion receive the Spirit, not only as the Spirit of grace and supplication, but also as the Spirit of wisdom and revelation in the knowledge of God and of Christ, and the things of the Spirit of God; as it is written of such spiritual Christians and true believers: "But ye have an *unction* from the Holy One, and ye know all things. I have not written unto you, because ye know not the truth : but because ye know it, and (ye know) that no lie is of the truth. These things I have written concerning them that seduce you. But the anointing which ye have received of him, (abideth) in you: and ye need not that any man teach you, (i. e. any new doctrine or article of faith which ye have not received) but as the same anointing teacheth you all things, and is true, and is no lie : and even as it hath taught you, ye shall abide in him," 1 John ii. 20, 21,—26, 27. And now, this being some part of the Scripture-account and character of the spiritual man, it is easy from hence, to discern who the natural man is; forasmuch as he is the very reverse of the spiritual, or at least he is one who is destitute of the characters which come into the true and exact definition of him who is truly spiritual. The natural man then is every one, man or woman, in their natural, unregenerate, or unrenewed state. He is one who has nothing but nature, and natural endowments and attainments. He is one who is possessed and influenced by the spirit of the world, and is full of the wisdom of this world ; big with arts and human sciences, but really destitute of the Spirit of God ; and so Jude describes them, Sensual, (ψυχικοὶ, i. e. natural or animal men) not having the Spirit. Whence they are as much beneath the least saint, as gracious and spiritual, **in God's account, as the brute or** animal is beneath a rational being; yea, there is as vast a disproportion betwixt the spiritual and natural man, in the scripture's-account and esteem, as there is between the first and second Adam, according to those words of the apostle; "The first man Adam was made a living soul, the last man Adam, i. e. Christ, was made a quickening Spirit. Howbeit, that, or HE, was not first that was spiritual, but that which was natural, and afterwards that which was spiritual. The first man is of the earth, earthy: the second man is the Lord from heaven. As is the earthy, such are they also that are earthy: and as is the heavenly, such are they also that are heavenly," 1 Cor. xv. 45, 46, 47, 48. Thus having given you the scripture-definition of the spiritual and natural man, I shall proceed,

Secondly, to give you the judgment of some of the learned and judicious, concerning this natural man, who as such neither can nor will receive the things of the Spirit of God, because they are foolishness to him. And the first shall be that of Dr. Whitby, on the place:—' The natural man here, says he, is one who acteth only by the principles of human reason and of worldly wisdom—who rejects revelation, and admits of no higher principle to judge of things by but philosophy and demonstration from the principles of natural reason.—The natural man is the same with the wise man, the disputer, the philosopher, the Greek.—He counts the things of the Spirit of God foolishness when propounded to him, because he doth not see them proved from principles of natural reason, by philosophical deductions, which is the wisdom he seeks after.' Now though that this is not a full account and description of the natural man, yet it is just and true, as to the drift and scope of the text. To which I will next add that of Mr. Samuel Clark, on the place:—' The natural man is the unregenerated person; one that has nothing but what he derives from the first Adam, viz. a principle of reason, though he be one of the most exquisite natural accomplishments, and has improved his reason to the highest pitch.—He has not ability, for want of a spiritual principle, to understand them spiritually, according to the nature of the things, and so to form a right judgment of them, no more than a blind man can see the sun: they being apprehended and judged of only by ability derived from the Spirit of God.' Now put both these definitions of the natural man together, and you have a true and full account of him. Yet I will proceed to add some others upon this place. Mr. Burkitt describes him thus:—' The animal man is one, who acts only by principles of human reason and worldly wisdom; who, though well furnished with intellectual and moral improvements, is yet destitute of the enlightening of the Spirit and the renewing grace of God.—Natural reason, by what helps soever assisted and improved, is altogether insufficient, without spiritual illumination, to apprehend supernatural and evangelical truth; not but that (as he well adds) the Spirit of God in the work of illumination and conversion makes use of our reason. Christianity doth not command us to throw away our reason, but to subjugate it; not to deny or disown our reason, but to captivate it to the obedience of faith; but the sense of the apostle, (adds he,) is, that a person of the most exquisite natural accomplishments, and one that has improved his reason to the highest pitch, cannot behold evangelical mysteries in their proper light, or embrace them in their verity and beauty, without the superadded aids and assistances of the Holy Spirit.' And agreeable to these is that of the great and judicious Dr. Owen upon this place;* 'Every man, says he, who hath no more than what is traduced from the first Adam is called ψυχικὸς; he is a living soul, as was the first Adam. The person therefore here spoken of is one that hath all that is, or can be derived from the first Adam; one endowed with a rational soul; and who hath the use and exercise of all his rational faculties.' But that

* Treatise of the Spirit, lib. 3. chap. 3. fol. 217, 218, 227.

which the Doctor afterwards quotes from St. Chrysostome, is yet more full, and to my purpose, which he renders into English thus:—' The natural man is he who ascribes all things to the power of the reasonings of the mind, and doth not think that he stands in need of aid from above; which is madness: for God hath given the soul that it should learn and receive what he bestows, or what is from him, and not suppose that it is sufficient of itself, or to itself. Eyes are beautiful and profitable; but if they would see without light, this beauty and power will not profit, but hurt them. And so the mind if it would see without the Spirit of God, it doth but ensnare itself.' Again, saith he, ' The natural man is he who lives in or by the flesh, and hath not his mind as yet enlightened by the Spirit; but only hath that bred human understanding which the Creator hath endued the minds of all men withal. The spiritual man is he who liveth by the Spirit, having his mind enlightened by him; having not only an inbred human understanding, but rather a spiritual understanding bestowed on him graciously; which the Holy Spirit endues the minds of believers withal.'

Thus it appears plain from the evidence of holy writ, and the concurring judgments of several of the learned and judicious, that the natural man in this text is intended of man as in his natural and unrenewed state, yet dressed up with all the advantages of nature and art; who thereupon is styled the wise, the scribe, and the disputer of this world: but these being altogether destitute of the Holy Spirit, both as a sanctifier and guide, God himself has declared in his word, that their wisdom and science is foolishness in his esteem. And now, as these are they to whom, for the most part, the things of the Spirit of God are of small account and esteem, so they are for a religion like themselves, i. e. all nature, and nothing else. These ascribe all the success of the word upon the hearts and lives of men in illumination, conversion and faith, to the power and efficacy of moral suasion upon the mind of him that sincerely endeavours to improve his natural reason and freedom of will; accounting it ignorance and enthusiasm to ascribe the success and effect of the gospel in conversion to the internal efficacy of Divine power, working in a supreme sovereign manner upon the hearts of men.

These, also, are for a religion without any mystery, but what a natural philosopher without the Spirit may explicate and comprehend; nor will these admit that any other power attends the gospel ministration, except that which is common to all, and may be resisted or complied with by a fallen creature, at his will and pleasure; nor are they for any other righteousness or obedience, as necessary for a sinner's justification before God, than that of sincerity; which a rational creature may and must perform for himself. These then are the natural men in the text, who would philosophize and reason us out of the doctrines of sovereign efficacious grace, and the necessity of the DIVINE ENERGY, in quickening and converting a sinner, dead in trespasses and sins. And the reason why these will not receive the things of the Spirit of God, is, because they are foolishness to them, and things of which they can form no true spiritual judgment; as it is said in the text—" Neither can he know them, because they are spiritually discerned:" and this, if there were no other, would of itself prove such a let and obstacle in the way of this man's faith and conversion, as moral suasion without Divine power could never overcome, and effectually remove. But there is still a

Second scripture-evidence, that moral suasion cannot convert a sinner to God, because of the inbred and deep-rooted enmity which is in the heart, and that principle of rebellion, which is in the will of every natural man and woman born into the world, in the ordinary way of generation: as is witnessed by this text; " The carnal mind is enmity against God: for it is not subject to the law of God; neither indeed can be," Rom. viii. 7. And would you know who the carnal minded man is? I answer, it is not to be interpreted of the sensualist or debauchee only, though it is eminently true of these, but it is the real state of all men; that is, it is not one, or two, or the generality of unconverted men whose minds are carnal, and filled up with enmity against God, and all that is truly and spiritually good, but it is the condition and disposition of all men by nature, till renewed by grace: and this appears from the argument which runs through several verses together, from verse the 5th; "for they that are after the flesh, do mind the things of the flesh: but they that are after the Spirit, do mind the things of the Spirit. For to be carnally minded, is death; but to be spiritually minded, is life and peace. Because the carnal mind is enmity against God: for it is not subject to the law of God; neither indeed can be. So then they that are in the flesh, cannot please God. But ye are not in the flesh, but in the Spirit, if so be the Spirit of God dwell in you. Now if any man have not the Spirit of Christ, he is none of his." In which it is evident, that to be after the flesh, is to be in a state of nature, and to be after the Spirit, is to be in a spiritual state: which spiritual state is a state of life and peace; whereas the fleshly state is a state of death and condemnation. In which state, says our apostle, it is impossible to please God. But, says he, you are not in the flesh, i. e. in the natural, carnal, fleshly state, but in a spiritual state, if so be the Spirit of God dwell in you; intimating they were so once, though now the case was altered: and in another place he speaks of this as being once the case of himself and others; " for when we were in the flesh, the motions of sins which were by the law, did work in our members, to bring forth fruit unto death," Rom. vii. 5. And thus all mankind are either born after the flesh, or after the Spirit. And accordingly, as our Lord testifies to Nicodemus, " That which is born of the flesh, is flesh: that which is born of the Spirit, is spirit," John iii. 6. In neither of which places is flesh to be taken for a loose, carnal, profligate, vicious life, but for the natural state and condition of all mankind, as proceeding from degenerate Adam, until they are renewed by grace, through the energy, and indwelling presence of the Spirit of Jesus: for he that has not the Spirit of God and Christ, so as to be born of God, is none of Christ's spiritual members. And now of all these natural men and women, who are born after the flesh, it is said, that their carnal mind is enmity against God: and that it is not subject to the law of God; neither indeed can be. That is to say, it stands at the greatest distance from God; as being contrary to, and being at enmity against his holy, righteous will: and this enmity, as an inbred principle, is full of vigour and activity, by which means hatred and rebellion are stirred up within, and work strongly, thereby alienating the affections from God: and hence it is that the apostle, when he is describing the degenerate, apostate state of lapsed, rational beings, throws this, among the rest, into their character, that they are "haters of God, proud, boasters, and inventors of evil things," Rom. i. 30. And as the carnal mind is enmity against the law of God, as pure and spiritual, so it is at enmity with the pure gospel, as it is a doctrine of free, sovereign, efficacious grace, in the hand of the eternal Spirit; who in his eternal, regenerating and quickening influences upon the hearts and souls of God's elect in effectual calling, is compared by our Lord himself, to the wind, which bloweth powerfully, and invincibly, when, and where it listeth; and is not subject to man's command or controul.

This is the doctrine and preaching that the carnal mind cannot bear, but rises up against, and daily encounters it, with all the zeal and argument that it is master of. Thus his affection and carriage towards the pure gospel, is much of a piece with that evil carriage of wicked, proud Ahab towards that faithful servant and prophet of the Lord, who would not temporize, nor flatter his prince in sin and delusion, "There is (says he to Jehoshaphat) one Micaiah by whom we may inquire of the Lord; but I hate him, for he doth not prophesy good concerning me, but evil," 1 Kings xxii. 8. Even thus the carnal mind hates the pure, spiritual law, and gospel too, because neither of them will flatter him; but on the other hand, like the true prophet of the Lord, they both speak evil, as he interprets it, of his present condition, and best performances, while in the flesh, or unregenerate state: in which state he cannot please God. As for the just and holy law of God, this curses him; for that his services are not perfect and exact, according to its requirements; for it is written, " cursed is every one who continueth not in all things written in the book of the law to do them," Gal. iii. 10. And the gospel, as it is the ministration of the gift of life and righteousness, committed to the Holy Spirit, to make the same effectual for the saving of all God's chosen ones, this blows upon, and withers his best performances, and stains all his pride and glorying in the flesh; as it is written, " All flesh is grass, and all the goodliness thereof, (כל חסדו, Col-khasdo, i. e. all its piety, virtue, charity, holiness and goodness; which are the glory of man, as the Septuagint renders it; even this glory and beauty of the creature) is as the flower of the field. The grass withereth, the flower fadeth;

because the Spirit of the Lord bloweth upon it: surely the people is grass," Isai. xl. 6, 7. Nay, the gospel proceeds further, and pronounces all the creature's righteousnesses, or best doings and performances, to be but as filthy rags, loss, dross, dung, and unprofitable. Thus the gospel, as being mighty through God, is ordained to pull down strong holds, and to cast down vain imaginations, or carnal reasonings; in order to bring every disobedient thought into obedience, and subjection to Christ; according as it was long since foretold in those words of the prophet, which for emphasis and certainty are twice recorded: "The lofty looks of man shall be humbled, and the haughtiness of men shall be bowed down: and the Lord alone shall be exalted in that day," Isai. ii. 11—17. Hence it is, therefore, that the carnal mind in the natural and unregenerate man cannot well brook the preaching of the pure unmixed gospel, no more than the spirituality of the holy law; and thus both of them serve occasionally to stir up, awaken and excite this inbred principle of enmity and rebellion, into an opposition to these things; as may be further demonstrated from a third scripture-evidence, which says that " the flesh lusteth against the Spirit; and the Spirit against the flesh; and these are contrary (or opposite) the one to the other; so that ye cannot do the things that ye would, "

Gal. v. 17. And though this text speaks of a believer, or converted person in whom only there are these two contrary principles and combatants, the flesh and Spirit, which are opposites and enemies to each other; and, like antipathies in nature, cannot possibly be made friends, so as to dwell at quiet in the same soul; yet, nevertheless, it doth also as fully evidence and confirm the matter in hand; which is, that in every unregenerate person there is a powerful and prevailing principle of contrariety, enmity and rebellion against the grace of God, and all that is good; so that if the gracious soul and spiritual minded man cannot do the things which he should, and would do, much less the unregenerate soul, while in its natural state, and destitute of God's grace and Holy Spirit, make any effectual stand against its power and prevalency: for if it is too strong for grace, it will be much more so for nature, as fallen and depraved; in whom, as St. James says, "There is a spirit that lusteth to envy." Which evil disposition and vigorous spirit, or law of sin, will prevail, and be too strong for the best inclinations and firmest resolutions of him who has nothing but his own power wherewith to engage against it.

Thus having, from the concurring evidence of divers scriptures, laid open the nature and prevalency of this second let and hinderance which lies in the sinner's way, and obstructs his converting himself to God, by the influence and effiacy of moral suasion, and the improvements of his reason and free-will, I shall proceed to the

Second thing proposed, and that was to shew you, that the inbred perverseness, enmity and contrariety which powerfully prevail in the souls of the unregenerate, are too powerful and prevalent to be mastered and removed by moral arguments. And this shall be demonstrated by some particular instances out of the word : and first of all, we will begin with the conduct of the whole world under the premonitions which were given them by Noah, the preacher of moral righteousness and justice to that world of ungodly sinners. How he found them, you may read in the 6th of Genesis, but more particularly in the 5th verse, where it is said, ' That God saw that the wickedness of man was great in the earth, and that every imagination of the thoughts of his heart was only evil continually.' Upon which God resolves upon an universal deluge, and gives orders to Noah to do two things, viz. first, to give warning to the world, and next to prepare an ark of safety for himself and family : both which he performed, and thereby condemned the world, and saved himself and his from perishing by the flood. That Noah was a preacher of righteousness, i. e. morality and justice, to the world, and that for 120 years, we are well assured from out of the Old and New Testament. How he succeeded, the event declares; which is also more particularly set forth in those words of Peter, in his premonition given to his countrymen, the Jews, just before the sad destruction of their temple, worship, city and constitution, both as to church and state, in which he tells them, "that God spared not the old world, but saved Noah, the eighth person, a preacher of righteousness, bringing in the flood upon the world of the ungodly." 2 Pet. ii. 5. And that they eternally perished, is also evident, I think, from what he saith, where he calls them, " the spirits in prison : which some time ago were disobedient, when once the long-suffering of God waited in the days of Noah, while the ark was preparing," 1 Pet. iii. 19, 20.

Thus then it appears plain, that as he found them so he left them; unpersuadable, disobedient, unbelieving, and impenitent. Now here was moral suasion used by God's appointment, but it had no saving effect upon them; for, like those spoken of by the prophet, "They refused to hearken, and pulled away their shoulder, and stopped their ears, that they should not hear. Yea, they made their hearts as an adamant stone, lest they should hear the law," Zech. vii. 11, 12. And as it was with these, so it would be with all mankind, wherever either the law or gospel is preached, if God did not work effectually therewith, by putting forth the exceeding greatness of his power : thereby circumcising the heart, and bowing the will, so as to make them willing in the day of his power: for it is he only, that works both to will and to do of his own good pleasure, in whomsoever he pleases : whereas the old world being left to themselves, as having these warnings, and admonitions ministered as unto them in word only, and not in power, they rejected them as foolish and unreasonable; as if only the offspring of a sickly distempered brain, or the dotages of an old enthusiast. But suppose they had really believed that the message came from heaven, and would prove eventually true, though it might perhaps have startled and affrighted them for a while; yet unless it had been set home with power upon their hearts, this terror would have soon worn off, and they would have been, but like that fair spoken young man, who at his father's bidding, said, "I go, Sir, and went not."

And thus as Noah's ministry, which lay altogether in moral suasion, and preaching up the duties of morality, had no powerful and saving effect upon the old world; so neither did that judgment, though great and universal, make any alteration in the frame and temper of the heart Godward, in the succeeding generations, who came on after the flood, nor in those which follow, to this day: for mankind was immediately as corrupt as ever; and so it remains a truth to this day, "That every imagination of man's heart is evil from his youth." Forasmuch as now, sin succeeds in the place of the image and law of God, which was once drawn and engraven in man's heart, in legible characters, which, as a contrary law written there, becomes the active and leading principle in man's soul; as is elegantly set forth in those words of the prophet, " The sin of Judah is written with a pen of iron, and with the point of a diamond; it is graven upon the tables of their heart," Jer. xvii. 1. Therefore moral suasion can effect nothing, as to an internal gracious change, which consists in razing out this law of sin, and in softening and removing this heart of stone, by giving a new and clean heart, and right spirit; in which heart God is graciously pleased by his own finger, or Holy Spirit, to write his laws anew.

But the insufficiency of this human method to convert sinners is further manifested, as I shall endeavour to demonstrate, from a

Second instance, and that is given us in these words of the Psalmist; "the wicked are estranged from the womb, they go astray as soon as they are born, speaking lies. Their poison is like the poison of a serpent: they are like the deaf adder that stoppeth her ear; which will not hearken to the voice of the charmers, charming never so wisely," Psal. lviii. 3, 4, 5. Which words do most elegantly set forth the depravity, evil disposition, and perverseness of fallen man; together with the craft and conduct of the impenitent, from the womb to the grave; as arising from a law of sin, and spirit of enmity and rebellion which is brought into the world with them.

In which words several things are remarkable, and to our purpose; as, first, here is a straying principle and estrangedness from God, that comes into the world with us; "the wicked are estranged from the womb, they go astray as soon as they are born, speaking lies." Plainly and fully teaching us, that sin is an evil disease, and vicious disposition brought into the world with us, and that we begin to transgress betimes. Hence we are justly styled "transgressors from the womb," Isai. xlviii. 8. Nor need any, for the solution of this supposed difficulty, have recourse to that old metaphysical whimsey of Pythagoras, afterwards espoused by Origen, concerning the pre-existence and fall of human souls, before they were confined to, and imprisoned in their terrene bodies for punishment and probation; who will but content themselves with the account given in holy scripture, concerning the rectitude of the first man and woman when created, and the occasion and sad consequence of their eating the forbidden fruit. That God made Adam upright, and that we all sinned in him, so as that, by one man's disobedience all were made sinners, is a doctrine plainly and fully taught in the holy oracles. And from hence it is, that all are begotten, and conceived in sin, as David for himself complains, and bemoans before the Lord, in these words; "behold, I was shapen (or begotten) in iniquity, and in sin did my mother conceive me," Psal. li. 5. For as Job says, "who can bring a clean thing out of an unclean? not one," Job. xiv. 4, " How then (says another) can a man be justified with God? Or how can he be clean that is born of a woman?" chap. xxv. 4. And again, " what is man that he should be clean? and he which is born of a woman, that he should be righteous?" chap. xv. 14. And now this, and much of the like language, being plentiful in the holy scriptures, we need not doubt but what is here spoken of the nature of the wicked and impenitent, is also as true of all others, viz. that all mankind are by nature children of wrath, being alienated and estranged from God; and begin to go astray in their evil, depraved imaginations and affections, before they can speak: and we all know, that no sooner do children begin to speak, but they tell lies, and shew a depraved, perverse and rebellious disposition. But then, here is also a second thing worthy of our notice, and that is, the parallel between the wicked and impenitent, both as to the principle from whence they act, and the craft by which they manage themselves. As, first, in that the wicked are sinful, spiteful and mischievous, like the serpent, from an internal principle. Their poison is like the poison of a serpent. That is, it is con-natural, inbred, and hereditary; being at first communicated with their nature and existence. And now, that by poison here, as it is applied to the wicked, is meant original sin, and that vicious disposition, and promptness to transgress and rebel, which appear betimes in those who have the advantages of the best education and examples, I think none will doubt, except such who never knew the plague of their own hearts.

But the chiefest resemblance between the serpent's poison and this original concupiscence and enmity against the pure and holy law of God, that is found in these impersuadable ones is, that as it is this lurking poison in the serpent's head, which being quickened and spirited by the vital heat, animates and pricks them forward, so as to make them fierce, cruel, and mischievous; even thus, this inherent, moral poison, and deadly mischievous venom of sin in man's nature, not only depraves the faculties, and disorders them in their several offices and operations, but also fills them with an evil disposition, and then prompts them on, to commit all those various acts of wickedness and rebellion, of which the world is full. And how this inward lust and evil concupiscence allures, entices, and draws away the heart, is set forth in these words; "Every man is tempted, when he is drawn away of his own lust, and enticed. Then when lust hath conceived, it bringeth forth sin: and sin, when it is finished, bringeth forth death," James i. 14, 15. And that there is an exciting power in this lust or evil concupiscence, which spurs the affections and mind forwards, in the most eager desire and thirst after evil things, is by another apostle excellently set forth to be the case of all persons before they are renewed by grace; "For, (says he,) when we were in the flesh, the motions of sin which were by the law, did work in our members to bring forth fruit unto death," Rom. vii. 5.

Thus then it is further manifest from the word, that sin is not an accidental distemper, which is catched or communicated like as some evil diseases of the body are said to be; nor is actual sin first learned from bad examples, though these, no doubt, do much confirm it, and render reformation more difficult. And that childhood, youth, and old age, go astray, more from principle than example, our Lord declares in these words; "For from within, out of the heart of men, proceed evil thoughts, adulteries, fornications, murders, thefts, covetousness, wickedness, deceit, lasciviousness, an evil eye, blasphemy, pride, foolishness. All these evil things come from within, and defile the man," Mark vii. 21, 22, 23. But then there is still a

Second resemblance between the wicked or unpersuadable, and the serpent's kind, viz. "They are like the deaf adder that stoppeth her ear: which will not hearken to the voice of the charmers, charming never so wisely." This creature, here translated adder, is properly the asp, and so it is rendered in several places of the Old Testament, and by the Septuagint in this place. In the Hebrew its name is Pethen, which some think to be the serpent called Python, both which names come from a word which signifies to persuade; and are given to this kind of serpent by the figure Antiphrasis, by which words and names have always a reverse or contrary meaning: thus, because she most craftily stops her ears, so that it is impossible to charm her, by the most skilful in that art, she is therefore called by such names, as by the aforesaid figure is sufficiently intimated, that she of all creatures is the most impersuadable: and therefore is an exact resemblance of a carnal mind, and rebellious will. And hence the wicked, being like this deaf adder, in the New Testament are styled Apeitheis, i. e. unpersuadable and disobedient; because they remain in the state of unbelief and impenitency, let preachers say and do all they can; and furthermore,

Doth this creature stop her ear, and thereby so craftily manage herself, as that all the cunning of the charmer by the force of charms can never take, nor hold her? Why, even so the wicked and unpersuadable are quite out of the reach and power of moral suasion, and the most rational arguments, unless set home by HIM whose peculiar work it is "to open the ears of men, and seal their instruction." But we will now pass on to some other scripture instances of this kind, which also further manifest the weakness and insufficiency of moral suasion when alone. The prophet Ezekiel was sent to preach to the backsliding, degenerate house of Israel, God's professed church and people; and how he succeeded in his ministry you will quickly hear. How he found them you may read in his commission; "And he said unto me, Son of man, I send thee to the children of Israel, to a rebellious nation, that hath rebelled against me; they and their fathers have transgressed against me even to this very day. For they are impudent children, and stiff-hearted: I do send thee unto them, and thou shalt say unto them, Thus saith the LORD GOD. And they, whether they will hear, or whether they will forbear, for they are a rebellious house, yet shall know that there hath been a prophet among them," Ezek. ii. 3, 4, 5. Thus he found them; and how he succeeded you may perceive by the account which God gives of their carriage and demeanor towards him, in respect of duty. " Son of man, the children of thy people still are talking against thee by the walls, and in the doors of the houses, and speak one to another, every one to his brother, saying, Come, I pray you, and hear what is the word that cometh forth from the Lord. And they come unto thee as the people cometh, and they sit before thee as my people, and they hear thy words, but they will not do them: for with their mouth they shew much love, but their heart goeth after their covetousness. And lo, thou art unto them as a very lovely song of one that hath a pleasant voice, and can play well on an instrument: for they hear thy words, but they do them not," chap. xxxiii. 30, 31, 32.

This Ezekiel was a golden mouthed orator, whose ministry they attended with delight: because it pleased their ears, and suited with their genius and inclination; and this, as some think, will go a great way towards conversion, but yet, his soft and oily words, hard arguments, and solid, rational discourses made no lasting, or saving impressions upon their flinty hearts, and stubborn wills; though delivered with all the art and advantage that moral suasion can pretend to. Thus we still see the weakness of this human method to convert sinners. But to close this argument with one instance more; we find him, who " spake as never man did," making much the same complaint, when upon earth; " Whereunto (says he) shall I liken the men of this generation? They are like unto children sitting in the market-place, and calling to their fellows, saying, We have piped to you, but ye have not danced : we have mourned to you, but ye have not wept," Mat. xi. 16, 17. That is, neither the ministry of John the Baptist, whose doctrine called for humiliation, mourning and repentance, nor the Messiah's more gladsome doctrine of spiritual freedom and redemption, attended with the promise of life eternal in the world to come, had any saving efficacy or influence upon their hearts. Thus then, let who will be the minister, and let his message be never so good, and though delivered with an angel's skill and tongue, yet none will believe the report, to the saving of their souls, unless the arm of the Lord be revealed; i. e. is made bare, and exerted, to make way for it in the heart, and upon the will, so as to fix it there. Thus then, as to the second let and hinderance of a sinner's conversion, which moral suasion cannot remove, I shall now proceed to a

Third hinderance that will obstruct the sinner, and hinder his conversion, until removed out of the way by a superior power; and that is, the dominion of sin, in its reigning and prevailing power; as being seated in the heart, will, and affections of the unregenerate; by which means he is a bond slave to this indwelling evil. And now,

This dominion and prevailing power of sin in and over the sinner, is the effect of indwelling sin, as it is an active principle, and propensity to evil; which is continually working in the affections and will; having in it the nature of a spirit for vigour and activity, and the force of a law, in respect to its commanding and coercive power; I say coercive, for sin, or evil concupiscence within, is a sort of compelling law in the scripture-language; and the believer, to his sorrow, experiences it to be so, according to that of the apostle; " I find then a law, that when I would do good, evil is present with me. I see another law in my members, warring against the law of my mind, and bringing me into captivity to the law of sin, which is in my members," Rom. viii. 21—23. Thus inward lust not only tempts, but overcomes, and carries the soul captive; yea, the regenerated soul is often thus overpowered and borne away: how much more then are the unregenerate liable to be overcome, who have no will, nor spiritual ability to withstand.

and oppose it. In the regenerate, sin acts the part of an enemy, by waging war against grace, and oft makes sad havoc in their souls, though not without opposition and resistance on grace's part; in which the mind and will, as sanctified, stand it out to the last, so that the Christian is carried captive, as by force of arms; whereas in the unregenerate, it always commands as a master and lord, and allures after the manner of a lewd woman, and thereby insnares and overpowers both the will and affections, and enslaves the soul; so that the unregenerate man cannot say with the apostle, "That which I do, I allow not: for that I would I do not; but what I hate, that I do," Rom. vii. 15: it being, on the other hand, his greatest delight and pleasure "to fulfil the desires of the flesh, and of the mind." Thus he is sin's willing servant, yielding himself to it with all readiness, according to those words of the apostle, "Know ye not, that to whom ye yield yourselves servants to obey, his servants ye are whom ye obey; whether of sin unto death, or of obedience unto righteousness," Rom. vi. 16. And so says another text; "For of whatsoever a man is overcome, of the same is he brought into bondage," 2 Pet. ii. 19. Even as our blessed Lord saith to the unconverted Jews in his day, who pretended to be freemen, and not at all enslaved; "Verily, verily, I say unto you, whosoever committeth sin, (i. e. in his daily practice with delight) is the servant of sin," John viii. 35. Thus it appears, from scripture-evidence, that sin hath a reigning and prevailing power in, and over the souls of the unregenerate, while it is seated in the heart, will and affections; whereby it allures, and prevails to the enslaving the man to some one outward or inward lust: there are also lusts and desires, or habitual inclinations in the mind, as well as in the flesh, both which the natural man is daily seeking to fulfil. These lusts are of two sorts; some are peculiar to the body, i. e. gluttony, drunkenness, and corporeal pollutions; and some to the soul; either in its animal or intellectual powers: those peculiar to the animal functions of the soul, yet not wholly exclusive of the intellectual, are passion, anger, strife, inordinate affections, and evil concupiscence. Those sinful lusts which are seated in, and peculiar to the rational soul, and which reign and prevail in its more noble faculties, are such as these; pride, covetousness, envy, hatred, malice, rebellion, error, heresy, idolatry, blasphemy, and the like; These all are seated in the mind, as on a throne, and reign, and so far prevail over the whole man, as to hold him in subjection to sin and Satan. It is true they do not prevail at all times alike, nor are all persons addicted to the same sins: some are most addicted to one sin, and some to another: and it is likewise observable, that one sin is hated, while another is the darling; as for instance, a man given up to covetousness, does, as it were, naturally hate prodigality, drunkenness, and lewd women; there being a contrariety in these evils, so that if one prevails, the other must give place: not but that all sorts of sins and lusts subsist seminally in the corrupt nature of man, and so they may be said to be, where they never did so much as once appear; yea, and new sins, new vices, and new vanities break forth continually, as from a never-failing spring. And furthermore, it is to be noted, that where the lusts of the flesh and of the animal soul do not reign and prevail, yet there the lusts and desires suited to, and seated in the intellectual mind, are not extinguished by external reformation, and strict morality: for in these persons, while in a natural state, pride, self-love and self-righteousness, error, idolatry and unbelief, do all reign and prevail, to the holding their souls in a state of bondage to sin, and alienation from God; notwithstanding all the pretences of loving and serving of Him, and seeking his glory. Thus Paul, while a strict Pharisee, though he accounted himself blameless, as touching the righteousness of the law, yet he was at the same time the chiefest of sinners; as himself owns and declares, being, before his conversion, " a blasphemer, and a persecutor, and injurious." Who verily thought that he ought to punish and persecute those who met together to worship God contrary to their established church, and the orders of the Sanhedrin.

Thus the evil propensity in man's heart to sin, and the imaginations of the thoughts of his heart will be evil continually; and, like waters in a spring, they will not only bubble up, but make their way, and take their own course some way or other, according to that of the prophet, "All we like sheep have gone astray: we have turned every one to his *own* way," Isa. liii. 6. "Every one turned to *his* course, as the horse rusheth into the battle," Jer. viii. 6 : in which texts it is observable, as I have hinted already, that mankind do not all of them take the same way, nor run the same lengths in sin and open profaneness; but yet every man is a sinner, and a servant to sin, before conversion. There are, indeed, open sins, which go before to judgment, even to man's bar : and there are others, which man's law cannot, or will not take cognisance of; these will follow after, and meet the authors of them at God's tribunal. And there are, indeed, hidden secret sins, which get the mastery and dominion over the man; against which, every saint, with David, ought to watch and pray; "keep back thy servant also from presumptuous sins; let them not have dominion over me;

then shall I be upright, and I shall be innocent from the great transgression," Psal. xix. 13.

From the whole it appears plain that sin has founded a sort of an usurped dominion and lordship in man's soul; and so far reigns by some one or other beloved lust, or secret heart-sin, as that it holds him in subjection; being the sin that doth easily beset him.

And now, this being the state and condition of all mankind, from their childhood and youth, even to grey hairs and old age, the grand question now returns, and is again to be debated, i. e. whether moral suasion, as being accompanied with the creature's sincere resolution and utmost endeavour, be sufficient to break off this external and internal dominion and prevalency that sin has over a man's heart, will and affections, without the aids and assistances of God's efficacious grace and Spirit?

Where, by the way, pray observe, the query is not how far moral suasion and reason, if attended to, and accompanied with a sincere endeavour, may prevail, so as to begin and further a reformation of life in those who are wicked and openly profane. Though upon this head it might be queried, how such, of themselves, should first come at this sincere inclination, desire, and will, to amend and reform: and then, how far this reformation from evil, and doing of good, can extend itself, without any auxiliary helps of Divine grace and power from above: but we will not immediately attend this, but pursue the grand query, viz. Whether moral suasion and reason, if improved, can make or create a clean and new heart, and renew a right spirit within the sinner, by removing the stone out of the heart, and the iron sinew of obstinacy and rebellion out of the will? And yet, this must first be done, before the dominion and reigning power of sin in the soul can be destroyed. The heart, affections, and will of man, by nature, are viciously disposed, and strongly inclined to evil, and to that only, being filled with enmity, pride and rebellion against God; so that some secret or open sin, or sins, as you have heard, prevail over him, and hold him fast by the affections and mind. And will any say, and pretend to prove it by scripture, or some other unexceptionable instances, that fallen man may recover himself out of the bondage of sin and moral corruption, without the grace of God, and work of the Spirit upon his soul? Let the man come forth, or be produced, that can say, It is by moral suasion and the use of my own free will and creature power, and not by the grace of God, that I, being a saint and sound convert, am what I am. This would be such a bold stroke against God's efficacious grace, and the internal work of the Holy Spirit upon the heart in conversion, and in making a soul truly and spiritually free from sin's reigning power and dominion, as even James Arminius, that great and noted champion for free-will, would have been ashamed to have uttered: and yet, it necessarily follows, that if man can, and doth do these things of himself, there is no need, nor room for the Divine power to exert itself, to effect so great and universal a change, as must be in him who gets the mastery over his own internal lusts and vicious habits.

And here, by the way, seeing the power of a rational creature, and the freedom of man's will, are so mightily exalted in this our day, as if there were really no need of the exceeding greatness of God's power to convert a sinner, and to work in him both to will and to do of his own good pleasure, I will, for your information, who have never read what was Dr. Arminius's judgment upon this point, give you his opinion concerning free-will, as he delivered it, by a writing under his own hand, to the High and Mighty States of Holland, and West Friezeland, in these words; 'Touching man's will, (says he,) I am of opinion, that he was endowed with knowledge, holiness, and other abilities, by his creation, whereby he was able to understand, estimate, consider, will and perform true good; even as far as the commandment obliged him; yet, not this without the auxiliaries of Divine grace. In the state of apostacy and sin, he is disabled of himself, and by himself, to think, will, or do any thing truly good; and stands in need of the renovating and regenerating power of God in Christ by his Spirit in his intellect, affections, will, and all other faculties, to impower him hereunto; but participating hereof, as freed from sin, he is able to think, will and do good; yet still as under the supplies of the grace of God.'*

Oh noble declaration! Would to God that none in our day, who follow him close in other points, had degenerated and fallen beneath him in this.

Thus far then we have gained the question and matter in debate, and that from a reputed champion for the free-will cause, that moral suasion and man's endeavours are weak and insufficient of themselves to effect a saving change, without ' the renovating and regenerating power of God in Christ, by his Spirit in his intellect, affections, will and all other faculties, to impower him hereunto.' To which words of Arminius, I will join a greater and more authentic testimony borne to this truth, by Him who cannot lie, in these words; "If the Son, therefore, shall make you free, ye shall be free indeed," John viii. 36 : plainly enough intimating to them, that unless he, by his Spirit, wrought out

* See his book entitled, The Just Man's Defence; as translated into English, by Tobias Conyers, page 112, 113.

this part of their spiritual freedom and delivery from the power and dominion of their indwelling sin, which held them in present bondage and subjection, there was none else could do it effectually. Thus having laid open, and demonstrated sin's dominion, and reigning power in the soul, to be an effectual let and hinderance to conversion, too strong for moral suasion and a fallen creature's ability to overcome and remove I shall proceed to the

Fourth let and hinderance mentioned, and that is, ' the present hold, and prevailing influence that Satan, as the prince and god of this world, has over all mankind;' especially while in a state of spiritual death, and under the reigning power and dominion of sin. And this is such another effectual let and hinderance, that all the art of reasoning, and power of a fallen creature, can never effectually overcome; nor can it possibly be removed, except by the energy of his Almighty power, whose peculiar work it is, to bind the strong man, and divide the spoil with him, by an effectual recovery of his lost sheep from among the devil's herd.

And now, for the opening and evincing of this, I shall shew you, in three particulars, wherein this Satanic hold, possession, and influence, do consist; and that moral suasion and human power cannot dispossess this enemy, or make him surrender and give up his present hold and possession of the sinner's heart, that so it may become " an habitation of God through the Spirit." The first part of Satan's hold and possession of man's soul is that of a conqueror. The second is that of a prince, yea, of a god, who governs and reigns, and is after a sort worshipped. The third is that of an invisible diabolic spirit, that doth work in and upon the heart in a wonderful, powerful, secret and undiscerned manner; by which means he hath the greater advantage over mortals, especially where he dwells in the heart before regeneration; because there he will keep firm and full possession, in despite of all that reason and free-will can say and do.

First then, this Satanic hold and possession, which the devil has of mankind, while lying in the ruins of the fall of the first Adam, is that of a conqueror: and their condition is that of prisoners and captives, held in, under the power of a strong hand: only there is this difference between them and the common sort of captives and prisoners, as has already been hinted; those, in corporeal thraldom and imprisonment, would gladly accept of liberty if offered to them; whereas these prisoners and captives to sin and Satan, love and choose to abide in darkness, and their present bondage-state. Which evil disposition and aversion to spiritual freedom, renders their case more desperate, and out of the reach of moral suasion.

And that Satan has such a possession of mankind, whereby he holds their souls in bondage and captivity, to sin and himself, is manifest, both from scripture and experience. Hence it is, that the elect, at effectual calling, are said to be " brought as prisoners out of the prison-house," Isai. xlii. 7: yea, " to be turned from darkness to light, and from the power of Satan unto God," Acts xxvi. 18. And our blessed Lord compares this hold and possession that Satan has of mankind, to that of one who dwells in, or possesses a house or castle: and in two parables he shews, and plainly declares the difference betwixt a partial and total dispossession, and the power that must be manifested and exerted in the effectual dispossessing of him : " When (saith he) the unclean spirit is gone out of a man, he (viz. the spirit) walketh through dry places, seeking rest: and finding none, he saith, I will return unto my house whence I came out. And when he cometh, he findeth it empty, swept and garnished. Then goeth he, and taketh to him seven other spirits more wicked than himself, and they enter in, and dwell there: and the last state of that man is worse than the first," Luke xi. 24, 25, 26. This departing of Satan for a season, is owing to the common operations of the

Spirit with the word, as the Holy Spirit is sent forth to be a Spirit of conviction to a world of sinners, wherever the word is purely and truly taught; upon which first entrance of the gospel, a reformation from the grosser sort of sins, and a sudden temporary profession often follow: but the Spirit of God, who did this, not entering in himself, as a Spirit of grace and sanctification, to take and keep possession for Jesus Christ; when Satan returns, and makes his next visitation, knocking at the door of the heart, he finds it empty and destitute of the Spirit of God, and of all sanctifying and saving grace; and though the house be swept and garnished, that is, in some measure reformed from gross immoralities and errors in religion, yet he likes it never the worse; and thereupon, not only re-enters himself, but brings with him a stronger power than ever, to secure himself therein, against any after attempts that may be made to dispossess him.

And thus it is with many a professor in Christianity; and of such as these, who are only *almost Christians*, it is that the apostle speaks, saying, " For it is impossible for those who were once enlightened, and have tasted of the heavenly gift, and were made partakers of the Holy Spirit, and have tasted the good word of God, and the powers of the world to come; if they shall fall away, to renew them again by repentance: seeing they crucify to themselves the Son of God afresh, and put him to an open shame," Heb. vi. 4, 5, 6. These professors of Christianity are all of them as empty houses, swept and garnished, but destitute of the indwelling presence of the Spirit of God, as the Spirit of grace and sanctification: so that they are yet " in the gall of bitterness and bond of iniquity," notwithstanding " their fair shew in the flesh." Thus then, it appears, that Satan has an internal hold and possession, and that he is oft in part, and only for a time, dispossessed.

I shall next shew you how Christ proceeds under the gospel-ministry to dispossess Satan totally, by not only casting him out, but by removing his people from under his power and dominion. And this is set forth more particularly in this parable of our Lord; " When a strong man armed keeps his palace, his goods are in peace. But when a stronger than he shall come upon him, and overcome him, he taketh from him all his armour wherein he trusted and divideth his spoils," Luke xi. 21, 22. The STRONG ONE is the devil; his palace is the world; his goods are mankind, while in a natural and unconverted state, which he possesses and retains in peace as his own; the "stronger than he," is the Lord Jesus; this his coming upon him, was twofold, first, by his death, resurrection, and triumphant ascension into heaven, and session at the right hand of God, upon which "angels and authorities and powers were made subject unto him," 1 Pet. iii. 22. Secondly, by the preaching of the everlasting gospel, being accompanied with the Holy Spirit sent down from heaven. By the former, "He spoiled, (i. e. disarmed,) principalities and powers, making a shew of them openly, triumphing over them in it," Colos. ii. 15: and by the latter he pursued the grand design, which was to divide the spoil with Satan, according to a prior engagement upon the Father's part, as it is written; "Therefore will I divide him, (i. e. the Messias,) a portion with the great, and he shall divide the spoil with the strong: because he poured out his soul unto death," Isai. liii. 12. From which text, by the way, you may observe that Christ is only to take a part, and not the whole; "he divides the spoil with the strong," by taking his own sheep from among the devil's goats; which before conversion lie mixed together, and are only known to the Father, Son, and Holy Spirit, until he, who is the "Good Shepherd, and knows his sheep by name," is pleased to call them out, and bring them into his own sheepfold. But then,

Secondly, Satan has not only made a conquest, and took present possession of mankind through the fall, by which means he keeps them in bondage and subjection; but he has also set up his kingdom in the heart, and also in this lower world amongst men, by which means he rules as a prince; yea, he is also worshipped as God: hence, in scripture, he is styled " the prince and god of this world," John xiv. 30, and chap. xvi. 11, and 2 Cor. iv. 4. And now, that he might more effectually secure himself in this his usurped dominion and diabolical kingdom among men, he has made the heart of man his principal seat and throne, and has possessed himself of the mind as a fort and garrison; where the rebellious *will* is sub-governor, and man's carnal depraved *reason* acts as chief engineer; whose battering-pieces can never be dismounted, nor the fortifications thrown down, and the castle made to surrender by any weapons but those that are truly spiritual and mighty through God. Which possession of the heart and kingdom among men, Satan will do what he possibly can to support and maintain, in despite of all that moral suasion can effect. And that he has mankind in possession and under his influence, by means of their being in bondage under the dominion and reigning power of sin, has already been declared.

How he came at first to found this his usurped kingdom and government, and by what crafts and methods he has supported and continued it among mankind, especially in the Christian world, to this very day, is what is now briefly to be laid open and considered; in which the real weakness and insufficiency of moral suasion, and the necessity of the Divine power and efficacy to attend the word for conversion will be still further evident.

Now for an introduction to this I shall take leave to remind you of a hint that was given to Adam upon the fall, that such a kingdom and government would be immediately set up among men, with the mystical serpent at the head thereof, as you may read in those words commonly called the first promise. In which fundamental promise of life and salvation, to be wrought out and completed by another hand, two different kingdoms and interests were foretold should be set up in the world, and carried on in opposition to each other, as the text sufficiently declares; "And I will put enmity between thee and the woman; and between thy seed and her seed: IT, (or rather HE,) shall bruise thy head, and thou shalt bruise his heel," Gen. iii. 15. Which terms are all mystical: the serpent is the devil; the woman is the church; her seed is Christ: the serpent's, or devil's seed, are the reprobate world; being those "whose names were not written in the Lamb's book of life, from the foundation of the world:" the serpent's head is his kingdom and power in and over mankind; which head of power and malice, and all his designs against Christ and the elect were crushed by Christ's death upon the cross: the heel of Christ is the church militant; the serpent's bruising this his heel while upon the earth, was a prediction of all the persecutions and troubles that the church and her seed were to meet with in all ages, from the death of righteous Abel, whom Cain slew, to the last stroke of Anti-christian violence that shall be offered to the least member of Christ's mystical body the church, while upon the earth.

And in these two brothers, Cain and Abel, the two different seeds and opposite kingdoms first appeared. The first and eldest did belong to the devil, i. e. he was one of his subjects: being the beginning and the beginner of the devil's kingdom, as he is prince and ruler, yea, and god of this world: for in him the world first began to be distinguished and separated from the holy and spiritual seed or church of Christ in Adam's family: which diabolical kingdom, set up and managed by Satan, who then began to be worshipped, was founded in error, will-worship, persecution, violence, and bloodshed. Now,

Cain not having a true, saving, and justifying faith in the promised seed, as prefigured by the typical sacrifice of the firstling of the flock, by the offering of which Christ was representatively and virtually " the Lamb slain from the foundation of the world;" he therefore neglected the institution of a bloody sacrifice for his atonement, and betakes himself to an unbloody one; by which he could not obtain acceptance with God, nor remission of his sins: thus he failed both in the matter and manner of his religious performances, and therefore was neglected and rejected of God. Whereas his brother Abel, keeping up to the institution, and exercising faith therein, he and his sacrifice were accepted; as it is written, "By faith Abel offered unto God a more excellent sacrifice than Cain, by which he obtained witness that he was righteous, God testifying of his gifts; and by it, he being dead, yet speaketh," Heb. xi. 4. And that the reasons why Cain's sacrifice was not accepted, were, because it was not right as to kind, nor was it offered by faith, is, I think, plainly hinted to him by the eternal WORD, who reasons with him thus; "Cain, why art thou angry: and wherefore is thy countenance fallen? (q. d. Why so cast down and dejected?) If thou dost well, (i. e. sacrificest right) shalt thou not be accepted? And if thou dost not well, (but goest contrary to, or besides the rule) sin lieth at thy door," (i. e. it is thine own fault,) Gen. iv. 6, 7.

Thus Cain, upon his not sacrificing aright, and not "worshipping in spirit and in truth," had his sacrifice and person rejected; for which he revenges himself against a justly offended God upon his own innocent brother, who was the spiritual seed and true worshipper: and so " he that was born after the flesh, persecuted him that was born after the Spirit," Gal. iv. 29. And the reasons why he slew his brother are given in these words; " Cain was of that wicked one, and slew his brother: and wherefore slew he him? Because his own works were evil, and his brother's righteous," 1 John iii. 12. Now one of the works here referred to was this very deed of sacrificing, upon which that quarrel arose, which ended in death; one of these being only a natural, but the other a spiritual worshipper; upon which Cain, the murderer, is immediately excommunicated and banished from the gracious presence of God in his church, which was in Adam's family; whereupon, as bearing the mark of God's vengeance, he wandered a considerable distance from the church and worship of God, where he lived by himself as a cast-away and exile in a separate and distinct state from the church.

Thus Satan's kingdom here on earth began, in this his own seed and subject; who, like his mystical father, the devil, was full of enmity and rebellion against God, and of hatred to his brother.

And so the church of God in Adam's family became separate from the world in Cain's family; and were in their after generations distinguished by these terms, i. e. daughters of men, and sons of of God: which, I think, is plainly enough expressed in the beginning of the sixth chapter of Genesis; "And it came to pass, when men began to multiply on the face of the earth, and daughters were born unto them, that the sons of God saw the daughters of men, that they were fair; and they took them wives of all that they chose." By daughters of men here, must be meant Cain's offspring, and the seed of such as were degenerated and gone off from the communion of the saints, and the public worship of God, as kept up in the church then in Seth's family; and the Sons of God must be the true church members who were distinguished by this epithet then, and for a long time after, even in the days of Job.

But then, we also find by this account, that although these two kingdoms and seeds, the church and the world, were for a while separated and distinguished, yet they were too soon mixed and made one again, by disorderly marriages; by which means the world was brought into carnal union with the church, and the professed church of God, in the far greater part, soon degenerated and became one with the world; which almost universal degeneracy and apostacy, was the sad occasion of that deluge, which was in the days of Noah.

And here, by the way, I heartily wish that all

true believers and church-members in our days, and the succeeding generations, would take notice and well consider the consequences of such mistaken steps in yoking of the spiritually dead and living together.

Thus much as to the original rise and progress of the devil's kingdom, set up in and among mankind, and as visibly beginning in Cain, the devil's first-born, the reprobate seed, in whom the aforesaid enmity first manifested itself in the highest degree; and by which he was sufficiently declared to be " of that wicked one." Which diabolical kingdom, as separate and distinct from the woman's other seed, the church and spiritual kingdom of the eternal word, continued and prevailed for above sixteen hundred years, " until the flood came and took them all away."

And then it began again in Noah's younger son Ham, the father of Canaan, and increased until it took in that vast number of Babel-builders; who after their language was confounded, and they scattered upon the face of the earth, gave themselves up to idolatry and superstition, and became immediate subjects to, and worshippers of Satan, by their idolatry: but Satan's principal seat and empire, as the prince and god of this world, was first erected and fixt at Babel; for there the first of the four monarchical beasts, and worldly empires began under Nimrod, whose name foretold him to be a rebel against God and his church. He was the first tyrant-king, a mighty hunter, or rather persecutor; whose kingdom began in confusion and ambition, and was supported by force and cruelty, and governed by tyranny and oppression; and whose religion with that of the rest of the world, that went off from the church of God, consisted only in error, superstition, and dæmon-worship.

Thus Satan ruled and governed among mankind, and was worshipped in those idols, as the God of this world, for above the space of two thousand years: "but when the fulness of time was come, god sent forth his Son, made of a woman, made under the law:" who, by his death upon the cross, broke the serpent's head; and having "spoiled principalities and powers, he made a shew of them openly, triumphing over them in it." After which he proceeded to break in upon the devil's kingdom, and entering his palace, he bound the strong man and took away his armour wherein he trusted; i. e. the worldly wisdom and vain philosophy which Satan then made use of, and divided his spoils: and through the weakness and foolishness of preaching by a company of mechanic preachers, full of the Holy Spirit and Divine wisdom, he not only brought all the wisdom of Greece and Athens into contempt, but, notwithstanding the opposition made by the powers of hell and the heathen emperors, he drove Satan from his temples and altars, and stopt the mouths of all his lying oracles, and by degrees put an end to dæmon-worship throughout all the Roman empire: according to that ancient prophecy, which saith, " And the idols he shall utterly abolish," Isai. ii. 18. Which combat of Christ and his apostles, and other gospel-ministers, with the dragon at the head of his kingdom of darkness, as assisted with legions of pagan-priests, and heathen-magistrates, vile and bloody persecutors; and the issue of that large siege of Christ by his gospel-ministry against Satan, and the rage and fury of the dragon upon his being worsted, and his after attempts made upon the woman and her holy seed, " which keep the commandments of God, and have the testimony of Jesus Christ;" are all most lively set forth throughout the twelfth of the Revelations.

After which victory on Christ's part by the gospel, and the fruitless attempts of the red dragon, by persecution, to root out the woman's seed, the old serpent played a new game, and effected that by craft and deceit, which he could not have done by force; and that was by setting up a succession of Antichrists at Rome, in the church and temple of God there; who, under the title and pretence of being Christ's vicars, have all along acted as the devil's deputies and chief factors for hell: even as it was foretold by the Holy Spirit, who also has described them at large, saying; "There must come a falling away first, and then that man of SIN, and son of perdition shall be revealed: who opposeth and exalteth himself above all that is called God, (i. e. above all magistracy and civil government,) or that is worshipped; so that he as God sitteth in the temple of God, shewing himself that he is God. And now ye know what withholdeth that he might be revealed in his time. For the mystery of iniquity doth already work: only he who now letteth will let, until he be taken out of the way. And then shall ὁ ἄνομ☉, that WICKED (i. e. lawless vile wretch) be revealed, whom the Lord shall consume with the Spirit of his mouth, and shall destroy with the brightness of his coming; even Him, whose coming is after the working (i. e. by the energy) of Satan, with all power, and signs, and lying wonders. And with all deceiveableness of unrighteousness in them that perish; because they received not the love of the truth, that they might be saved. And for this cause God shall send them strong delusion (i. e. an internal, operative and efficacious error; which shall blind their minds, and deprave their reason to that degree) that they should believe a (most gross and palpable) LIE, (i. e. transubstantiation) that they all might be damned who believe not the truth, but had pleasure in unrighteousness," 2 Thess. ii. 3, 4,—6, 7, 8, 9, 10, 11, 12.

Thus the devil, as Prince and God of this world, set up his kingdom a third time in the world: which kingdom and power of darkness, Christ, the Lamb, broke in again upon, and in a great measure ruined it, by his glorious and powerful appearing and presence with those two eminent instruments of the reformation, Luther and Calvin, and those who assisted and succeeded them in the furthering of the same: upon which Satan at the first raged, and acted the part of the bloody dragon over again, for a considerable time, in raising bloody persecutions, massacres, plots and conspiracies against the reformed religion; but this not succeeding, he took another method, viz. to corrupt the principles and practices of the reformed, by raising a standing army of learned men, to preach and write against the doctrines and principles upon which the reformation was begun; and upon which it subsists and stands, and by which only it can be maintained and continued in the world.

These have entered into a new war and fresh engagements against the Lamb, and his virgin company and followers: and have their several leaders, who are men of as different principles as are their faces, and who engage against the several parts of sacred truth, with different and quite contrary designs.

Some are battering and bantering all religion, under the name of priestcraft; others are setting themselves to oppose and assault all revealed religion, as unnecessary and troublesome to the more learned and polite part of mankind: some are resolved, if possible, to expunge the true scripture-doctrine of the ever-blessed Trinity, by imposing and substituting another falsely so called, which is nothing else than old Plato's Tritheism revived again: and many there be, though from different principles, who do daily attack the true and proper divinity, and distinct personality of the eternal Word and Holy Spirit; while others make it their province and chief business, to rave against and stigmatize the Protestant faith and doctrines of original sin derived from Adam, as it comes upon all men, in its guilt and pollution, to condemnation; and of the imputed righteousness of Christ, as being put upon a sinner for his justification and acceptance before God, through faith; accounting and calling it imputed nonsense. And many of these are also employed and spirited by Satan, to assault and banter all the doctrines of sovereign free grace: and others there be, and those not a few, that employ their abilities against all spiritual experimental religion, advancing furiously against the doctrine of efficacious grace, as in the Holy Spirit's hand, and the assertors of the necessity of Divine power, in the exceeding greatness thereof, to be exerted in an invincible, efficacious manner upon the heart, will, and affections of a sinner, while dead in trespasses and sins; thereby bringing him into a state of regeneration and conversion to God, and so to a true, saving and justifying faith in Christ Jesus, as accompanied with a repentance unto life.

And by the instrumentality of these it is, that Satan supports and defends the several parts of his kingdom of darkness among mankind; blinding the eyes of some, and prejudicing and prepossessing the minds of others, so as to turn many from the faith; "tossing them to and fro, they being carried about (or whirled round) with every wind of doctrine, by the sleight of men, and cunning craftiness, whereby they lie in wait to deceive," Ephes. iv. 14.

Thus Satan keeps and maintains his present hold of mankind, while in an unconverted state, they being goods and subjects in his possession and kingdom; which kingdom is called the power of Satan and the power of darkness, because it is a state of bondage and darkness, which holds men in subjection, by an influence it has on the minds: hence men by nature are said to love and chuse darkness and bondage rather than light and liberty by Jesus Christ; nor will all the moral suasion or rational arguments that either men or angels can use, bring these dead sinners to life; nor make or enable them to circumcise their own hearts and rebellious wills; nor can they remove themselves out of Satan's power and kingdom: No, it is God, and God only, " who delivers us from the power of darkness, and translates us (out of the kingdom and possession of Satan) into the kingdom of his dear Son," Col. i. 13.

Thus much for the second part of our argument, shewing the real weakness and insufficiency of moral suasion in conversion, unless accompanied with efficacious grace, and the exceeding greatness of God's mighty power. I shall proceed to a

Third argument, and that is to be taken from the energy of Satan upon and in mankind, both good and bad, which, according to its nature and extent, through the Divine permission, is great; and in the unregenerate it greatly hinders their conversion and faith, until it is removed out of the way by Him who only can bind the strong man, and take away that defence in which he trusts; and so delivers his out of the devil's snare, that were taken captive by him at his will.

And here if we were but fully able to trace the way of this serpent, and could we at once, or by parts, view all his subtle wiles, and crafty methods to beguile, deceive, and ensnare poor souls, by his internal and undiscerned influence upon the minds, affections, passions, and imaginations of men and women, we should, no doubt, stand amazed at the depths of Satan, and the methods of this evil one.

And hence it is, that we read concerning him, that as he is "the prince of the power of the air," so he is "the spirit that now worketh in the children of disobedience," i. e. in those that are in a state of unbelief, Ephes. ii. 2; and that Satan, after a sort, has an internal hold of, and influence upon the minds of men in a state of unregeneracy, by which means he works powerfully, and prevails upon them so as to keep them in blindness and bondage, is further evident from those words of the apostle Paul, who saith; "But if our gospel be hid, (i. e. veiled or concealed) it is hid to them that are lost. In whom the God of this world hath blinded the minds of them which believe not, &c." 2 Cor. iv. 3, 4. And here, if you will but regard the full import of the expression, you will find it is full, and to my purpose: for that he is first said to be in those whom he thus blinds; in whom this denotes internal possession; then it is added, that

" he blinds the minds of them that believe not;" this denotes efficiency, and that he has a way to work upon the minds and passions of mankind, and yet they perceive it not: not that Satan infuses sin into the faculties, as the Holy Spirit works or creates grace in them, in and at the time of regeneration and effectual calling; but he works upon the passions, and stirs up the corruptions, like as the wind by its violent motion agitates the waters of the sea, especially near the shores, to that degree as to stir up the mire and dirt, which before lay still and unperceived at the bottom; and so it is written, " But the wicked are like the troubled sea, when it cannot rest, whose waters cast up mire and dirt," Isai. lvii. 20.

And now, the methods that he, "the god of this world," takes to work thus upon the minds of men, so as to blind the understanding and reason, are manifold and various; sometimes he doth it by stirring up their inbred lusts, corruptions, passions, and blind zeal, to rage against and oppose the pure gospel, by casting in vain reasonings into the mind, and raising new objections against it; or through misrepresentation of the gospel and the true ministers thereof, by covering them with slander and reproach, or by setting them all in a false light, and unseemly dress; thereby prejudicing the minds of men, and hardening their hearts, and then making use of their depraved reason and acquired abilities to defend against its doctrine and efficacy.

But, that I may set this internal working and influence of Satan in and upon the minds of mankind, in a full and clear light, I will give you some scripture instances of his secret and unperceived way of close conjunction with, and working upon the soul; whereby he not only suggests and injects thoughts and fiery darts into the mind, but also entices, excites, and prevails so far, if permitted, both upon good and bad, as to bring them to say and do that which once they abhorred the thoughts of: and yet they perceive not that these first motions come from him.

It is true the instances I shall give are somewhat extraordinary; but that I think adds the more strength to the argument; for if he works to such a degree, through the Divine permission and limitation, upon one, or two, or more, he can upon all, if permitted; and if he can manage so artfully and powerfully upon those in whom he does not dwell, how much more may he be supposed to have a powerful influence into the retaining them as prisoners and bond-slaves, in whom he may be said both to dwell and reign? The first instance then that I shall give you of Satan's unperceived power and influence upon the heart or mind, shall be that of his exciting David to number the people, as it is written; "and Satan stood up against Israel, and provoked David to number Israel," 1 Chron. xxi. 1. That is, he stood up against Israel as an adversary and accuser, seeking an occasion and leave to break in upon them; he knowing they had greatly sinned and provoked the Most High, as appears by comparing this part of the story with that other text where the fact is first recorded; "And again the anger of the Lord was kindled against Israel, and he moved David against them to say, Go, number Israel and Judah," 2 Sam. xxiv. 1. In this last text we find the reason of this just judgment on God's part, as in the former we find the malice, efficiency, and instrumentality of Satan, by God's permission, bringing the same about; and this he did by suggesting something that was pleasing and taking with him, in order to stir him up thereto; what it was, whether that thereby he might know the number of his subjects, and men fit to bear arms upon any emergency; or whether he suggested the necessity or advantage of entering upon a new war with his neighbours or professed enemies, it is all uncertain to us; yet something pleasing and advantageous there must be to make it take with that good king.

But besides this his first suggesting and darting the pleasing thought and project into David's mind, he added force and fervency to the temptation. "He provoked David to number the people of Israel;" which expression represents temptation in its strength and power; not a power to force the natural liberty of the will, but yet a force powerful enough to excite corruption, and thereby raise his ambitious desires to such a degree, as to overpower grace, and carry the good man away into sin as a captive or prisoner of war. And yet Satan managed it so artfully and secretly, that David never perceived that it came from him. But for further proof that he has such a secret and undiscerned way of enticing and prevailing upon the minds of men, take a

Second instance in the case of Ahab; whom God, as a just judgment and punishment upon himself, family, and people, for their joint sins, would have to fall in battle at Ramoth Gilead: for you are to remember, that God in punishing the wicked, reserves to himself a right and liberty of chusing their delusions, and giving commission to the instruments of their ruin, to execute his judgments upon them; as appears plain in that account given by the true prophet of the Lord, who declares, that by the way of vision he saw "the Lord sitting upon his throne, and all the hosts of heaven standing round about him; and the Lord said, Who will persuade Ahab, that he may go and fall in battle at Ramoth Gilead? And there came forth a spirit, (i. e. a fallen angel, one of the tempting devils) and stood before the Lord, and said, I will persuade him; and he said, Wherewith? And he said, I will go forth, and I will be a lying spirit in the mouth of his prophets. And the Lord said, Thou shalt persuade him, and prevail also; go forth and do so. Now therefore behold, the Lord hath put a lying spirit in the mouth of all these thy prophets: and the Lord hath spoken evil concerning thee," 1 Kings xxii. 19—23.

Thus, by a second instance, it appears plain that Satan hath a nearer and more effectual way to a man's heart than men are aware of; whereby he can after a sort slip into the heart and mouth, without our privity; as I trust to shew more fully by and by; not that he at any time uses our tongues without our consent, but his suggestions come in so unawares and agreeably, that a man looks upon them and approves them as his own. And I might add, if he could so speedily, and with success, tempt and effectually seduce pure innocency, what may we expect? whose corrupt nature is as subject to catch and embrace allurements and temptations to sin, as the dry tinder and powder are to receive the spark that falls upon them. And Satan being a thorough artist in natural philosophy and physiognomy, he cunningly suits his temptations with the present circumstances, temper, and inclination: and like the skilful fisher, he always baits his hook with a proper fly.

And now from these two texts we may gather up these three truths: as first, that God makes use of Satan's temptations and seducements, both of the good and bad, to accomplish and bring about his own eternal counsels and just judgments upon sinners. Secondly, we learn hence that Satan, under the Divine permission and limitation, has both art and power in tempting; and though he has no power to force, yet he can allure, excite, and move the passions and affections by suggestions and injections from himself, or by proper instruments, in such a manner, as that none, without Divine assistance preventing them, can deliver themselves from being ensnared, and overcome. And,

Thirdly, we learn hence, that such is his sleight and skill, that he can tempt, entice, seduce, and overcome, either by his own secret suggestions and allurements, or by the help of instruments fitted for his purpose, in such an undiscerned manner, as that neither the tempted, nor those by whom he seduces, know or perceive that it comes from him.

But for a further and fuller proof of this invisible influence and power that Satan has to tamper with the heart of man, let us briefly survey a few instances more of this kind, as recorded in the New Testament; and the first shall be in that reproof and advice given by Peter to his Master, as it is written; "Then Peter took him, and began to rebuke him, saying, Be it far from thee, Lord; this shall not be unto thee. But he turned, and said unto Peter, Get thee behind me, Satan, thou art an offence to me; for thou savourest not the things that be of God, but those that be of men," Matt. xvi. 22, 23. I think nothing need be more plain and full than that the devil was at the bottom of this, and made use of Peter as an instrument to dissuade " the Lord of life and glory," from going up to suffer at Jerusalem; that so he might, if possible, prevent the breaking of the serpent's head upon the cross, according to the first promise and early prediction in Paradise.

And now, can we think that Peter perceived in the least that this grave advice given to his Lord and Master came originally from hell? And that in this he was actuated and influenced from Satan? Or that this was first contrived and suggested to him by the devil, before it was uttered by his tongue? Verily no; he would have abhorred the counsel himself had he perceived the author, and its evil tendency to prevent salvation being wrought out for sinners.

Again, take a second instance of Satan's unperceived way of seducing and dealing with the hearts of mankind; and that is in the case of Ananias, who was detected by Peter in these words ; " Ananias, why hath Satan filled thine heart to lie to the Holy Ghost, and to keep back part of the price of the land ?—Why hast thou conceived this thing in thy heart? Thou hast not lied unto men but unto God," Acts v. 3, 4. Here again it is intimated plain enough that Satan first put the suggestion into Ananias's heart: it being agreeable to his covetous disposition, who probably thought it highly reasonable to keep a secret reserve for himself and wife, for private uses and other occasions; therefore he immediately consents to the suggestion; and so having lust conceived in his heart, it then came forth into act, and was covered with a lie. Thus it appears that the devil is the author and father of all those monstrous conceptions and births of sin in men's hearts, although those in whose hearts this cockatrice egg is laid and hatched, think not, nor perceive any thing of it.

I will proceed to a third instance, in which we read concerning Judas Iscariot, that Satan first put that hellish thought and contrivance into his head; for it is said, " supper being ended, (not the Lord's Supper, but a private supper at Simon the leper's house, in Bethany, about two days before the Passover, as appears by comparing

Matthew's and Mark's history with this,) Satan having put it into the heart of Judas Iscariot, Simon's son, to betray him. He then having received the sop, went immediately out unto the chief priests, and agreed with them, to deliver Jesus into their hands, &c." John xiii. 2—26, 27—30, compared with Matt. xxvi. 14, and Mark xiv. 1, 2, 3,—10, 11. Now that which I would here take notice of and remark, is this expression; viz. " Satan having put it into the heart of Judas Iscariot, Simon's son, to betray him;" by which it is further manifest and confirmed, that Satan has a secret way of practising upon men, and knows how to set on foot any bad design in and among mankind; he has a way to inject contrivances into our minds, and then he doth his utmost to hurry us on to a speedy execution of his hellish projects; our corruptions, carnal passions, and affections, alas for us! are like the dry tinder or sulphureous powder, which are ready to catch hold of and embrace the least spark of fire; and it may be said of these, as well as of the tongue, " that they also are set on fire of hell." But I will conclude this part of my proof concerning Satan's hold of and influence in and over mankind, with a

Fourth instance, viz. that of Peter's denying his Lord and Master, of which he was premonished in these words; " Simon, Simon, behold, Satan hath desired to have you, that he may sift you as wheat; but I have prayed for thee that thy faith fail not," Luke xxii. 31, 32. Satan, it seems, had begged hard for all the twelve apostles, but by the Divine permission he was only allowed to try an experiment upon two. Judas was indeed the devil's own, yet he could not tempt nor possess him without leave from above: the other was Christ's own, in a more peculiar manner, being given to him to be saved by him; and therefore the latter is prayed for and recovered, while the other being the son of perdition is left in the hands of the devourer.

But now as to Peter, he being one ordained to eternal life, and also a true believer, therefore he is recovered and converted anew; yet here behold human weakness and frailty! he is forewarned once, and again, but is bold and resolute; yet as bold as he was, and notwithstanding all his resolutions and solemn protestations to stand by his Master, and, rather than fail, fight, and die for him, Satan was too cunning and strong for all his freewill and present stock of inherent grace. And here observe the metaphor made use of by our Lord to express the manner and consequence of the temptation; it was " to sift them as wheat" in a sieve; not that it was Satan's design to fan, or cleanse, by making a separation of the chaff from the wheat; no, he rather sought to have destroyed the other eleven with the son of perdition: but God had a more glorious end and gracious design. Thus, then, as the sieve by moving the wheat put therein, and agitated to and fro, disturbs the whole, and fetches up the chaff or bran that lay undiscerned before; even so did this dispensation upon the disciples, but on Peter more especially, fetch up and discover that inbred, hidden corruption, and evil disposition, which lay hid and unperceived before. And Peter being thus for a while (though still under the care of God the Saviour, to secure and recover him again, as by a new conversion) left to be sifted and influenced by Satan, he not only denies his Lord and Master, but he confirms this his unkind denial with lies, oaths, and cursings or imprecations upon himself, if he so much as knew the man. Good Lord, what is man, if left but a little while to himself and Satan!

I shall now, having produced these instances of Satan's power and influence in tempting, and man's weakness and real insufficiency effectually to resist the same, reassume the former question, and conclude my argument upon this head.

If Satan has indeed such an effectual power to tempt and seduce even the best of saints, and such a secret unperceived way of filling the heart with evil projects, and sinful excuses, nay, with lies, oaths, blasphemies and the like; and if he has a real influence and power to blind the minds of unbelievers, and to fill their hearts with prejudice against the gospel and person of the only Redeemer and Saviour, what then can a man do while in a natural, dead, unregenerate state? Who of himself has neither will nor power to deliver himself, nor yet to flee by faith to another, for succour and salvation, as the scriptures most evidently teach: of what effectual use then can moral suasion be, to make the devil leave off defending, and let go his prey? Will he be afraid like a bird? or let go his hold, though a multitude of shepherds should be raised against him? verily no, he will esteem their keenest arguments as straw, and the creature's resolutions as rotten wood; man's arrows will never make him flee; he will laugh at any, who without spiritual weapons and power, shall dare to approach him. For he reigns, and rules as king over all the children of pride.

Thus much as to the real weakness and insufficiency of moral suasion, though assisted by the fallen creature's best endeavours, to quicken and savingly convert himself to God, by making himself a new and clean heart and right spirit, or to deliver himself out of the power of sin and Satan.

CHAP. IV.

Proving that the Will of Man in true Conversion and Faith is not forced, nor its natural Liberty in the least infringed, but is by the Grace of God made truly free.

I shall now proceed to the third head, in which I am to make it evident, That in true conversion and saving faith, as they are effected by the Divine power, working in an effectual and invincible manner upon the heart of man by the word, the WILL of man is not forced, nor is its natural liberty or freedom in the least infringed; but on the other hand, that noble faculty is, by renewing grace, made truly and spiritually free.

There are indeed some, and they are not a few, who clamour, and cast reproach and contempt upon the doctrines of sovereign and efficacious grace, and also upon the internal renovating efficacy of the Holy Spirit upon the hearts of God's elect, on pretence that these doctrines are really injurious unto man's free-will, and tend greatly to spiritual sloth and licentiousness: imagining, it seems, that the Spirit of God cannot work in an efficacious and invincible manner upon the heart of man in conversion, without doing violence unto the natural freedom of his will: but that this is a mistake and causeless clamour, I hope to make appear, and also to demonstrate that free grace, and the Divine power, are the best friends and assistants to the will of a fallen, depraved creature. For it is plainly manifest from scripture and experience, that it is only efficacious renewing grace, as clothed with Omnipotence, that can and doth force Satan out of his present hold and possession in man as in an unregenerate state: and by knocking off the fetters, and unloosing the bonds of sin and Satan, by which the will and affections were bound and enslaved, sets the soul at liberty, and makes the will of man free indeed.

The will of man, I grant, was at its first creation made morally free, and disposed to good: but by means of the fall it became enslaved to sin, through a strong propensity and love thereunto; and cannot be made free (and inclined to love God above all, and steadily to adhere unto his revealed will as the only rule of faith and obedience) but by the power and influence of efficacious grace, as it is revealed and applied to the soul, for its conversion, by the Holy Spirit. And now, that I may set these things in the strongest light I am capable, I shall proceed, First, to lay down something by way of premise. Secondly, give you a brief account of the several names, and various operations of the faculties belonging to the human soul. Thirdly, shew you how, and upon which of these faculties sin made its first entrance, thereby seizing and overspreading the soul to such a degree as that the understanding became dark, the reason became depraved, and the will perverse, rebellious, and enslaved to sin; the imagination also became vain, and the affections sensual, carnal and vile. Fourthly, I shall shew you, that in effectual calling and conversion, as these are effected by "the exceeding greatness of his mighty power" in and upon the heart, will, and affections, God always deals with his elect as rational creatures, and in such a manner as effectually secures the true natural liberty and freedom of the will; while he also brings about and accomplishes all his eternal purposes and designs of mercy, and love towards those whom of mere grace he did choose and predestinate in Christ Jesus unto eternal life and glory, and that before the world began.

First of all then, by way of premise, you are to remember and consider that there is a twofold liberty of the will; the one is physical or natural, which freedom is essential to it, and cannot be subject to coercion or force, without doing injury thereunto; and there is also a moral freedom, which once consisted in an inclination and propensity to good: but this moral freedom and disposition to love, and choose good and hate evil, were lost through the fall and disobedience of the first Adam; it being only a moral quality, or created virtue in the will, and as such was subject to be lost through the mutability of the creature. But then,

Secondly, I premise that that moral freedom to good, which was lost in the fall, may be, and is restored, by the renewing grace of God, and his exceeding great and efficacious power put forth in and upon all those whom he calls, justifies, and saves, "according to the eternal purpose which he proposed in Christ Jesus our Lord:" it being very manifest from the word, and the experience of mankind, that God can, and doth work upon, overrule, and turn man's will which way soever he pleases. And hence it is, that in effectual calling and the conversion of the elect, God is said, "to work in them both to will and to do of his own good pleasure;" even in such a measure and degree as "to make them a willing people in the day of his power." And with respect to his government among mankind, the wise man tells us, that "the king's heart is in the hand of the Lord: and he turneth it as the rivers of water," Prov. xxi. 1. And now as the king's heart and will are at God's disposal, so also are the hearts and wills of all mankind in the Lord's hand to alter and dispose, to sanctify and renew; yea, and to soften or harden; either by giving or withholding the sanctifying and softening influences of his grace and Holy Spirit, as he pleases; for I hope there is none in our present day who will contend for such an absolute and unlimited freedom in man, as if he were thereby wholly independent of his Maker, and not subject to his Sovereign disposal and controul; for this would be the way, I think, to make him more than a creature; nay it would be no less than subjecting the Creator's will to his creature's, by leaving all the eternal purposes and decrees of the Supreme Being, to be overruled and determined by the precarious choice or management of man's unstable will; which to assert, is not only antiscriptural, but the greatest affront against his sovereignty and government, who " worketh all things according to the counsel of his own WILL," Eph. i. 11. And who also saith unto Moses, " I will be gracious unto whom I will be gracious, and I will shew mercy unto whom I will shew mercy," Exod. xxxiii. 19. From whence the apostle Paul infers, whether justly or injudiciously I leave others to say, " So then it is not of him that willeth, nor of him that runneth, but of God that sheweth mercy," Rom. ix. 16—18. And now if these things be granted, as I think they must, or else the plainest and fullest scripture-evidences must have their testimony invalidated, and their sense wrested and depraved, then the more difficult part of my work under this head is finished; the truth contended for being thereby granted me, viz. That God can and doth alter, incline, sanctify, renew, and dispose the heart or will of man, both before, in, and after conversion, which way soever he pleases, and that without hurting or infringing that natural freedom and liberty which is essential to it. I shall therefore now proceed,

Secondly, to give you a brief account of the several names and various operations of the faculties belonging to the human soul. And in order thereunto, I must remind you that MAN, that little world as the philosophers call him, is, according to natural philosophy and the sacred writings, distinguished into body, and soul, and spirit; as is plainly expressed by the apostle, in his pious wish and apostolical benediction, who prays, " the very God of peace sanctify you wholly; and I pray God your whole spirit, and soul, and body, be preserved blameless unto the coming of our Lord Jesus Christ," 1 Thes. v. 23, compared with Heb. iv. 12. By body is here meant the material, corruptible part of man taken at first from the earth: by soul is meant the animal life, and the several functions thereof; which though they be more noble in the rational than in the irrational or brutal creatures, yet they bear a resemblance to, and have an affinity with the beasts, whose soul, the wise man says,

" descendeth downwards into the earth," Eccles. iii. 21. and chap. xii. 7 ; whereas this soul, as in man, being in union to, and one with the rational or intellectual spirit, as the wise man observes, " ascendeth upwards, even to God who gave it :" and by spirit in this aforesaid threefold division, is meant the intellectual or rational part of man, which bears a near resemblance to its Maker, and is his created image in man. Thus the soul, as being distinct from the spirit, is properly the sensitive faculty, being the present seat of all the sensitive appetites, passions, and affections, so far as they be common unto the animal or sensitive world : and the spirit is the rational or intellectual faculty, and consists of the understanding, reason, and will. The animal soul, or sensitive faculty, as some call it, has three distinct functions, viz. imagination, affection, and memory; and these may be styled the inferior or subordinate powers of the human soul. The first of these, viz.

Imagination, which is styled the cogitative and roving faculty, is, as to its use and office, more principally seated in the brain; and is an active, busy principle, never idle, nor at rest night nor day; it being always at work when we are asleep, forming ten thousand monstrous, nonsensical, and foolish ideas, which though incoherent and confused, we ofttimes remember when we awake :

the occasion of which disorder and incoherency is, because reason or judgment, the balance and regulator of the roving fancy, is then at rest: and in those who are delirious it is weak and out of order, and cannot perform its office.

The natural office, and present inconstancy of this faculty, as in a human soul, are by a person of quality thus described; 'The imagination (says he) is the purveyor or hunter of objects for the affections; sometimes set on work by them, and controuled by them, and sometimes by reason; sometimes obeying one or both, and sometimes neither; sometimes inciting and enticing the affections, and leading them away captive, without regard of reason; and sometimes it is won to take part with reason against the affections.'

And furthermore, it appears consonant and agreeable to the scriptures, that this faculty is not only fickle and inconstant, but also depraved and corrupt, both in its work and office in the soul, even from the womb unto the grave: for it still remains a truth as much as ever, that "every imagination of the thoughts of man's heart, (considered as unsanctified and destitute of God's grace) is only evil continually," and that from his youth: "for as a good man (i. e. one sanctified and in a state of grace) out of the good treasure of the heart bringeth forth good things; so likewise an evil man, (i. e. one in his natural state, and unsanctified) out of the evil treasure of his heart bringeth forth evil things." But this is not all, for this cogitative faculty is not only disorderly, unstable, and evil in its work, but also in its influence upon the affections and the other superior powers, beguiling and captivating them to evil: its place, indeed, is to be handmaid to the affections, and always ready to be under the controul and government of reason; for lack of which subjection, I may say of the imagination, as to its evil influence upon the other powers of the human soul, as St. James says of the tongue among the members of the body; "behold how great a matter a little fire kindleth. The tongue is a fire, a world of iniquity among our members, it defileth the whole body, and setteth on fire the course of nature, and it is set on fire of hell." And even thus it is with this faculty; for from this disorder and evil influence proceed all that sin and wickedness which is in the world; of which I shall say more in its place.

Affection is next to be considered, as another in-inferior power of the human soul; common indeed, in a lower or higher degree to all sensitive beings; but in man it is more excellent than in any of the animal part of the creation, in which it is little or nothing more than bare sensation and instinct; for affection in man is essential to the immortal and intellectual spirit, though seated in the animal soul, as to its present function; being that by which he is capable, and that after a rational manner, to love, desire, joy, fear, grieve, mourn, hate, be angry, and the like; these are carnal, and sensually inclined and disposed to evil through the fall: but if this faculty of rational sensation or affection in human souls be considered as to its natural use and end, it is only the soul's capacity to receive impressions from the senses, and to be wrought upon by objects from without itself, or even by itself, in such a manner as to excite love or hatred, desire or aversion, joy or grief, anger or pleasure, and all their concomitants; upon which account these affections may be called the feet of the soul, by which she runs out after those things she loves and desires; or by which she, after a sort, flees from those things which she loathes, hates, and is afraid of. They are also her hands, by which she joins herself to, and embraces things agreeable and delightful, or by which she, as it were, thrusts from her things to which she has a dislike and aversion.

These passions and affections, at first creation, and before the fall, were innocent and free from perturbation, and disorder, and wholly subject to reason, as their comptroller and guide: whereas now, since the fall of the first Adam, they are fickle and uncertain, and wrought upon, and deceived oft times, both by the imagination and outward senses; so these also work as strongly and forcibly upon the more noble powers, and are frequently too strong for reason; and by supplying its place, carry away the will against all reason and judgment, to be of their side; from whence it comes to pass, that persons under the strongest convictions walk in the " lusts of the flesh, fulfilling the desires of the flesh and of the mind,"* Ephes. ii. 3. And hence it is, that persons of an ungoverned fancy, great passions, and strong affections are the most liable to be deceived and imposed upon by imagination and passion mixing together; by means whereof the judgment is blinded and misled; and with such, cogitation and affection pass for solid reason and judgment. Whereas in truth, reason, if attended to, as weak and blind as it really is through the fall, would, in a thousand instances, soon detect the fraud, and lead the person out of the present error and deceit of calling " evil good, and good evil, and putting darkness for light, and light for darkness; bitter for sweet, and sweet for bitter," Isai. v. 20. And here I might add another deceit which obtains amongst many, whose affection prevails and is headstrong, and whose fancy

* Θελήματα, the wills of the flesh and of the mind; for that these passions are headstrong, and carry the will away with them.

and imagination usurp the place of solid judgment or reason; and *that* is, such as give way to a pretended secret impulse, contrary to reason's dictates and scripture-revelation; and are unaccountably troubled, or as they think privileged with dreams, apparitions, voices, and revelations, &c. and all from this moral distemper and depravity, viz. imagination and affection supplying the place of reason, than which nothing is more irrational. Thus, as to affection and passion, there is a

Third subordinate power in the human soul, and that is memory; this is the collective and recollective faculty, which, considered passively, is nothing but the impresses of things from without or within, represented to the mind in such a manner as to fix some lasting ideas therein, and so it is the soul's power of retention, by which she retaineth more or less of the ideas of those things she hath conversed with by one means and another: and thus she may be said to keep a journal or register within herself, of all her thoughts, words and actions, as well as of the more remarkable and material passages and occurrences she has met with in her journey through the present world; and though now the soul, in the crowd and hurry of secular affairs and terrene enjoyments, may forget or lose the present sight or sense of her own words, thoughts, and actions, especially as to those that were vain and immoral; yet in the great day all these will stand in order, and come up in remembrance, and be eternally fixed upon the minds of those who perish: but this only by the bye. It must, indeed, be confessed, that though memory is a sort of storehouse of excellent use, when well furnished, yet it is too much like a leaking vessel, especially as to the things which are good: for these for the most part quickly leak out or run beside: and to this it is thought the apostle doth allude, when he saith; "therefore we ought to give the more earnest heed to the things that we have heard, lest at any time we should let them slip," or flow out,* i. e. as liquors do on all sides through a leaking vessel, Heb. ii. 1. The things they had heard were the doctrinal truths delivered in the apostles' ministry, as they were preachers of the gospel, and publishers of the glad tidings of life and salvation, through a crucified and exalted Redeemer: and to

* Παραρρυῶμεν of παρὰ and ῥυω, to leak and flow out as liquor; and the apostle here, to me, seemeth to refer to Solomon's exhortation, Prov. iii. 21, and Ephes. iv. 21, in which he alludeth to the טטפת totaphoth, that is frontlets, which God commanded, Deut. vi. 8, to be bound on the head between the eyes; which being put on at prayer-time, they were thence called the tephilloth, from tephillah, a prayer; but both the Chaldee paraphrase and Septuagint translation render the word in Proverbs, by a word which signifieth, to flow down or leak out, as waters out of a vessel not firm; and our apostle retaineth this metaphor as most proper.

let these go, through a careless or apostatizing spirit, is very dangerous: this is indeed done, when the precious truths themselves, which are of the utmost importance, are not taken in and attended to, with a due regard, so as to " sink down into the heart, and fix upon the mind," Luke ix, 44, chap. viii. 15, and chap. ii. 51. The words by which these truths were conveyed to the mind may indeed be forgot, nor is it greatly necessary that we should always retain them, but the things we have heard and learned ought by no means to be forgot nor deserted: for that is criminal, and of fatal consequence to the hearers, as is afterwards intimated in the second and third verses. And here, by the way, for the instruction and benefit of some who complain of a bad memory, let me tell you, a man may have a great and strong memory, as to the retaining the words of a sermon or long discourse, and yet be an unprofitable hearer, and one, that in the sense of the Holy Spirit in this text, may be said to let the things slip; when they either regard not the truths themselves, so as to receive them in the love of the truth, and live the things or doctrines they profess; or when they let them go by way of desertion and apostacy, as many of the Hebrews did, or at least were in danger of. Thus the word preached to one of a weak memory may purify and enrich the soul, though little of the discourse, verbatim, be retained: whereas, as I before said, another who can carry home and repeat the whole sermon, may never receive the doctrinal nor practical truths delivered in the love of them. Take then the whole of your duty in this point, in the words of the same apostle, as I think, in another place; " The gospel which I had preached unto you, which also you have received, and wherein ye stand; by which also ye are saved, if ye keep in memory what I have preached unto you, unless ye have believed in vain," 1 Cor. xv. 1, 2; that is, made a profession of the Christian religion to little or no purpose, with regard to your soul's eternal welfare. Thus as to the memory, and its usefulness, where it is weakest in the Christian, it yet retains the truths as a rich treasure and precious jewel, though the particular words and the pleasantness of the sound are lost, and quite gone out of the mind. Perhaps this long stay upon that text in the Hebrews, may be justly styled a digression; but I thought it at this time necessary, because I have heard the complaint of many a gracious soul with concern, about the badness of their memory, to whom this sound distinction of retaining the truths, though we let go the bare words, may be of solid use and comfort. And so I shall proceed,

Secondly, to give you the names, distinctions,

and use of the more noble and superior faculties, with their relation and dependence upon each other; and that the understanding and reason, or power of reasoning and making judgment, are really two distinct faculties, I trust to make appear.

And the first I shall name to you is the understanding, which considered, as ofttimes it must, distinct from the soul, and as one of her mental operations, either in or out of the body, it is her eye, or visive power; by which she discerneth, converseth with, and judgeth about the nature of things, and the physical and moral difference betwixt them, whether considered visible or invisible, as to the body. And as the eye is to the body, so is this faculty to the soul; if the eye of the body be clear, and in a good light, it is of excellent use and benefit; but if it be dark it is of little or no service: and thus it is with the eye or eyes of the mind, if that is dark, as it is in all, through the fall and other accidental causes, the person is, in a metaphorical sense, said to be blind; and so he can only guess at and grope after spiritual things, as the scripture abundantly testifieth; of which in its proper place. There is, indeed, a twofold way of giving notice of things to the understanding, whereby she is able to form some proper, though inadequate ideas of things visible and invible; the one is by the senses, which are without, and seated in the body. Hence by the help of the eye, the understanding taketh in, and conceiveth aright, as to the place and distance, and different shape and colour, and the like, of material bodies; as the sense of feeling helpeth the understanding to the knowledge of their different qualities and accidents, whether light or heavy, hot or cold, hard or soft, wet or dry, &c. and so are the taste and smell of things suited thereto; and so the ear, as to the difference of melody, or ungratefulness of sounds: and thus, from the visible works of creation, " the invisible Being and Former of all things," Rom. i. 20, and his invisible attributes, such as power, wisdom, goodness, and might, in some good measure have been clearly seen and understood: but, besides, there are other notices both of God and of the nature and tendency of actions morally good or evil; and they are from the indelible law of nature, as at first writ plainly upon the tables of Adam's heart, chap. ii. 15. and from him with their nature transmitted and left, as to some remainders of it, down to his posterity; but of these things I am not now treating: this then shall suffice, That the understanding, considered as a faculty, is the soul's eye, or visive power, by which she discerneth one thing from another, in order to form a true judgment, as to their nature and morality.

The second superior and more noble power in the soul of man, is that discursive faculty called REASON. This faculty is, I confess, for the most part confounded with the understanding, as though they were not two distinct powers in the soul; but if we will rightly and justly distinguish, the understanding is only the eye or visive power, as has been shewed, and reason is that faculty by which we search and sift out the nature, truth, or mystery of things within the sphere of reason; and by ratiocination infer and deduce one thing either truly or falsely from another: and so understanding is the light and evidence of things natural and moral, as faith and the word are the evidence of things which are purely Divine, and depend upon revelation only. So that if this mental eye, the understanding, be dark or deceived, then reason, like a judge misinformed and imposed upon, errs in judgment, and gives a false sentence. This Divine reason, the image of its Maker in man's soul, was first set up at our creation, as God's deputy or viceroy therein, to superintend, govern, and moderate the other faculties, and all actions of human life, Gen. i. 27, compared with chap. ix. 6, and with 2 Pet. i. 4. How it came to be displaced, and something falsely so called fixed in its room, I shall lay open in its proper place: as also how still at times in the unregenerate it performs that function in man, of judging and reproving: for which it obtaineth the name of conscience, which also with relation to the present discharge of its function may be called good or evil. Its principal work it has to do at present, is, as I said, to moderate and controul the roving fancy, and ruder passions of the soul, which since the fall are like a tumultuous mob and rabble in a riot and rebellion against the higher powers, and thereby settle, order, and compose them, that they may not usurp reason's place, and so seduce the will to be always on their side. Which leads me, in the

Third place, to consider that noble and superior elective power, called the will. This faculty in its office or order takes place last, upon the sentence that either doth or should come from reason rightly informed; and it hath two parts, elective and negative: and thus the will ought always to follow reason as its guide, and not be at the beck of wild fancy, or the disorderly affections and unruly passions: for this were to "follow a multitude to do evil," Exod. xxiii. 2. And here it may not be altogether amiss to throw in a scripture-distinction between the elective and executive power: since one is distinct from, and may be where the other in a great measure is wanting; else what meaneth that of the apostle, " with me to will is present, but how to perform that which is good, I find not." Rom. vii. 18. And again, " It is God that worketh in you both to will, and to do of his own good pleasure," Phil. iii. 13. Thus, we find freedom of will, even where the will is spiritually renewed and sanctified, is not sufficient for the performance of that which is good without superadditional power from above: for allow the will its perfect liberty, either of choice or negation, yet that faculty is not so far absolute as to do what it pleaseth: and that because the other faculties, i. e. imagination, affections, and passions, will not only incline towards and hanker after other things, but act in a way of opposition and rebellion both to reason and will, as renewed and sanctified but in part. So that I think the true state of the controversy about the freedom of man's will, is not about its physical liberty, of which none can justly doubt, but about its moral freedom, and executive power of performing the thing assented to as good. And now whatever executive power the will might have before the fall, as being perfectly subject to reason and all the rest of the powers in a state of order and subjection, yet no such power is at present to be found, no not in the most sanctified and mortified saint on earth: for were the saint once got thus far, that as to holy and spiritual acts and performances, he could do as he would, perfection would soon follow: for what else hindereth now, but real impotency, through the remains of the old man still lodging in the members, who, by his influence, often raiseth disorder and rebellion amongst the lower powers, against the government and dominion of grace, which is "the kingdom of God set up in man's soul at regeneration and conversion," Luke xvii. 21, compared with Rom. xiv. 17; whereby both enlightened and sanctified reason, and the law of grace in the soul, are served as the soldiers and ship's crew serve their head officers and commanders when they have opportunity, and are resolved to mutiny and rebel; that is, they first overcome and bind the leading officers who will not come into their measures, and then they steer the vessel whither they please, while their commanders can do little else than shew their dislike and bear a protest against them: and that this is oft the case of the regenerate who are in part renewed and sanctified, is manifest both from scripture and the saints' experience; being feelingly, and to the life expressed by the great apostle in those words: "I find then a law, that when I would do good, evil is present with me: for I delight in the law of God after the inward man; but I see another law in my members, warring against the law in my mind, and bringing me into captivity to the law of sin, which is in my members," Rom. vii. 21, 22, 23. And now this is so far from not being the case of a saint or regenerate person, as some have pretended, that it really is not, nor can it be the complaint of any other but the regenerate man: for he only it is that can say that he delighteth in the law of God after the inward man; and that with him to will is present, though he findeth little or no strength for the performance of the good desired and delighted in. From whence I think it appears very clear from scripture and experience, that though the elective power is in the will, yet not the executive, so that while the flesh lusteth against the spirit, we cannot do the things we would: nor can we at all times leave those things undone that we would not do; but this, I trust, will be set in a stronger light in another place.

There still remaineth something to be spoke, according to my former promise, concerning the nature and office of conscience; not that I shall trouble you with the etymology and derivation of the word, but only let you know what I apprehend it to be, and of what use and dignity in the soul of man. Some indeed make it a distinct faculty, by making understanding and reason to be one and the same thing, then conscience supplieth the proper place of reason; indeed if I thought, and were willing to place it as a distinct faculty, I should call it the soul's power of self-reflection and censure: for, with submission, conscience is not so much a self-knowledge, as the soul is privy to all its past actions, as it is a power of self-judging; and so of self-acquitting or condemning. It is a court of equity set up in man's soul under his sovereign lord and legislator, the King of heaven, to whom of right he doth belong: and so it is but another distinct office of reason, as God's vicegerent, to act as judge: for hereby a judgment is made of past actions as to their morality, whether good or evil: and accordingly the man is either condemned or acquitted in a judicial manner: hence the apostle saith, "if our hearts, (i. e. conscience,) condemn us, God is greater than our hearts, and knoweth all things," better than they. 1 John iii. 20, 21. And so though conscience may err, and censure wrong, as oftentimes through mistake it doth, yet the sentence shall not be binding in heaven, nor ought it to hinder our addresses by unfeigned faith and prayer: but then, argueth he, if our hearts or consciences do not condemn, but on the other hand acquit us, then "we have boldness in his presence." Thus, conscience is the candle of the Lord set up in man's soul, by which he searcheth and exposeth to public view, all the chambers of the belly, * Prov. xx. 27; that is, all the secret, dark recesses of the soul's habitation in the body, as she is said to dwell and operate either in the heart or reins, or any other part. An "evil conscience," in the scripture-sense of the word, is a guilty accusing conscience, not yet sufficiently sprinkled, pacified, and cleansed with the blood of Jesus, as the sin-atoning sacrifice; and till this is done it can do nothing but condemn the sinner," Heb. x. 22, compared with ch. ix. 14. A good conscience is that which hath nothing to lay to a man's charge as to things immoral and offensive, either against God or man; as is evident from that of the apostle, in his defence before the governor Felix: "And herein do I exercise myself to have always a conscience void of (scandal or) offence towards God and man," Acts xxiv. 16. And thus as an accusing or acquitting conscience is occupied about the morality of past actions; so a weak, tender, scrupulous conscience is busied, and turmoileth itself about the lawfulness or unlawfulness of things called by some indifferent, and not expressly declared in the written word to be morally evil in themselves. Hence every Christian not be-

---

* חפש khaphas, signifieth a most exact search made by ransacking, as we say, every hole and corner in a room. So it is used Obadiah 6, compared with Jerem. xlix. 10. So Prov. ii. 4, and 1 Kings xx. 6.

ing wise enough to know how far his Christian liberty, as to these things, reaches and extends, one believeth that he may eat any thing, Rom. xiv. 2; another who is weak, i. e. through a scrupulous conscience, only eateth herbs: and some, says he, at that time, though they eat meat, eat it as a thing sacrificed to an idol; and so their conscience being weak is thereby defiled: and therefore every one, as he ought to regard the welfare of his brother, should take great heed not to lay a stumbling block or snare in the way of them that are weak and of a scrupulous mind. 1 Cor. viii. 7, 8, 9.

Thus much as to conscience, and as to the several distinct faculties, and their function and order of operation in the great soul of man. I shall now proceed to the

Second branch of this general head; and that is, to shew you how sin was first conceived in man's soul, and by what means it at first seized, overspread, defiled, and subjected all the rational powers under its tyrannical dominion. And now, that I may set this in a true light, it is needful that I first shew you in what capacity our first parent Adam stood, as considered in his upright estate, and first act of disobedience in eating the forbidden fruit: and then, secondly, lay open to you the subtlety of Satan in the method he took to seduce our first parents: in the latter part of which story it will plainly appear how SIN made its first entrance, and gradually seized on and enslaved the whole man. As to the

First of these, that is, in what capacity our first parent, Adam, stood both before and in the act of disobedience, it appears to be that of a covenant-head and undertaker for all his posterity, as to life and death, and eternal happiness or misery: and this is evidenced both from scripture and reason: in that we find he and his posterity in him were not only turned out of Eden, and debarred the use of the fruit of the tree of life, but both he, and we in him, were subjected to the curse of the law, which took place first upon him, and then on us as considered in him, and as descending from him; and that because he did not continue in obedience to the law and revealed will of his Creator. And accordingly the scriptures teach, that by the offence of that one man, Adam, judgment came upon all men to condemnation, i. e. to damnation, for that is the consequence of every transgression and disobedience; and now whether we read it through the one offence, as coming or being imputed, to all men; or that through the offence of one, judgment, i. e. the sentence, came upon all men to their condemnation, it is still much the same: for the text, with its coherence and context, fully proveth that Adam, a figure of Christ, as the second

Adam, stood in the capacity of a covenant-head and public person; else death, judgment, and condemnation could not immediately seize such as never actually transgressed; wherefore, as says the Holy Spirit, by one man sin entered into the world, and death by sin, and so death passed or seized on all men, not only because all have sinned, but in him, i. e. in that very man, all have sinned: for by this one man's disobedience many were made sinners. And here by the way note the apostle's change of the time in the two different acts of imputation on God's part:* for he it is that fixeth both the acts of the two Adams by way of imputation to their proper offsprings and federal members. As to Adam's act, he doth not say they will be sinners, i. e. by imitation, but they are made sinners, that is, reckoned and accounted so in the eye and sentence of the holy law, and that by that one man's first act of disobedience: whereas of the others, who relate as a federal seed and spiritual offspring to the second Adam the Lord from heaven, he says, by his obedience, they shall be made righteous, i. e. when they believe: for look, as natural generation is the instrumental means and way of conveyance both of pollution and

* The 1st is in the 1st aorist, κατιςάθησαν, they were fixed, or made sinners: and the 2d is in the 1st future καταςαθήσονται, they shall be made righteous: and both of them are in the passive voice of καθίςημι, whose theme is Ἵςημι.

guilt from the first Adam, so faith in Christ Jesus is ordained by God to be the mean by which that righteousness becometh ours : but yet our apostle doth not stop at natural generation as the mean of conveyance, as if men were not sinners in God's account before; but he by this expression, "by one man's disobedience many were made sinners," intimateth that all mankind were so reputedly in God's account: for that they were all in Adam's loins considered as a covenant-head; and so they all sinned in him, and fell with him in a much more proper sense than that of Levi, who is said after a sort to have paid tithes to Melchisedeck in Abraham's loins, forasmuch as he was seminally there when Melchisedeck met him, Heb. vii. 9. 10. Thus much as to Adam's fall, and how we, according to the Holy Scriptures, are justly said to have fell with him, and sinned with him : for that he being our federal head, and we in his loins, we also eat the forbidden fruit, and were turned out of all, and subjected to misery, death, and condemnation. I shall now proceed,

Secondly, to shew you the crafty method the devil took when he set upon our first parents; and how, and by what means lust and sin were first engendered, and found an easy passage into, and conquest over the most noble powers. This method, then, which the devil took was peculiar, and adapted to the very nature, coherence, and influence both of the persons and the order of working of the human powers one upon the other; which is like that of an engine or machine, which, if one principal wheel be moved, though in a disorderly manner, all the rest of the wheels are thereby put into the like disorderly motion: for the devil being well skilled in natural philosophy and physiognomy, first set upon the woman, as the man's weak side, knowing that where the affections are the strongest, and the passions soonest raised, there judgment is the weakest; and that, if he had once seduced the woman, the work was as good as done; for that she would soon complete the rest by alluring charms and importunities peculiar to the sex. And so he accordingly applies himself to the woman when alone, as we may rationally enough conclude, that so Adam, her covenant-head and guide, might not be present to dissuade nor hinder, by resisting him in his first attempts. And so it was, the man neither heard the parly nor felt the fatal deadly blow and conquest upon his dearest part the woman, till half himself was gone, and she engaged (Oh cowardly foe, and cruel harbinger of death, and every deadly ill!) to betray the other part into the enemy's hand, by enticing and persuading her husband and head, like her, to yield. Thus, it is plain, the devil knew aforehand which was the " weakest vessel," 1. Pet. iii. 7 ; and that there was none so proper nor capable to work upon the man's affections, and steal away his heart by the magic of her natural pleasing charms and resistless importunities, as she, his bosom friend, and one without whom he could not possibly be completely happy nor useful in this world : and yet with whom he could not live one hour comfortably, but as he complied with her soft and winning temper and importunities. And thus, though the man was by his wife enticed and persuaded to eat, yet the scripture telleth us, " That Adam was not deceived, but the woman being deceived, was first in the transgression," 1 Tim. ii. 14. And now how the woman came to be deceived, and so to fall into the sin of eating the forbidden fruit, is next to be considered. And thus we read the devilish serpent began with the woman; " Is it true, (good woman) that God has said, Ye must not eat of every tree in the garden ?" To which she replies, " We may eat of the fruit of the trees of the garden : but of the fruit of that tree which is in the middle of the garden, God hath said, Ye shall not eat of it, neither shall ye touch it, lest ye die." This latter part of the answer was very likely a charge given to her by her husband : and it is what the wise men among the Jews called the hedge or fence set about the command to keep men far off from transgression; because the coming near, first to view, and then to touch and handle the fruit, is the very beginning of transgression. Well, to this her answer the serpent replies; "Ye shall not surely die: for God doth know, that in the day ye eat thereof, then your eyes shall be be opened: and ye shall be as gods, knowing good and evil." Thus, basely insinuating that God deprived them of a peculiar blessing and benefit, in denying the free use of that tree: in which he both lied and deceived; first he told a lie, in that he said that God knew that they should not certainly die; and hence he is said to be a liar and murderer from the beginning, John viii. 44, and therefore called the father, i. e. the first inventor and teller of a lie. And then, secondly, as he was a liar from the beginning, so also was he a deceiver in these words, " ye shall be as gods," Gen. iii. 5, because in Hebrew the speech is very ambiguous and doubtful; for כאלהים * Ce-lohim, may

---

* כאלהים which is rightly rendered as God's, i. e. angelic spirits, who are so styled, both considered as good and bad, in these texts, Psal. xcvii. 7. and Heb. i. 6. For all the angels of God who are there commanded to worship the Son, as being truly God as well as Man, must be construed of the evil as well as good, according to 1 Pet. iii. 22, compared with Phil. ii. 9, 10, and so the Greek interpreters render it ὡς θεοὶ, as gods, and the Chaldee Targums say Cerabrebin, as princes or great potentates, or Cemal-achin Rabrebin, the mighty angels.

be taken either for God the Creator, or for angelic spirits; he indeed intended it of himself, and his companions in iniquity, who knew good by being once good and happy, and afterwards evil by becoming evil and miserable, through his apostacy from God: but the woman being deceived, thought he meant and intended it of a being like her Maker, which puffed her up with an ambitious desire of bettering her estate, by equalizing, in some measure, her Creator. Hence the devil, in allusion to this story, is called the old Serpent and Deceiver, yea, the murderer from the beginning; for that he thus basely murdered our first parents, and all their posterity in them.

And now the woman being thus deceived and imposed upon by the devil, she begins with gazing on the forbidden fruit, and then proceeds to reasoning and debating within herself after this manner; 'the tree, though prohibited, is fair and beautiful, and its fruit is charming and pleasant to the eye, and cannot but be good for food, and therefore much to be desired; especially seeing, as is plainly enough intimated in its very name, it is a fruit whose tendency and effect, if eaten, is not to hurt the body, but is to improve the soul by making its eater wise: and what! since thus to be wise as this, is brave indeed, who would reject the benefit, and slight this generous offer and opportunity to be made for ever? And seeing wisdom is the most excellent and desirable of all created good, what bad consequence can there be in being wise? Sure none; but suppose there should any evil, deadly accident happen, is not the remedy at hand, and the tree of life prepared as an antidote? Get ready therefore, it is but putting forth the hand and taking and eating also of that, and we shall live for ever.' Some such reasoning and debate, no doubt, there was, before the will was brought to yield to the concupiscence begot in the affections, through her first feeding the passions by pleasing fancies taken in at the eye.

And here I might venture to say, her false way of reasoning and deducing inferences from significant names, and the devil's false proposition, undid both her and us; and so will it fare with all those, who by the vain art of ratiocination lean upon their own reason, and trust to their own understanding and capacities as to things divine. And thus it was that sin entered into the world, and death, judgment, and eternal condemnation by sin. Eve, she gazeth on the pleasing alluring fruit, until its beauty, by cogitation, deluded the fancy with a false shew of good; and these awakening the passions, inflamed them on a sudden: and upon this there was engendered a strong appetite or desire in the affection-part of the soul; we call it LUST, the Jewish Rabbies call it YETSER HARAY, the evil appetite, or the concupiscible faculty: and now nothing being wanting but the will, this also, through the aforesaid abuse of the art of reasoning, is presently obtained, by the presenting a false good to the more noble faculties, upon which darkness seizeth upon the mind or understanding; and reason thus imposed upon, giveth false judgment; or rather at this very instant imagination and passion out-voted reason, and drowned her stiller voice in the soul; and by displacing her, they got the reins of the will into their own hands, and so enticed and drew the whole man into sin; which latter part is excellently set forth in that of James; " every man is tempted, when he is drawn away of his own lust, and enticed. Then when lust hath conceived, it bringeth forth sin: and sin when it is finished, bringeth forth death," James i. 14, 15. That is, thus lust or this concupiscible appetite being engendered as aforesaid, in the heart, the seat and bed of the affections and passions, and being a sort of vital, powerful principle, by the apostle called the " law of sin in the members," Rom. vii. 21, 23, 25, because of the pleasing, powerful motions it causeth in the flesh,* though in the unregenerate it is seated chiefly in the mind; this, I say, spurreth and prompteth the soul forward, till it is drawn aside from its guard and duty Godward, and the will is enticed or allured, as by a bait, to consent to the lusting appetite: and this conjunction of the carnal affections and will, is that by which means sin is conceived; lust is its male parent, and the will is a female which cannot be forced, but must be deluded and won over by fair or false pretensions; and no sooner hath the will yielded, though it be but to cast an eye, or but just to touch the object or pleasing bait, but sin immediately is in the heart conceived; as saith our blessed Lord, "He that looketh upon a woman so as to lust after her, he hath committed adultery already with her in his heart," Matt. v. 28.

Thus, I have endeavoured to lay open to your view something of the way and manner of sin's entrance, and how it made it's progress, and by degrees corrupted and subjected the whole man. Let us then, for a conclusion of this second branch, take a short survey of all the powers of the soul as

* Τὰ παθήματα, Rom. vii. 5. is not only an affection or inclination to sin, but it signifieth the boiling, pricking motions and strong passions of sin, or evil appetite, which as it were spurreth the flesh and mind forwards, first to consent, and then to act.

now defiled and enslaved. And first, as to the imagination or cogitative faculty, God hath declared, as you have already heard, that every imagination of the thoughts of man's heart is evil and only evil, and that from its youth, Gen. vi. 5, and chap. viii. 21. And then, as to the affections and natural passions of the soul, these are declared to be carnal, sensual and earthly: these were that part of David, which, as he complained, cleaved to the dust, Psal. cxix. 25. Yea, these are the loins of the mind that want to be girded up as long garments, which otherwise hanging loose about the feet, will hinder our activity in the ways of God, Luke xii. 35, and Ephes. vi. 14, and 1 Pet. i. 13. And then, thirdly, as to the memory, it is become an evil treasury and store-house, readily retaining evil things, but letting slip the best. And then, fourthly, as to the understanding, this is the dark, yea, blind part of the soul, Rom. i. 21. and Ephes. i. 18: and so great is this blindness and darkness of man through the fall and the consequences thereof, that it is expressed in the abstract, darkness, i. e. to the highest degree. And thus, in the fifth place, reason is depraved, and, as I have sometimes thought, served just like Samson by a beloved lust, which proveth a Delilah to entice and betray: and then being captivated and made stark-blind, like him, it serveth only to gratify the affections making them and others sport. And sad it is to see, though it is very observable, that many men of the brightest genius, and who are the greatest pretenders to reason, are, for the most part, the furthest from the practical part thereof; being, as to spiritual things, stark blind and mad: some being Sceptics, Deists, and Heretics, and the rest Atheists, or somewhat worse. And lastly, as to the will, this is so far from being in the state of liberty pretended, that it is really a captive, drudge, and slave, sold under sin: and ready at all times to shew its real backwardness to good, and forwardness to evil. Yea, it is obstinate and rebellious, as has been shewed at large. And now this being man's present state, I am, in the

Third place, to shew you how victorious grace and Almighty power, when invincibly put forth upon the soul, make a gracious conquest without offering any violence to the will, or infringing any thing of its just liberty and privilege; according as it is written: "Thy people shall be willing in the day of thy power," Psal. cx. 3. This day of a Mediator's power, is the gospel-day of efficacious grace upon the hearts of his chosen people; who are *his* by donation and purchase as to right, before they are *his* by conquest, and the marriage-contract at the time of effectual calling: the gospel-ministry is the instituted means that God hath ordained, being accompanied by the Spirit, to make the same powerful and efficacious to the hearts of his elect, both for renovation and salvation. For as Adam's sin began in hearkening to the voice of his wife, so the soul's return begins in God's circumcising and opening the ear: and the first thing that Messias bespeaks under the ministry is the ear, as it is written; " Hearken diligently unto me, incline your ear, and come unto me, hear and your soul shall live," Isai. lv. 2, 3. Hence faith is said to come by "hearing, and hearing by the word of God," Rom. x. 17; that is, the word preached first openeth the ear and heart, and then it worketh faith, which produceth obedience. For as sin entered by the outward senses, so likewise does grace; and as the forbidden fruit seized the imagination first, and then the affections and passions being wrought upon, they, as you heard, wrought upon and prevailed over the other more noble powers, thereby bringing over the will without force, from an approving and choosing of good to a greedy liking of, and consenting to evil; even so now in God's recovering of the sinner, he beginneth by the ear in hearing, or the eye in reading, to work upon the cogitative faculty; and by that means he first moveth and worketh upon the affections and passions of the soul, so as to open and incline the heart to attend the instituted and appointed means of grace, and to approve of and have some stirrings and desires after that which is good; and then shining with more light into the dark understanding, he, by degrees, discovereth to the soul both the misery and sinfulness of his present state of bondage and wrath, so as to make it weary of itself and its present condition: and now by an Almighty power he forms the new birth of grace, and also spiritual vital principles and dispositions: and the man is immediately newborn; " Not of blood, nor of the will of the flesh, nor of the will of man, but of God: who of his own will begets him with the word of truth," John i. 13, and James i. 18. And now from the affections thus wrought upon, and the heart thus sanctified by, and impregnated with, the vital and vigorous principles of grace, the man begins, like the prodigal, to come to himself; now it is he begins to use his reason aright, and communing with his own heart, he reasons and argues with himself after this manner; 'Why sit I still and quiet, and how can I rest night or day, while I am in such a miserable state, and perishing condition? If I continue in this present state I am undone for ever. If I go to the creature or the law for help and relief, and think to depend upon my own wisdom, ability, and righteousness, I shall certainly perish eternally. I have heard of a dying Saviour, I have heard of an atoning sacrifice, and of a justifying righteousness, wrought out by Christ, the Surety and Mediator of the new and best covenant, established upon better and more suitable promises than those under the law. I have also heard that with " Jehovah there are mercy, forgiveness, and plenteous redemption, that so he may be feared," Psal. cxxx. 4, 7. Yea, methinks I hear Him now calling to me, " Awake thou that sleepest, and arise from the dead, and Christ shall give thee light," Eph. v. 14. And again, " Let the wicked forsake his ways, and the unrighteous man his thoughts, and let him return unto the Lord and he will have mercy on him, and to our God, for he will abundantly pardon," Isa. lv. 7. I will therefore now arise, and venture, like the prodigal, upon the mercy and clemency of a tender-hearted and compassionate Father, who concerning his sons and daughters, has thus testified, " That he delighteth not in the death of a sinner," Ezek. xviii. 23, 32: thus then will I expostulate with him, " Father, I have sinned against heaven, and in thy sight, and am no more worthy to be called thy child," Luke xv. 18, 19; however, suffer me not to perish with hunger. " Behold I come unto thee; for thou art the Lord my God," Jer. iii. 22. " Take away iniquity, and receive me graciously, so will I render to thee, the calves of my lips," i. e. eternal praise and thanksgivings, Hosea xiv. 2:

I henceforth renounce my own righteousness in point of justification and acceptance; and come to thee for the change of raiment: all confidence in the flesh and creature performances I reject, as that which can administer no comfort nor relief; and only desire to be found in Christ, and not in any filthy garments and rotten rags of my own. And now, Lord, seeing this is the only door of mercy and hope set before me in the word, here I come to knock, and wait till I have admittance; being resolved to die at that door whose motto is, "And him that cometh to me I will not cast out," John vi. 37, upon any account whatsoever.'

This, my friends, or something like it, is the language of the heart of one under the Spirit's quickening efficacious work, in the day of power, or gospel-efficacy. Thus by the preaching and reading the word of God, the ear and heart are opened, and the affections touched and made to move after Christ; who, in this his day of efficacious grace upon the hearts of his chosen, worketh in them first to will and then to do; drawing them with the cords of love, and bands of the man Christ Jesus, fixed to the heart, the seat of all affections, love, joy, and desire. Thus the devil entices and allures to sin; and does he do it without forcing the will? So doth Christ under, and by the gospel allure and persuade, and make willing in the day of gospel-power and efficacious grace. Yea, and could the devil prevail by craft to draw off the will when it was wholly bent and inclined to good? And shall not Christ be allowed to have power and wisdom enough so to prevail and persuade, as thereby to bring the will back to its former freedom and inclination to good, and that without force or constraint? Yes, of unwilling he makes willing, not by forcing, but by sanctifying and renewing the soul in all its powers: for so it was long ago foretold, That God would persuade Japhet,* i. e. the Gentiles, and they should dwell in the tents of Shem, i. e. Jesus Christ, Gen. ix. 27: for Shem there, is put for Messias, as being both his father and type, as he was afterwards styled Melchisedeck, being King of righteousness and peace. And thus it is plain from scripture and every gracious soul's experience, that the will of man may by another be excited, persuaded, and inclined either to good or evil, by creature-arguments; how much more then by the Mediator's superior power and efficacious grace? The will of man being mutable as well as free, and subject to these several alterations before it is eternally fixed to good; as first it was created good and upright, inclined to good only, but mutable; so, secondly, at the fall it received a wrong

---

* Japht Elohim lejepheth, God shall persuade Japhet. The word Japht in the *future* is of פתה, he persuaded, allured.

bent and bias, an evil disposition seizing it, by degrees it grew more and more degenerate, obstinate, and inflexible to good, yet still mutable. In the beginning of conversion by grace it receiveth a gradual change, and becometh at first partly willing, and in part unwilling, of which more by and by. In the further work of the Spirit according to the new creature, it is effectually gained over to God, and the love and choice of good, and refusing the evil, yet so as that through the imperfection of sanctification and the remaining of the old man and body of sin and death, it ofttimes relapseth, being carried away by sudden temptations and spiritual decays.

It being too much like what is said by astrologers of the planet Mercury, viz. that it is good with the good, and bad with the bad; so that Reuben's motto suits with it, " unstable as water," Gen. xlix. 4. And this is the case of all the faculties: for that none of them are completely sanctified; but in the will it is more discernible as to the struggles and combats that are commenced and continued in the souls of the new-born, between the carnal unrenewed and the spiritual sanctified part of the soul, commonly called the flesh and spirit. But a time remaineth when the whole spirit, soul, and body will be thoroughly and completely sanctified : and then this fickle, inconstant faculty, together with the affections, will be eternally fixed to good in a state of perfect and endless bliss and happiness. And now to close this head, I shall entertain you with something out of holy Augustin,* being penned by himself in his book of Confessions, as the matter of his own experience as to the first work of God upon his soul, in working in him first to will, and after that to do of his own good pleasure. His words are these; 'The new will but now beginning to grow in me, by which I desired, disengaged of all other loves, freely to serve thee, and by which I wished to enjoy thee, O my God, the only certain pleasure, was not yet able to master the former will strengthened with age. So these two wills of mine, the one old, the other new, one carnal, the other spiritual, combatted one another, and in their disagreeance, rent and divided my soul. Thus I understood, myself being the experiment, that which I had read; how the flesh lusteth against the spirit, and the spirit against the flesh: and it was I that was in them both: but more, I in that which I allowed in myself, than in that which I disallowed; because for the most part I rather suffered it against my mind than willingly acted it.' Upon which, addressing

* Augustin's confessions in the English edition, lib. viii. chap. v. ix, x, xi.

himself to search out the mystery of this conflict and contrariety within himself at this his first conversion, he thus begins to expostulate and reason with himself: 'From whence such a monster? And how can this be? The mind commands the body, and is presently obeyed; the mind commands itself, and is opposed; the mind commands the motion of the hand, and so speedily is it executed, as the obedience is scarce distinguishable from the command: the same mind commands itself to will this or the other good, and yet it doth it not. Whence such a monster? And how can this be? It commands, I say, that it should will a thing which it could not command unless it willed it first; and yet that is not done that it commands. The mystery is this; indeed it is not wholly willing, therefore doth it not wholly command; for it only so far commands as it wills: and so far as it willeth not its command is not done, because the will is not wholly inclined to do it. To will, and yet to will in part, therefore is no monster; but a sickness and infirmity of the mind, which cannot entirely arise when lifted up by the truth, because it is counterpoised by vicious custom. For when I thus deliberated to enter upon the service of my Lord God, as I had long designed, it was I that willed, and I also that nilled it. I was the same I who as yet neither fully willed, nor fully nilled it; and therefore was in contention with myself, and divided and rent from myself; but this rent in me was indeed made against my will; and therefore it was no more I that wrought this distraction, but sin that dwelleth in me, from the punishment of that first more freely committed offence; inasmuch as I am a son of Adam. Thus sick in mind, and thus tormented, I was accusing myself much more severely than formerly, and tumbling and winding to and fro in my chain, till I had wholly broken it off; a small piece only of which now held me, and yet it held me still. And thou, O Lord, pressest sore upon me in my inward parts with a severe mercy, redoubling the lashes of fear and shame, that I might not give over stretching, and lest I should not break off that thin piece which now remained, and so it should grow again upon me, and bind me faster than ever. For now I said within myself, ' Come, let it be done presently, just now let it be done:' and already in a word I began to league with thee; and already I almost did it: but quite did it not: for there still hung upon me these trifles of trifles, and vanities of vanities, i. e. sinful motions, which plucking me by the vesture of the flesh, softly whispered to me, 'will you then thus forsake us? And from this moment shall not this nor that be lawful for you to do any more for ever?' Thus they somewhat retarded me, that I made not due speed to catch away myself, and shake them off and to spring from them whither thy grace called me; whilst a strong custom of them said unto me, ' thinkest thou that thou canst, for ever henceforth, live without the practice of such things?' I indeed blushed exceedingly, that I yet continued to hear the whisperings of these toys, and to hang in suspense; such was the contest acted within, in my heart only, between me and myself. But thou, O Lord, wert good and merciful, and thy right hand sounded the profundity of my death, and drew out of the bottom of my heart that abyss of corruption, summed up in this : to will all that thou wouldest, and to nill all that thou wouldest not. But then (adds he,*) where was all this while, during so many years, and out of what low and deep retreat of my soul didst thou thus in a moment call forth, that my (now indeed) FREEWILL, wherewith I should submit my neck to thy easy yoke, and my shoulders to thy light burthen, O Jesus Christ, my Helper and Redeemer? How sweet upon a sudden became it now to me to want the sweets of those toys! And what before was my fear to lose, how was it now my joy to dismiss! For thou, the true and supreme sweetness, didst expel them from me, and didst enter in thyself instead of them. Now my mind was freed

* Lib. ix. chap. 1.

from those consuming cares of getting honour; and now my infant tongue began to converse with thee, my ambition, my riches, my salvation, and my Lord God.'

Thus far St. Austin, as to this part of his experience relating to God's working in him first to will, and then to do; and with respect to the struggles and conflicts in the will itself, in the beginning of his conversion to God, before it was made so far free, and at liberty as to act with a full consent of mind: all of which are effected by the sweet efficacious and powerful work of the Spirit in conjunction with the word, upon the heart of Christ's people in the day of power. And thus I have laid open to you something of the nature and distinct use of the several distinct faculties in the soul of man, and their dependance and influence upon each other; as also how sin made its first entrance upon them by the outward senses working upon the affections, and they upon the will till it came over to them by consent: and I have also shewn that even this is the very method God takes to recover his by the ministry of the word, through the ear, working upon the heart; and by his grace and Spirit begetting a new life and disposition in the will, he by degrees looseth the bands and breaketh off the chains that held it down fast as a slave and captive to sin and Satan;

and so restores it to its former freedom and propensity to good, and by his mighty power engaged, secureth it from a total and final elapse: and this is done without the least coercion or abridgment of its natural freedom; crowning the work at last with a perfect freedom from sinful dispositions, and an everlasting stability in glory without any alteration of the nature and true physical liberty of free-will.

Thus, having gone through and dispatched this third head in the method proposed, I shall now dismiss it, and pass on to the next.

CHAP. V.

Shewing the Passiveness of Men in several Parts of the Spirit's Work upon their Hearts, both in and after Conversion.

THE fourth head in order to be taken into consideration, is to manifest in several instances that a person may, in a true and proper sense, be said to be really passive in some part of the Holy Spirit's work upon the heart, both in and after conversion. In which I shall endeavour to lay open and demonstrate, that there is a passiveness of soul under some parts of the Holy Spirit's work in and after effectual calling and conversion: at which time the man is first a patient under the Spirit's hand before he is able to be a doer of his will. Hence we are said to be " his workmanship, created anew in Christ Jesus," Eph. ii. 10, in order to the right spiritual performance of any good works, which God hath foreordained us to walk therein. And now the method I shall take to set this in a true and full light shall be,

First, to shew you that man is really and truly passive in his receiving of the Holy Spirit, as the Spirit of all effectual conviction and saving grace.

Secondly, that the soul is really passive in its receiving vital union with Christ, as the head and root of all life and spiritual strength and fruitfulness.

Thirdly, I shall demonstrate from out of the Holy Scripture, that a man is really passive in the great work of regeneration, or the new birth, as it is effected by the Spirit and the word.

Fourthly, that there is a real passiveness of soul in the first beginnings of all spiritual motions of grace in order for the repeated acts and exercise thereof.

First of all, I am to shew you that every man is passive in his first receiving of the Spirit of God, as the Spirit of all powerful conviction and saving faith. In which two things will be needful; as, first, to shew you that Christ doth first apprehend and lay hold of the sinner by the Spirit, as the Spirit of powerful conviction and grace, before ever the sinner in good earnest seeks after him, as it is written; "I was found of them that did not seek me; I was made manifest to them that did not ask after me," Rom. x. 20. And then, secondly, I shall lay open to you somewhat of the Spirit's special work upon the soul, in which it will appear to be passively held under conviction, and that at first entirely against its will and inclination.

First, then, it is very manifest, both from scripture and experience, that God beginneth first to seek after and layeth effectual hold of the sinner, in order to convince and convert him, before ever he setteth out after God in a way that is right and acceptable; even as the good shepherd first goeth after that which is lost, seeking of it till he find it, and then he bringeth it home upon his own shoulders rejoicing, Luke xv. 4, 5, and compared with Ezek. xxxiv. 11, 12, 13. And this is usually done by and under the ministry of the word; for it is only under the gospel that the Spirit of God is given to the elect at effectual calling, in order to convince and convert them to the Lord. Hence the word is said to take hold of, or as it were seize and arrest them, in order to prevent their persisting in sin and open rebellion, and thereby secure the sinner's return. And to this end the Spirit of God is not only promised and given to attend the ministry of the word, but the Spirit is also given, and sent forth to make a seizure and take possession of an elect vessel, so as to enter, and dwell in the heart: and this indeed is the great specific difference betwixt the transitory convictions of the Spirit and word in the ministry, as wrought upon an auditory in common, and those lasting and powerful saving convictions which are wrought by the same Spirit upon the hearts of God's elect in their effectual calling; in the former, the Spirit is no indweller, but worketh only in a transient way, and as at some distance; but in the latter he secretly and powerfully possesseth himself of the heart, and so remaineth and abideth by, and watcheth over and secureth his own work begun in the heart till he hath perfected the same, as it is written; " Being confident of this very thing, that he who hath begun a good work in you, will perform," i. e. perfect and finish the same, Phil. i. 6. Hence we find it to be a promise peculiar to the new covenant, that God will put his Spirit within his people to dwell, inhabit, and possess them as a spiritual house and temple, Ezek. xxxvi. 27. And from this indwelling of the Holy Spirit in God's people, as an inhabitant, the apostle formeth a strenuous argument against fornication and idolatry; "What, know ye not that your body is the temple of the Holy Spirit, which is in you, which ye have of God, and ye are not your own?" 1 Cor. vi. 19. So again, it is written concerning believers; " Ye are not in the flesh, but in the Spirit, if so be that the Spirit of God dwell in you. Now if any man have not the Spirit of Christ, he is none of his," Rom. viii. 9.

Thus then it appears from scripture, that there is such a thing as the Spirit's possessing of and dwelling in a child of God, in such a manner as is peculiar to him only, and which is the greatest characteristic and best evidence of his being so: and it is also plain from scripture, that the Spirit is given to dwell in an elect soul, first as a spirit of conviction and efficacious saving grace, in order to effectually convince the soul, and regenerate the man: in which first reception and work of the Spirit, as now dwelling in him, he is wholly passive, and is wrought upon without his consent, nay, contrary to his present inclination: which bringeth me next to consider, and lay open to you in its proper order, something of the Spirit's work under this head of conviction, and the distinct steps thereof, as begun and gradually carried on upon the soul; in which much of the man's passiveness, as to that part of the Spirit's work, will appear; forasmuch as the Spirit of God, when he at first seizeth the soul, and taketh possession thereof for Christ, as a Spirit of powerful conviction and saving grace, he findeth an unwillingness to be saved in God's way; and the man at first resisteth the Spirit's motions, convictions, and reproofs, till he is effectually made willing in the day of his Almighty power. And now, in order thereunto, the Spirit first giveth the soul a repeated survey of its past and present sinful life. Secondly, as a Spirit of conviction, he giveth the soul an astonishing conviction and sight of his own vileness and guiltiness before God, and the wrath and vengeance he has deserved. Thirdly, he giveth the soul a humbling view of the corruption and uncleanness of his nature, as to the filth, depravity, perverseness, and deceit therein, all which make up the plague of the heart. Fourthly, he convinceth the soul of its real impotency and disability to perform that which is truly and spiritually good and acceptable before God. Fifthly, he convinceth the soul of the real need and necessity of saving faith in Christ; and of the pernicious effects and damnable nature of the sin of unbelief. As to the

First of these, it is manifest from the word and experience, that the Spirit of God beginneth in a way of conviction of sin, and carrieth on that work by a mighty power, setting home the terror and killing part of the law, though in some more and in others less: and in some the bondage-part and terror is not only sharper, but longer than it is in others. And this is done that the soul may be thoroughly humbled, and savingly cast down before God, as it is written; "For the lofty looks of man shall be humbled, and the haughtiness of men shall be bowed down, and the Lord alone shall be exalted in that day." Thus then, the law is of use under the gospel to convince of sin: for, as saith the apostle as to his own experience, "By the law is the knowledge of sin," Rom. iii. 20. "Nay, I had not known sin but by the law. For without the law sin was dead. For I was alive without the law once; but when the commandment came, sin revived, and I died; and the commandment which was for life, I found to be unto death. For sin taking occasion by the commandment deceived me, and by it slew me," chap. vii. 6, 7, 8, 9, 11, 12, 13. And this was done that sin might appear, as we say, in its own colours; hence he adds, "Was then that which is good made death to me? God forbid. But sin, that it might appear sin, wrought death in me by that which is good; that sin by the commandment might become exceeding sinful." That is, that sin by this means might appear in the sinner's eye to be, as indeed it is, excessively sinful, vile and heinous. Thus in conviction; the straight and strict rule of the holy law being laid home to the crooked lines and perverse actions of a sinful life, the disproportion is the more discernible and self-evident; and the innumerable swervings aside, sinfulness, and short-comings in the best performances begin to appear, and stare the awakened sinner in the face; and like a ghost continually haunt and affright him : yea, those pleasing childish faults, which in childhood and youth are overlooked as harmless and innocent, do now, under the present conviction, appear in the glass of the holy law to be monstrously great and culpable; for as the least star, though scarce discernible, is really many thousand times bigger than it is vulgarly accounted, even so sin now appeareth to the soul in the least act infinitely affronting to God, and of such a demerit as that the sinner can never possibly atone justice, nor give an equivalent satisfaction for it: and the soul begins to say, as he of old in another case; " Innumerable evils have compassed me about, mine iniquities have taken hold upon me, so that I am not able to look up; they are more than the hairs of my head, therefore my heart faileth me," Ps. xl. 12. And again, " Mine iniquities are gone over mine head : as a heavy burden, they are too heavy for me. My wounds stink and are corrupt, because of my foolishness. I am troubled; I am bowed down greatly; I go mourning all the day long: for my loins are filled with a loathsome disease: and there is no soundness in my flesh, because of thine anger; neither is there any rest in my bones because of my sins," Ps. xxxviii. 4, 5, 6, 7, 8. And what occasioneth all this pain and uneasiness in the flesh and mind, you read in that he saith, "Thine arrows stick fast in me, and thy hand presseth me sore," ver. 2. But this is not all; the next work of the Holy Spirit, as the Spirit of conviction of sin, is in the

Second place, to give the soul, now under his awakening power and efficacious conviction, an awful humbling sight and sense of its own vileness and guiltiness before God, and the wrath and eternal vengeance due to it upon that account. And this is done and effected by the Holy Spirit's representing to the soul the real true merit and desert of sin, and the curse that is justly pronounced upon the sinner for every transgression and disobedience; thereby letting forth the fire of the law, or setting it home in the penal part as to its sentence: and this killeth the man, as we say, outright. Hence the law, in this its work and office to terrify by its rigour and curse, is called the "ministration of death and condemnation," 2 Cor. iii. 7. 9, or rather of eternal damnation, as it is a killing letter engraven on the tables of stone. And then it is that sin beginneth in the conscience to be armed with a deadly sting, as you read, "The sting of death is sin: and the strength of sin is the law," 1 Cor. xv. 56. Every sting or bite of a venomous serpent is attended with deadly poison, which entering into the wound or wounds the sting makes in the flesh, immediately poisons and inflames the wound, and fills the flesh with pain and cruel deadly torture; so that it is then with the awakened sinner as it is said of the wicked in another case, " Terrors beset him round about, and make him afraid on every side," Job. xviii. 11. " Now he travels in pain, and a dreadful sound is in his ears, even in the midst of all his outward prosperity: yea they prevail again him as a king ready for the battle," ch. xv. 20, 21, 24. Which terror of conscience, and its effects of horror, shame, and guilt, through the apprehensions of eternal wrath and misery due, I cannot better nor more fully represent to your minds than in the words of St. Austin, which in English may be thus expressed: ' Alas! miserable and most wretched is he, whose own conscience torments him, because he is not able to flee from it: most miserable man is he who daily expects his own damnation, which he cannot possibly escape, unless God removes it. He is most unhappy who is sensible of his eternal death:

yea, most extremely miserable is he whom continual horrors scorch by reason of his own unhappiness.'*

This is a lively description of a soul struggling under conviction, and the wracking, griping pains of an awakened guilty conscience, when sin, guilt, law, and apprehended wrath meet together. It is true this is but legal sorrow, but yet as such it tendeth to death and bondage, and, if not prevented, would sink the sinner down into deep despair and death eternal, as it often doth in the reprobates: who being left to themselves, either fall into despair or a phrensy, under which delirium they are oft suffered to lay violent hands upon themselves, as many a professor has done. Thrice happy then are they who by the Spirit and word, are led forth out of this bondage-state of apprehended wrath and guilt by a right way; being directed and enabled like him who being pricked or stung at the heart, cried out, "What must I do to be saved?" Acts xvi. 30, 31. And was immediately answered, "Believe on the Lord Jesus Christ, and

* Heu! miserum nimisque miserum quem torquet conscientia sua, quam fugere non potest; nimis miserum quem expectat damnatia sua quam vitare non potest, nisi Deus eripiat. Nimis est infelix cui mors æterna est sensibilis; nimis ærumnosus quem torrent continui de sua infelicitate horrores. *August.* de Contritione cordis. Inter Opera.

thou shalt be saved. But this is not the whole of the Spirit's work in conviction; for he further proceedeth, in the

Third place, to give the soul a humbling view of the corruption and uncleanness of his nature as filthy, depraved, perverse, and deceitful: all which put together make up the plague of the heart. And this is done first by leading the soul into itself, as the prophet was by the Spirit led through the hole in the wall into Israel's idolatrous chamber of image-work; where he beheld the form of every creeping thing and abominable beast, and all the idols of the house of Israel pourtrayed upon the wall, Ezek. viii. 10. Thus the soul is led to see that in its heart are to be found the seeds of every sin: all sins, lusts, and iniquities in their roots, seed, and principles, being in the heart, as in a seed-plat ready sown, which only want room and opportunity to come up and appear. Hence it is, that so soon as the seeds of sinful folly and vanity have spent themselves in childhood and youth, a new succeeding crop of sin and vanity cometh on, and so continues through all the ages and courses of this sinful life: so that sin now appeareth to the man to be that monstrous hydra with many heads, that no sooner is one lopped off but two more appear in its room. And now it is, that not only the sinful pollution of depraved nature does begin to appear in a true light, but also the depravity and perverseness, treachery, and deceit of the heart; so that the soul can feelingly say, "The heart is deceitful above all things, and desperately wicked, who can know it?" Jer. xvii. 9. And then,

Secondly, the Spirit in conviction leads the soul in some measure to trace these branches and streams up to the root and fountain where they grow, and from whence they proceed; thereby discovering that sin is the leopard's spot and Ethiopian's skin brought into the world with us: and like as the blackmoor derives his nature from his parent, even so we derive sin from our parents as the mean and way of conveyance, but from Adam the first federally, not by imitation but imputation. Thus David affirmeth concerning himself, "behold I was shapen (or begotten*) in iniquity: and in sin did my mother conceive me," Psa. li. 5. So that sin is, as we say, bred in the bone, and brought forth into the world with us; and as one well querieth, "How then can he be clean that is born of a woman?" Job xxv. 4. For as Job saith, "Who can bring a clean thing out of an unclean? Not one," chap. xiv. 4. And now, as that which is born of the flesh is flesh, so that which is born of sinful flesh is

* חוללתי kholalti, I was beggotten.

undoubtedly sinful: for as is the cause so is the effect, and as is the root so is the branch: for a corrupt fountain cannot send forth pure streams. And by this time the soul, who is thus convinced and humbled under the mighty hand of God, is fully cured of, if before inclined to, the Pelagian error; for he finds sin doth not come by imitation, but by propagation and communication; and that it is all first in the heart as in the embryo, before it is in the act as a birth perfected and brought forth; as our Lord, who best knew, teacheth; " That which cometh out of the man, that defileth the man. For from within, out of the heart of men, proceed evil thoughts, adulteries, fornications, murders, thefts, covetousness, wickedness, deceit, lasciviousness, an evil eye, blasphemy, pride, foolishness. All these evils come from within, and defile the man," Mark vii. 20, 21, 22, 23.

And as the sinner appears vile and odious to himself, so he is fully convinced in time, by the Spirit, in the

Third place, of his own impotency and disability, to perform any thing that is truly and spiritually good and acceptable to God; either according to the strict requirements of the holy law as the first covenant of works, or as to any other requirements under the gospel-dispensation: for he now begins to find by experience, that in him, as carnal and unregenerate, there dwelleth nothing that is good. Hence, then, the sinner stands convicted, that all he doth or can do is unclean, and therefore utterly insufficient to render him acceptable to a holy God, before whom he considereth himself now standing, guilty and defiled. It is now with him as with those who were ceremonially unclean under the law, all that they touched and did were like themselves, unclean. As you may read at large in the xvth of Leviticus, the moral use and signification whereof is plainly taught in the holy scriptures, of which take an instance; "Thus saith the Lord of hosts, ask now the priest, saying, If any one bear holy flesh in the skirt of his garment, and with the skirt do touch bread, or pottage, or wine, or oil, or any food, shall it be holy? And the priest answered No. Then said the prophet, If any one that is unclean by a dead body, touch any of these, shall it be unclean? And the priests answered and said, It shall be unclean. Then replied the prophet and said, So is this people, and so is this nation before me, saith the Lord; and so is every work of their hands, and that which they offer there is unclean," Hag. ii. 12, 13, 14. From whence it is very observable, that holiness is not to be communicated from one thing to another in such a way as pollution is; this appears plain, in that the holy flesh doth not make that holy which it toucheth: and thus then, though Adam was restored by grace, and renewed, and that before ever he knew his wife, yet it was the polluted image of his fallen nature, and not the new holy image of Christ that he conveyed to his offspring: and so it was as a sinner, and not as a saint, that he is said to beget a Son in his own image and likeness. And so holy believing parents beget sinful polluted children: for they beget according to nature, and not according to grace. And now this being the case, all that the unclean toucheth and doth, is unclean, and all that they offer to God is unclean, as it is written and confessed by the church; " But we are all as an unclean thing, and all our righteousnesses are as filthy rags," Isai. lxiv. 6. This then being the sinner's case, he now standeth before God, at least in his own apprehension, as Joshua the high priest did, "clothed with filthy garments," Zach. iii. 3; which must be removed from him, and the best robe put on, or he is undone for ever: for he finds himself utterly insufficient to perform any thing good or acceptable, much less is he able to do any thing by which God should become a debtor to him; and yet so it is, men, till fully convinced and humbled, will be attempting to work for justification, life, and acceptance, thereby going about to establish their own righteousness.

Indeed one would have thought, if they had not

heard nor read the contrary, that mankind who pretend to own themselves to be sinners, out of modesty, if there were no bible to instruct and teach them, should at all times acknowledge both before God and man, that when they have done the most and best they are capable, they are nevertheless " unprofitable servants," Luke xvii. 10. And sure I am, that Job's language better befits sinful men than the rant of some, both in the pulpit and from the press: that good man had no such good opinion of himself, nor his own performances, had they been better than they were, especially when he was to stand before his Judge; " If I were righteous, (says he) I would not own it," so as to fetch an argument or plea from thence, Job ix. 15; " If I be righteous, yet (says he) I will not lift up my head," chap. x. 15. No, David's plea best suits and becomes a convinced sinner. " Answer me in thy righteousness, and enter not into judgment with thy servant: for in thy sight shall no man living be justified," Psal. cxliii. 1, 2. And again, " If thou, Lord, shouldest mark iniquity, O Lord, who shall stand? But there is forgiveness with thee that thou mayest be feared," Psal. cxxx. 3, 4. Thus the convinced sinner lieth down in self-abhorrence and shame, and crieth out in good earnest, unclean and undone!

Thus then, the Spirit of God, as the Spirit of conviction, both emptieth and levels the vain creature man, in order to famish him out of all self-sufficiency, and glorying; and then the Holy Spirit carries the conviction still further, and to perfection; as I am to shew, in the

Fifth place, by convincing the soul of the real need and necessity of true saving faith in the Lord Jesus, and of the pernicious effects and damnable nature of the sin of unbelief: first, with respect to the need and necessity of faith, this appeareth to be the one thing necessary; forasmuch as without it it is impossible to please God. Now faith is to be considered first as a moral duty, and so the law requireth faith, as well as mercy and justice, as our Lord declares, as one of the weighty matters and of the greatest moment, Matt. xxiii. 23. Thus, as a necessary moral duty, "He that cometh to God (in an act of worship) must believe that he is, and that he is a rewarder of those who diligently seek him," Heb. xi. 6. But this is not enough; for there must also to this be added a gospel-justifying saving faith, which under the Old Testament carried the true worshippers to look to, and worship God through the promised seed as the only way of our recovery from sin, as to its reigning power, and the curse and misery entailed thereby; and also as that which can alone restore man unto Divine fellowship: and under the gospel it is a grace that dealeth with God by Christ, as having borne our sin, and satisfied Divine justice by removing the wrath and curse due, and bringing to the faithful, by way of obedience, an everlasting righteousness, for the justifying poor sinners. So that now the need and necessity of this gospel-faith appears in that, in the second place, the soul, thereby is convinced now, that his work and duty is not to work for life, righteousness, and acceptance with God; but to believe for righteousness, by laying hold of it as in another, being of mere grace provided for him, according as it is written; " To him that worketh, is the reward not reckoned of grace, but of debt. But to him that worketh not, but believeth on him that justifieth the UNGODLY," Rom. iv. 4, 5, 6. Thus David is said to describe the blessedness of the man unto whom God imputeth righteousness without works. And though this doctrine of God's justifying the ungodly who believe for righteousness, instead of working for it, by a righteousness of his own providing, imputing, and accepting, goeth down very hardly with such as are not savingly humbled and cast down; yet to a soul thus far savingly convinced, this is the one thing necessary: forasmuch as now he seeth that this is the chief work, the work of works, to believe aright. This is what Christ calls " The work of God," as being the most excellent and acceptable to him; and without which the sinner can neither be justified nor saved: for so it is written, John vi. 29. " Go preach the gospel to every creature," i. e. to all mankind, of what nation, state or condition soever. " He that believeth, and is baptized, shall be saved; but he that believeth not shall be damned." And this believing is a believing on Christ for righteousness unto life, as it was long ago foretold concerning gospel converts. " Surely, shall one say, in the Lord have I righteousness and strength. In the Lord shall all the seed of Israel be justified, and shall glory," Isai. xlv. 24, 25. Thus, then, he stands, under this further work of the Holy Spirit upon his soul, convinced, that it is impossible to be just or righteous in God's account but by faith; as this text in the Romans sufficiently demonstrateth; for if God justifieth the ungodly, who do not work for righteousness, but believe and lay hold on it, as in another; that is, in Christ as their righteousness before God; then there is no way now of being righteous in God's account but this. But then the need and necessity of faith still appears to this soul, in that the Holy Spirit further convinceth him of the necessity of a constant life of faith in Christ; first, because without it he who is "just cannot live," Hab. ii. 4, and Heb. x. 38; it being ordained by God as that grace by which we depend on, and abide in Christ as members of living influential head, and branches engrafted into this holy fruitful root, CHRIST. Is Christ's fulness our store and treasure? It is only received and lived upon by faith. Is he our living bread? He is only received and lived upon by faith. Doth his blood cleanse from all sin? No application to be made to it but by faith. Is Christ our new and living way, by which we may at all times have liberty and free access to the Father? Why, there is no drawing nigh but by faith. Doth the royal law of Christ call for holiness both in heart, lip, and life? There is no true evangelic holiness and purity of heart, but as faith dealeth with the blood of sprinkling: which blood, when thus apprehended and applied, hath a healing, as well as cleansing virtue in, and a powerful influence upon the heart; so as to promote gospel-holiness and purity of life, without which none shall see God. And doth the gospel call for love and obedience to Christ from them who follow him? No obedience is acceptable to God, nor rewarded by him, but that of faith, as it runneth through and influenceth all the practical part of the Christian's life in love and gospel-duty.

But this is not all; for as the Spirit convinceth of the real need and necessity of faith, so also doth it, in the second place, of man's real impotency and inability to believe aright, to the saving of the soul. Most men and women, upon the first hearing of the necessity of faith in the Lord Jesus Christ, look upon it as a small matter, even the least part of religion, and that which is the most easy requirement in the whole book of God: and just as it is with children and ignorant persons, who, while they look upon others doing business, or hear the directions given, they think it is easy, and may be performed without any great matter of difficulty; but the attempt discovereth their ignorance and misapprehension: so here, let a person be but thoroughly convinced of the need of faith, as that upon which, by the ordination of God, all turneth; let him but know the true nature and use of faith, and once attempt in the face of ten thousand discouragements from within and without, from sin and Satan, and from the flashes of a Sinai-law and lashes of a terrified accusing conscience; I say, let a soul under these disadvantages, as every awakened sinner besure is, but once attempt to believe, by laying firm hold of the promise of mercy, free and full pardon and justification to life, as it is held forth in Christ Jesus ministerially, and then let him tell me whether it is so easy a matter to believe and keep fast hold in spite of all this opposition and discouragement: and that at a time when innumerable enemies and evils beset the soul around, and the surging waves and billows of realized wrath and guilt go over the head, and the waters come into the soul, as into a vessel at sea, which in the midst of a violent storm has sprung a leak at bottom. Ah sure! to such a soul, faith is no such easy or cheap thing as some imagine. It is therefore only men's ignorance makes them to think or talk of faith as some easy thing; and as if it was no more than a moral duty and act of the rational creature, assenting and consenting to this and the other revealed truth and proposition laid down or to be evidenced and demonstrated from the word; whereas it is, as I have shewed under the first head, a new created principle of the new creature, and is to be found only in the souls of the new-born; who are born from above, "Not of the will of the flesh, nor of the will of man, but of God." And so the soul standeth convinced that this " faith is not of ourselves, but is the gift of God," Eph. ii. 8; and must be wrought in it by the energy or operation of God, by the same power which raised Jesus from the dead, and set him in our nature at the Father's right hand. Thus as to the soul conviction of the need and necessity of faith, and of its own impotency and inability to believe aright until it is renewed by regenerating grace; and this grace of faith as a new creature-principle is created in the soul by the power and operation of God. And now it is also, that on the other hand, the soul beginneth to discern the odious nature and evil tendency of the sin of unbelief, first, as that it is a sin of a monstrous size, the greatest of all sin, and the root of all evil; and that it nourishes and confirms all other sin, by keeping up the spirit, life, and dominion thereof in the soul; there being more evil wrapt up in this one sin than in all other actual transgressions. It being the master-sin and ringleader of all, and a root bearing gall and bitterness, from whence all other actual sins and apostasies proceed. This put Adam upon running away from God, and Cain upon murdering his brother: yea, as the apostle on the other hand speaks concerning faith, that it was at the bottom, and ran through whatever the saints of the Old Testament did; so may we justly say of unbelief, that it lieth at the root, and hath had a powerful influence in promoting all the evil that ever was committed in the world among mankind. This it is that setteth and keepeth the soul at the greatest distance from, and enmity against God; this runs through all the best moral and religious services of men in a natural state, and mars all they do; this spoils all religion and duty, and turneth it into sin. Hence it is that " the sacrifice of the wicked is sin," Prov. xv. 8; as also his ploughing, chap. xxi. 4, and all the other parts of his civil employ. Thus all that he doth is sinful and defiled, and that for lack of faith. Yea, this is the sin, that as it is the most capital, so is it the most condemning. Unbelief is that sin which through all ages, but especially under the gospel, is the most dangerous and provoking, as the apostle argueth with the Hebrews; "To whom sware he that they should not enter into his rest, but to them that believed not? So we see they could not enter in, because of unbelief. Let us therefore labour to enter into that rest, lest any man fall after the same example of unbelief," Heb. iii. 18, 19, and chap. iv. 11. But that which makes the sinner's case still worse and harder to be cured is, that this sin of unbelief is seated chiefly in the will as in its throne, from whence it easily commandeth and swayeth all the other powers. Hence enmity, rebellion against, and apostacy from God are the very bias and evil propensity of the will; which till it be cured by grace, and overcome by Almighty power, it is with every man and woman as Christ complaineth, "Ye will not come to me that ye might have life," John v. 40. Man's moral impotency lying chiefly in the lack of a will or heart to come, so as to believe in Christ to the saving of the soul. Thus I have gone through this first part of the Spirit's passive work in beginning, carrying on, and holding the soul under conviction till he is thereby emptied and humbled; being brought to a thorough sight and sense of his sinful, miserable, helpless state, and damnable condition, as under the curse of the law occasioned by the fall of the first man Adam. I shall crown and conclude this branch with something pertinent and confirming, from the experiences of two great men, as they were first written by their own hands, and afterwards for the benefit and encouragement of others brought to public view.

The first shall be that of St. Austin, as I have transcribed it out of the English copy.

* 'Let the arrogant deride me, and those not yet savingly cast down and broken by thee, O, my God: but let me continue to confess unto thee my disgrace to thy praise. Permit, I pray thee, and grant unto me, with a present memory, to repass through all those past circles of my error, and from thence to offer to thee the sacrifice of joy; let them, the strong and the mighty, laugh at us, then, whilst we, the infirm and poor, confess unto thee.—Thou, O Lord, didst (amidst this discourse of Pontianus) turn me about towards myself; and tookest me from behind my back, where I had placed me, whilst I had no mind to observe myself; and thou didst set me before my own face, that I might see how crooked, how ugly and deformed a thing I was, covered over with filthiness; and I beheld, and abhorred, but found no

---

* Augustin's Confessions, lib. iv. ch. i. and lib. viii. ch. 7.

way to fly or run away from myself; and if I endeavoured to turn away my sight from so loathsome a spectacle, still thou didst bring me again before myself, and thrustedst me before my eyes, that so I might discover my iniquity, and hate it. Not that I had not known it before; but I dissembled it, connived at it, and forgot it. And now the more ardently I loved those, who so piously and ardently resigned themselves into thy hands, to receive their total cure from thee, the more detestably I hated myself, when compared with them. And now was the day come in which I was laid naked to myself; and my conscience began to reproach me. Thus was I inwardly corroded, and extremely confounded with horror and shame.' And now that it was the guilt, horror, and trouble of an awakened guilty conscience, as arising from the conjunct views and apprehensions of sin, wrath, and judgment to come, that thus wracked and tortured him, appears from these and the like expressions which lie scattered about in his book of Heart-Contrition, of which I will give you just a taste.

' * Truly my sins are an abyss, for they are in-

---

* Vere abyssus peccata mea sunt, quia incomprehensibilia profunditate, & inestimabilia sunt numero & immensitate. O Abyssus abyssum invocans! O peccata mea, tormenta quibus me servatis abyssus sunt, quia infinita & incomprehensibilia sunt. Est & tertia abyssus, & est nimis terribilis; Judicia Dei abyssus

comprehensibly profound, and their number and immensity are unaccountable. O deep calling upon deep! O my sins, the torments in which ye keep me are an abyss, because they be infinite and incomprehensible. There is also a third abyss, and it is most terrible; the judgments of God are a great abyss, for they are hidden beyond all sense. All these abysses are terrible to me on every side, for there is fear upon fear, and sorrow upon sorrow. The abyss of God's judgments is over me, the abyss of hell beneath me, the abyss of my sins is within me. That which is above me I fear, lest it should rush in upon me, and plunge me with my abyss into that which lieth hid under me.' Thus St. Augustin.

The next I shall present you with shall be something to our present purpose, out of the experience of the late Dr. Thomas Goodwin;* whose memory will be precious, and his works a public blessing, and sweet to such as have a spiri-

---

multa, quia super omnem sensum occulta. Hæ omnes abyssi terribiles sunt mihi undique, quia timor super timorem & dolor super dolorem. Abyssus Judiciorum Dei super me, abyssus inferni subtus me, abyssus peccatorum meorum est intra me. Illam quæ super me est timeo ne in me irruat; & me cum abysso mea in illam quæ subtus me latet, obruat. Lib. de Contritione Cordis, inter Opera August. Cap. ix. As quoted by Dr. Owen in his Discourse on the Holy Spirit, Fol. pag. 302.

* Vol. V. in the Doctor's Life, page vii. viii. ix.

tual taste, and their senses exercised to discern between good and evil. 'Upon the hearing of Dr Bambridge preach, (says he,) I was as one struck down by a mighty power. The grosser sins of my conversation came in upon me, which I wondered at, as being unseasonable at first; and so the working began, but was prosecuted still more and more, higher and higher: and I endeavouring not to think the least thought of my sins, was passively held under the remembrance of them, and affected; so as I was rather passive in it all the while than active, and my thoughts were held under, whilst that work went on.—In all this intercourse, and those that follow to the very end, I was acted all along by the Spirit of God being upon me, and my thoughts passively held fixt, until each head and sort of thoughts were finished, and then a new thought began and continued; that I have looked at them as so many conferences God had with me by way of reproof and conviction. My thoughts were kept fixed and intent on the consideration of the next immediate causes, of those foregone gross acts of sinning; an abundant discovery was made unto me of my inward lusts and concupiscence, and how all sorts of concupiscences had wrought in me; at which I was amazed to see with what greediness I had sought the satisfaction of every lust. And these lusts I discerned to have been acted by me in things that were most lawful, answerable to that saying in scripture, "the very ploughing of the wicked is sin:" and by the clear light thereof the sinfulness of my sin was exceedingly enlarged; for that light accompanied me through all and every action that I could cast my remembrance upon, or that my view went over. And by and through the means of the discovery of those lusts, a new horrid vein and course of sin was revealed also to me, I saw lay at the bottom of my heart in the rising and working of all my lusts; namely, that they kept my heart in a continual course of ungodliness; that is, that my heart was wholly obstructed from acting towards God any way, or from having any holy or good movings at all. God having proceeded thus far, I perceived I was humbled under his mighty hand, as James speaks, with whom only and immediately I had to do, and not with my own bare single thoughts; but God continued orderly to possess my thoughts with a further progress, as to this subject; I being made sensible of God's hand in it, and myself was merely passive: but still God continued his hand over me, and held me intent to consider and pierce into what should be the first causes of so much actual sinfulness; and he presented to me as in answer thereunto, for it was transacted as a conference by God with me, the original corruption of my nature, and inward evil constitution and depravation of all my faculties, the inclinations and disposedness of my heart unto all evil, and averseness from all spiritual good, and acceptableness unto God. Hence I was convinced that in this respect I was flesh, which was to my apprehension as if that had been the definition of a man, "that which is born of the flesh is flesh." And here, says he, let me stand a while astonished, as I did then; I can compare this sight and the workings of my heart arising from thence to be, as if I had in the heat of summer looked down into the filth of a dungeon, where, by a clear light and piercing eye, I discerned millions of living crawling things in the midst of that sink and liquid corruption. How much and deeply did I consider, that all the sins that ever were committed by the wickedest men that have been in the world, had proceeded from the corruption of their nature; or that the sins which any or all men did commit at any time, were all from the same root; and I by my nature, if God had left me and withdrawn from me, should have committed the same, as any temptation should have induced me into the like. But what much affected me was a sight and sense that my heart was empty of all good; that in me, that is, in my flesh there dwelt no good, not a mite of truly spiritual good: as the scripture describes true inherent grace, to be some good in us towards the Lord our God, which none of my goodness nor ingenuity was which I boasted of. Thus at present I was abundantly convinced. But next I was brought to inquire into, and consider what was the original cause at the bottom of all this forementioned sinfulness, both in my heart and life. And after I had well debated with myself that one place Rom. v. 12. "By one man sin entered into the world, and death by him, and passed upon all men, in whom, or in that, all had sinned:" that it was in him they all sinned, for they had not in and of themselves sinned actually, as those that die infants, after the similitude of Adam's transgression; which limitation is cautiously there added by the apostle, to shew that they had not actually sinned of themselves, but are simply involved in his act of sinning: and that sin wherein we were all involved, as guilty of it, is expressly said to be the disobedience of that one man; this caused me necessarily to conceive thus of it, that it was the guilt or demerit of that one man's disobedience that corrupted my nature.'

Thus, as to the work of the Spirit as a convincer of sin, in all which, the man is really a patient under God's mighty hand, and held down to the sight and consideration of those things which at first are very unwelcome to him. This then is the first instance of man's passiveness in order to conversion,

i. e. in his receiving the Spirit as a Spirit of conviction of sin; by which he is seized and arrested in his soul, and laid hold of and possessed by the Spirit on Christ's part, in order to bring him, by a true and living faith, to lay hold of Christ for righteousness and life. I shall now proceed to a

Second instance of the Spirit's work upon the soul in effectual calling, in which the soul is wholly passive; and that is in the act of quickening the soul by giving and effecting a real, spiritual, vital union to Christ, as the head and root of all spiritual life and grace; from whom every member of his body, being thus spiritually and vitally one in him, receiveth all the necessary supplies of nourishment and edification suited to the new creature-life and motions: and as the Spirit of God and Christ knits or ties this vital knot of everlasting union betwixt the soul and Christ; so he himself becometh the eternal vital band, by which they two being "joined to the Lord, become one Spirit," 1 Cor. vi. 17, as truly and properly as the union between husband and wife, by God's ordination, make them one flesh. Upon which it is, that every truly regenerate person is a member of Christ, considered as head, and the whole collection of believers are styled his body, to which he, as a second Adam, becometh a quickening Spirit; as it is written, "The first man Adam was made a living soul, the last man Adam was made a quickening Spirit," 1 Cor. xv. 45. Which constitution of Christ as a second Adam in our nature, and as a life-giving head, hath a special regard unto the elect; of which number only he is the covenant-head, and to whom only he becometh a quickening Spirit; first in their effectual calling and regeneration, at which time he by his Spirit first apprehendeth and joineth himself to them, and they to him, in order of nature, though not in time, before ever there is the least principle of life or gracious disposition in them; much more before there is one vital gracious act of faith, love and new obedience performed by them: for as there must be life in the principle or habit, before it can be in the act; so there must be union to Christ as a head before there is life in the member: for as well may we imagine a branch cut off from the old wild olive, to have good juices in it received from the good root before it is grafted in, as to pretend that any have a life of grace or faith before spiritual vital union to Christ. How this is effected, and exactly when it beginneth, I will not pretend to be positive in; it being much more hidden and mysterious than the way of the Spirit of man in its first entrance into, and quickening the body before it is born into the world; the which, whatever men pretend, is to mortals inexplicable. But

However that be, we are sure we are as passive in our being quickened by, and from our life-giving head and spiritual Adam as we were in our first union to, and quickening in our natural parent: for as a life-giving Spirit, he first conveyeth life from himself into us by his Spirit which he giveth to us: and this very life is our union, even as life is the band uniting and tying soul and body together, so life and union are coeval. This vital union of the soul to Christ, considered as real and spiritual, is set forth and illustrated in the scriptures by the similitudes of members and head, and root and branches; whose life and motion, growth and fruitfulness proceed from the head and root to its members and branches considered as in a vital union, from whence communion followeth. Thus the whole body natural, and so consequently every individual and particular member, being fitly joined together, and compacted, by means of the several muscles and ligaments which bind and tie the joints firm and close together, is supplied with proper nourishment in every part through the arterious vessels by a secret energy peculiar to it: and thus also it is between every such united soul and Christ, as also betwixt him and his whole mystical body, who by certain invisible spiritual bands having nourishment ministered, increaseth with the increase of God. Thus, as to the nature and effects of spiritual vital union to Christ; the manner of which, as performed upon us and effected by the Holy Spirit, is excellently set forth by our apostle under the similitude of grafting or inoculating and budding of fruit trees or other choice plants; in the performance of which there is excision, transition, and embodying or joining with the new stock, so as to become one with it: and this, under the gospel, as mystically applied to Christ as a head, and vine or root, is first political and external only, and also spiritual, internal, and indissoluble. Thus, after this first sort of union to Christ as the head of the Jewish church-state and religion, and afterwards that of the Christian church-state under the gospel, the unbelieving Jews as the natural branches were said to be broken off, to make way for the Gentiles as adopted branches to be grafted in; who also stand no longer in this political relation and union to Christ, as the head of the Christian church-state, than, by a sound faith and agreeable obedience, they shall professedly hold the head, which is Christ, Rom. xi. 17, 21: and thus, if any single person or community of men, professing the Christian religion, shall cast off either their professed faith, or subjection to Christ as head, they also shall be cut off, and cast as unprofitable branches into an unclean place, according to Christ's own words, Rom. xi. 20, 22. "I am the true vine, and my Father is the vinedresser and owner. Every branch in me that beareth not fruit he taketh away; (i. e. pruneth off by Providence or church-censure;) and every branch that beareth fruit, he pruneth it, that it may bring forth more fruit," John xv. 1, 2. Thus, the Gentiles professing the Christian faith, being joined in church-relation and fellowship, were said to be cut off from, or out of the wild olive tree, and grafted into the good," Rom. xi. 24; which is also called translating them out of the power of darkness, or kingdom of Satan, into that of his dear Son, Coloss. i. 13. But then you are to understand, that besides this political ingrafture, in point of Christian profession and church-relation to Christ as a political head and king, there is still a more secret and invisible union of the elect to Christ, as a spiritual head and root of influence and grace; which he himself styleth a "being in them and they in him," as fruit-bearing branches, which can bring forth no spiritual fruit, but as in a vital union with the vine-root, John xv, 4, 5, compared with chap. xvii. 23. And as this union is real and not imaginary, and more than political and nominal, so the manner of it, as begun and perfected by the Holy Spirit, is somewhat like this of ingrafture, and the soul's union to the body, wholly mysterious and passive. For what body ever quickened itself, or what scion or bud ever cut itself off, and removing itself from its old root united itself to the new? No more did ever one soul by any act or performance of his unite himself to Christ in this spiritual vital union of head and members, root and branches being one. There is, indeed, another union arising out of this, which is effected by an act on our part, and that is faith-union; and this is the conjugal and marriage-union, but this must flow from the former, and can by no means be the same, nor the cause thereof: of which conjugal union, and how effected on the soul's part, I have already spoken something, as it fell in my way, under the first general head.

This, then, is a second instance of the Spirit's work upon us in our effectual calling, in which we are properly said to be passive. A

Third instance followeth; and that is, in his beginning and perfecting the new creature, called the new creation, regeneration, or the new birth, performed by the Spirit alone in the heart, and upon the whole man in effectual calling and conversion; "For we are his workmanship, created in Christ Jesus," Eph. ii. 10. I know this part of the professing world abounds with men bold and daring enough to make a jest of the Spirit's work and office in the church, and upon the hearts of God's elect in and after conversion; who by their cunning, in which, as to the evil part, they abound, lie in wait to deceive silly, unwary, and unstable souls. Some of these seem resolved we shall have no more in our bible than what suiteth with their principles; nor no more of gospel-mystery in the Christian religion, either as to its author and object of worship, or as to its doctrines of grace, and divine energy upon the hearts of the saved ones, than they the learned can account for as rational, and demonstrate as plain as any of the elements in Euclid. But in this they shall proceed no further than shall be for his glory, who esteemeth this their "turning things upside down but as the potter's clay," Isai. xxix. 16. This part of the Spirit's work in an efficacious manner upon the heart, as to its passiveness, with respect of us creatures, who are his workmanship, is in the sacred scriptures set forth by divers metaphors and similitudes. Thus, it is called "circumcising the heart to love God," Deut. xxx. 6. which in another text is called "taking away the heart of stone, and giving an heart of flesh," Ezek. xxxvi. 26. Which is also called the new heart, and a clean and right spirit. This in the New Testament is called the new creature, regeneration, or a being born again; which new birth is said to be of the Spirit and of God; as it is written concerning the sons of God, who so received Christ Jesus the Lord, as to believe savingly in him, that they were born, " not of blood, nor of the will of the flesh, nor of the will of man, but of God," John i. 13; " who of his own will (as St. James saith) hath begotten us by the word of truth," James i. 18.

And out of this part of the Spirit's supernatural and efficacious work upon the hearts of God's elect in effectual calling, it is, that faith and every other grace, spiritual duty, and performance do arise; it being his workmanship in and upon our souls.

This passive, yet efficacious work of God upon the hearts of his people in effectual calling and conversion is what our Lord taught Nicodemus under the similitude, of a new birth; " Verily, verily, I say unto thee, except a man be born again, he cannot see the kingdom of God;" that is, says he, except a man is born of water, and of the Spirit, he cannot enter into the kingdom of God, John iii. 3. Some there are indeed, who boldly and positively affirm that this new birth is water-baptism; and that our Lord calleth this baptism a new-birth, in allusion to the Jewish custom, and celebrated doctrine concerning the proselytes and their infant-seed, who were not admitted without being first washed in water; and then both they and their seed thus initiated, and their released servants when they had thus taken up their freedom in Israel's church and commonwealth, were said, it seems, to be as children new-born: for that now all their old relations were relinquished and forsaken for these new privileges. To which supposition I have this to say, that although it should be granted that there was such a practice brought in, and kept up in the Jewish church, as to the mode of making and receiving proselytes and their infant-seed into communion with them, yet that this was by them styled a new birth in our Saviour's time, and afore, doth not at all appear; first, for that Nicodemus, a teacher and ruler among the Jews, and one of the chief, seems by his questions and replies never to have met with this term, nor nothing like it; whereas, had it been a known phrase and customary speech, though but with the rabbins, he would in all likelihood have heard it; but most certain, according to his misapplication of it, he had never before heard of a metaphorical birth, or of any other way of being as a child new-born, but as coming out of the mother's womb; nor was he easily led into it, but still after its explanation, not at all understanding it to lie in water-baptism, he adds, how can these things be? But secondly, it is manifest, that whatever might be the practice of the Jews towards their proselytes and servants, when admitted to all privileges with them, both sacred and civil, yet the phrase is not, that I ever yet heard of or found, to be met with till a much later date, i. e. in a celebrated author* of the Jews, who wrote about 500 years ago: and to me it looketh more likely to be a phrase picked out of the New Testament by the rabbins, as are divers others of their phrases and expressions, than that our Lord should borrow it from them, and one of their chief masters know nothing of it: but be that as it will, for it is not worth contending for, as to any advantage to their cause who like to use it; let the custom be never so ancient, and the phrase common and known to the Jews, yet our Lord intended and taught something higher and more mysterious than water-baptism; though it is not to me improbable but he might allude thereto; but that baptism is the new birth, either in the whole or in part, or contributeth any thing thereunto, this to me is heterodox and antiscriptural; and as to the judgment, or rather misrepresented sayings, of the ancients, they are of little weight with me in this case: for at best they were but men subject to error, as appeareth in many no-

---

* Rabbi Moseh Maimony, in Issure Biah, per ד׳, he saith, Goy shenithgayar, veyebed shenishtakhrar, hare, hu cekaton sheuolad. That is, a Gentile who is newly become a proselyte, and a servant newly made free; behold he is as a child which is new born, &c. For that, as he adds, he now relinquisheth all his old relations, &c. for these his new ones.

torious instances, and so not to be at all relied upon, as consonant with the written word: but in fact, we know but little of what the ancients really held, taught, and practised; for that most of their works, if not all of them, before they came to us, fell into ill hands, who new moulded and modelled them, and made them to say what they pleased. He that will make me believe that the great St. Austin had such a veneration for the *relics of departed saints, and believed they wrought such miracles as he and others report, must hold me excused if I either think St. Austin in this a weak, credulous man, or else that he is grievously belied and misrepresented. Thus, when the ancients call baptism their regeneration, I verily believe, to do them justice, they only meant it in a figurative way, and not that the passing under that ordinance of unregenerate, ungracious, and ungodly, made them regenerate, godly, righteous, holy, and good. If they did so intend it, they were in this, as well as in divers other things, erroneous, and not to be followed nor relied upon. And to suppose our blessed Lord intended this being born again, of water-baptism, is to represent him in plain English, saying thus: 'Verily, verily, I say unto thee, Nicodemus, except thou, and the rest of thy countrymen

---

* Austin's City of God, lib. 22. cap. 8. fol. 883, 885, 886, 887, 888. And his Confessions.

the Jews, and also the Gentile nations, and their infant-seed, like your proselytes, be baptised with water, neither thou, nor they shall ever to go to heaven.' Or in a shorter way thus; 'Verily, verily, I say unto thee, whosoever is baptized, shall be saved, but he that is not, shall be damned.' From which mistake and abuse of Christ's words came in that old and still remaining error—without baptism no salvation. Even as of old, and of some places to this day, if we are not imposed upon by historians, they did and do administer the other ordinance of the supper to their infant-seed, from the like mistake of another text; " Verily, verily, I say unto you, except ye eat the flesh of the Son of man, and drink his blood, ye have no life in you: whoso eateth my flesh, and drinketh my blood, hath eternal life, and even he dwelleth in me, and I in him," John vi. 53, 54, 56.

The true meaning of both which texts seem to have been hid from and mistook by the antients; or else, as I said, they are misrepresented. But be that as it will, our Lord meant a higher birth than that of water in this text. There are some who would fain join the spiritual birth with baptism, and make us believe, that while the priest is just wetting the child's face, and signing the forehead, the Spirit of God at that very instant is washing the heart, sanctifying and renewing the soul;

or else they, on the other hand, think that water applied in due form by one who is regular, and in holy orders doth, as by an instrument, regenerate, and ingraft the child into Christ, as a living member and real heir of life and glory. But as baptism hath no such promise annexed to it, so, on the other hand, I persuade myself there is not so much as one single instance to be given of any one person, adult or infant, that came to baptism unregenerate, and devoid of grace, that ever received the Spirit, and true regeneration and renovation under that ordinance : and the reason is, it was never appointed to give grace, or to be the mean of conveyance thereof, nor the season of first bestowing the Spirit : for as to the adult, it always supposed grace to be first wrought, before they have any right or just claim; and as to those who pass under it without faith and regeneration by the Spirit upon the soul, it adds no grace, whatever it may do of external privilege; but leaveth the person just as it found him, as to the internal part of sanctification. Simon Magus was no more regenerated after his baptism than before; it left him as it found him, " in the gall of bitterness and bonds of iniquity," Acts viii. 23 ; though where it is applied to, and complied with by the faithful, it is of singular use and advantage for the increase of faith and comfort.

The true meaning and excellency of the water and Spirit in the new birth, are not to be sought for in the element of water of baptism, but in the blood of Jesus, and the grace of the Holy Spirit coming in the virtue of that blood by the ministry of the word; and by a secret power working on the heart so as to sanctify and cleanse, renewing it thoroughly; and inlaying it with all needful grace and holy principles, as being the water God promised to sprinkle his withal under the gospel-covenant, in allusion to the water of purification and blood made use of for cleansing under the law. Hence the apostle; as rightly evangelizing and expounding that water and blood, carrieth it to the blood of Christ under the gospel, saying; "If the blood of bulls and goats, and the ashes of an heifer, (i. e. being mixed with spring-water) sprinkled upon the unclean, sanctifieth to the purifying of the flesh; how much more shall the blood of Christ, who through the eternal Spirit offered himself without spot unto God, purge your consciences from dead works, to serve the living God?" Heb. ix. 13, 14. And hence, as that water prepared for to sprinkle the unclean, as you read in the 19th of Numbers, was called by the Jews, and the Septuagint Greek, the water of sprinkling, the apostle justly styleth its antitype " the blood of sprinkling," Heb. xii. 24. This then is the water of the new birth, and not the element used in baptism, with which we are said to be washed in regeneration, as distinct from the renewing of the Holy Spirit. In both of which we are really as passive as the clay in the hand of the potter. But this is not all; there is still a

Fourth instance in which the truly regenerate are passive; and that is in all the first and after repeated actings of grace, God, or Christ-ward: for though it be true that it is man who believeth and repenteth, &c. yet not one vital spiritual act can be put forth without the previous influences of the Holy Spirit. The Holy Spirit, as he dwelleth in, and presideth over his own work in and upon the heart of the regenerate, is to this his work, both as to preservation and regulation, as the main spring in a watch or mathematical movement; not that either the man or the new creature is a machine without life or will, but through the imperfection of the Spirit's work there still remaineth in this frail state an insufficiency; and though there is a will to good, and a desire after a more exact spiritual life and conformity, yet how to perform the good desired the regenerate findeth not, but as God worketh in him to perform of his own good pleasure. Hence the spouse petitioneth that she may be first drawn by the beloved, and then she promiseth to run after, in the free exercise of faith, love, and obedience, Cant. i. 3: and thus, when the fresh and renewed gales of the Spirit, like the wind upon the " garden of spices," breathe upon and excite the soul, the graces of the new creature, like the unbound atoms of the spices, flow forth and give a goodly scent, Cant. iv. 16. There is not one gracious soul without this passive and previous influence of the Spirit, can put forth so much as one vital spiritual act of faith or repentance. No, take a saint when in an unbelieving frame, or when under the sad effects of a backsliding spirit and spiritual decay, and if he would give all his substance for power and liberty to believe, and repent, even to a thorough evangelical act, as sometimes he hath done, it is not at present to be come at, but must be asked, waited for, and expected in God's own way and time. Thus there is more of the Spirit of God, as to his efficiency and energy, and kind assistances in every gracious act and spiritual duty, that some are aware of, or care to own : it is true, there is enough of ours in every performance to spoil it, and render it unacceptable, were it not for the tender mercies of a loving Father, and the infinite merits of a Redeemer; and yet the worst duties, and lowest acts of the saint are better and more acceptable to God than the best performances of the unregenerate : and that because there is habitual life and grace in the subject, and both a federal and vital, as well as marriage-union and relation to Christ, who always liveth and mediateth for him above, and dwelleth in him by the Spirit; nay, and though it is scarce discernible, there is something of the Spirit, and also of the new creature, in the meanest and lowest performances of the saints, which still denominates them spiritual; whereas the best of those who have not the Spirit are dead and carnal. But this is not all; that which I here chiefly aim at is, that as there is something of the Spirit in the meanest and lowest of the believer's services, so in every duty spiritually discharged, "the preparation of the heart and answer of the tongue are from the Lord," even the Lord the Spirit, Prov. xvi. 1. The Holy Spirit, my brethren, doth not come and work faith in a poor creature to day suppose, and then go his way, and leave the man to use and manage these and the other graces as well as he can; nor doth he bestow spiritual gifts upon his churches and particular persons for the benefit of the whole, and then leave their use and management to the skill and activity of the creature; no, he abides in his, and is "a Spirit of wisdom, and of might, and of counsel, and of the fear of the Lord;" Isai. xi. 2, and chap. xxviii. 6: that is, he supplieth the soul with these, and he directeth and exciteth to the use of the same, And this continued assistance of the Holy Spirit, and his repeated work in and upon the heart, proceed from the vital union; that as the tree in its branches putteth forth its bud and blossom, and yieldeth its fruit in its season every year from new incomes sent up from its root, so the believer yieldeth spiritual fruit in its proper season, more or less, oftener and sooner, according to the fresh incomes of spiritual life and grace from Christ, his root; for without him the believer can do nothing," John xv. 5 ; that is, he can not bear fruit, but as he receiveth daily grace for grace, out of Christ's stores; and by this means it is that God fulfils all the good pleasure of his goodness in us, and the work of faith with power, 2 Thess. i. 11: and it will be worth your time to observe how the apostle ascribes all that godly zeal and spiritual vigour and activity which were manifest in his ministry, to the special energy of the grace of God, and as managed by the Spirit : " By the grace of God, (says he) I am what I am : and his grace which was bestowed upon me, was not in vain ; but I laboured more abundantly than they all : yet not I, but the grace of God which was with me," 1 Cor. xv. 10. Mind it, he doth not say that it was the grace of God in him, as meaning it of inherent grace formerly received and wrought in him by the Spirit; but he saith it was the grace of God that was with him, meaning, no doubt, the special additions of grace thrown in upon all occasions; being an auxiliary supply reserved in Christ, and handed forth suitably and seasonably in the time of need; and this passive influence and energy of the grace and Spirit of God working in and upon him in his ministry, as well as with it, he expresseth thus in another place; " Whereunto I also labour, striving according to his working, which worketh in me mightily," Coloss. i. 29; which, according to the words of my text, is the working of his mighty power in us who believe. Thus, I have from the holy scriptures and the saints' experience endeavoured to evince something of the passive work of the Spirit of God upon the hearts of his elect, both in and after effectual calling and conversion, as the first in all that is good, in which it appeareth man is first wrought upon and moved, before ever he can move so as to perform one spiritual act or duty. I shall, leaving this, proceed to the next head.

CHAP. VI.

Shewing the absolute Necessity of the exertion of Almighty Power, and invincible and efficacious Grace in the Conversion of a Sinner.

V. GENERAL head proposed, was to demonstrate from the doctrine and evidence of the holy scriptures, that there is an absolute necessity for the exceeding greatness of God's almighty power, to be invincibly and efficaciously put forth upon the heart and soul of man, to effect his conversion, and bring him to a saving faith in the Lord Jesus.

Something of this has indeed been more than touched upon already, under the several foregoing heads; but there still remains something further to be spoken to under this head, more fully to demonstrate the necessity of such an exceeding greatness of Almighty invincible power in conversion: and the proof shall be of two parts; the first shall be taken from those scripture-metaphors, which more than intimate the necessity of invincible, efficacious grace in effectual calling. The second sort of evidence shall be taken from scripture-instances of conversion, in which the power and efficacy of omnipotent victorious grace stand manifest to all.

First of all, the scriptures do abundantly declare and set forth the state of man by nature, through the fall, to be a state of death: and conversion from this state is set forth and declared to be a spiritual resurrection to light and life. And now this death, which through the fall hath seized upon all mankind, is to be considered, 1st, as it is a state of condemnation and wrath: so it is death in a law sense; the sentence of death and damnation being passed upon all men, for that all have sinned. 2dly, This death is to be considered in a metaphorical sense. And so as death, corporal, is the privation of all life, sensation and power; so death, metaphorically and spiritually considered, is the privation of the life of God in his image, as it was once to be found in the great soul of man. As to the

1st Of these, it hath been already spoken to under the head of Conviction of Sin. In which it was declared to be one part of the Spirit's work and business, in order to conversion, to give the soul a full conviction of the misery of his present state with relation to the fall of Adam; as how by that one man's single act of disobedience in eating the forbidden fruit, sin and death entered, and seized upon him as a covenant-head, and all his offspring as then considered in him, and sinning with him: and hence judgment and condemnation passed as to the sentence upon all men; for that they were made sinners by this his single act of disobedience. Hence it is, that according to the doctrine of the holy scriptures we are declared to be the children of wrath by nature, as fallen under the righteous curse and sentence of the holy law: and so in this sense we are dead. But then this is not all; but,

2dly, There is not only the sentence of death eternal that we are fallen under, but there is a state of spiritual death, as the holy scriptures manifest; which consisteth in a privation of the image of God once in the soul of man, which consisted not of holiness and uprightness as qualities only, but as vital principles seated in the heart and will; by which man was then naturally inclined to love and serve his Maker with all his heart, soul, and strength; which principles of righteousness and obedience, as flowing from love and duty, together with their qualities of holiness and integrity, were lost in the fall; and a contrary or reverse image succeeded, consisting of evil principles and dispositions; whereby man is said to be alienated from the life of God, and estranged from the womb. Which is more than of holy to become unholy, or of an innocent to become a sinner; there being in our nature not only a privation or total absence of all good, consisting of the very principles of life, inclination and power of performance; but instead thereof there is the real presence of all the evil principles of sin, moral corruption and degeneracy, as well as pollution, guilt, and deformity. And hence, as the body upon the absence of life necessarily tendeth to corruption, even so in this kind of death, seizing the soul upon the fall, the image of God, so far as it consisted of holy pure principles and dispositions to good, is not only lost and evil, vicious principles and inclinations seated in their place, both in the affections and will; but there is from hence a further progressive decay and degeneracy both in the soul and life: so that although no one man, woman or child, is more dead than another, yet the effects of this death which has seized and dwelleth in all the powers of the intellectual soul, are more manifest and visible in some than in others; as in dead bodies some look fresh, fair, and beautiful for a while, others are immediately corrupted and nauseous both to the sight and smell, according as the principles of death and corruption work more powerfully and speedily, or slower in them. And even so it is in this spiritual or metaphorical death in the soul, this death worketh more powerfully in some than in others, and so the degeneracy and apostacy increaseth to a greater degree. And now, as in Adam, all are alike fallen, and become sinners, and alike dead in sin, so all are alike as to impotency and inability, to help themselves out of this present state. They have all power and will enough left to destroy themselves, if I might so say, over and over again by repeated acts of sin and rebellion against God; not only by breaking the holy law, but also in slighting, neglecting, yea, contemning and rejecting the gospel, as it is the only revelation of the way of life and salvation.

In a word, this death consisteth of impotency or inability, and of indisposition and contrariety in the WILL: and upon account of the first it is, that our Lord saith, "No man can come to me, except it were given him of my Father," that is, except the Father draw him," John vi. 44, 65. Here is impotency or inability: and as to the other part of this death, as it consisteth of contrary principles seated in the will, whereby it is prompted to resist and oppose, he saith, " Ye will not come to me, that ye might have life," John v. 40. Thus it appeareth that one part of this impotency is lack of will, as well as lack of ability; and both these are our fault in the eye and sentence of the holy law; and not only our moral fault, but also our punishment: even as the principles of lust brought into the world with us seminally, or which by degrees breed and put forth evil motions in our flesh and will, are our real fault, and render us sinners in the eye of God who judgeth the heart; notwithstanding they are, as to their being and first motions in our heart, quite out of our power to remove or cure.

And now this being our case and state by nature, the cure is harder than that of fetching a dead and decayed putrified body to life and perfect soundness: forasmuch as in the dead body though there are impotency and indisposition, yet there are no opposition, enmity, and rebellion to be overcome as here; so that the power of God in the exceeding greatness thereof is here absolutely necessary: for nothing but omnipotence can raise the bodies out of their grave, much less such who are dead in trespasses and sins; for much sooner might the dry bones in the prophet's vision gather together, and place and fix themselves in their proper form and order, and the body restore itself to life, and its members to their proper functions, Ezek. xxxvii. 5, 6, 7, 8, 9, 10, than those who are dead in sin, and under the dominion of this spiritual death, can come forth, into a life and state of grace, until a supernatural invincible power hath first wrought efficaciously in and upon them, so as to make them spiritually alive. And as in the prophet's vision there was an invisible omnipotency working with his prophesying or preaching, as the alone efficient cause of that resurrection, both as visionarily represented to him, and afterwards made good upon that people; so the gospel-ministry is the ministration of life and power, not only declaratively but efficiently: forasmuch as God thereby, as in the first creation, not only commandeth but worketh by a creating power; which leadeth me,

Secondly, to consider this work of a sinner's conversion, as represented in scripture by that of a new creation; in which we are said to be " his workmanship, as created anew in Christ," Ephes. ii. 10. We were, as creatures, his workmanship in the first framing our bodies out of the clay, and our spirits of that which did not before exist: and in this our formation we were created in Adam as our head and root; and agreeably and by way of analogy we are in our renovation and new birth his workmanship, he being the efficient, as potter, and we the clay: which new creature subsisteth in Christ as its influential head and root. Nor is this to be interpreted of a metaphorical creation as into an office, place, or privilege only, but it is a power working in and upon the heart, so as to give those things, as to the principles of grace and a new life, a real existence and being in the heart and soul of man, where there were none before. And hence, as the first man is said to have been created in his Maker's image and likeness, as to the moral rectitude of his soul, as well as on some other accounts; so this new man is also said to be "created in righteousness and true (or substantial) holiness, being renewed in knowledge after the image of him that created him," Eph. iv. 24, and Coloss. iii. 10: in which the new creature is the subject, and righteousness, holiness, and knowledge are the principles constitutive of his very nature and being, and not loose or adjoining accidents or qualities: and he is called the new man, for that this work is in and upon the whole soul and intellectual part of the creature, man, so that he is considered as a rational intellectual creature: and not as a creature only; for so a stone, clod, or worm, may be said to be a creature, but not a man. And let them profess what they will, and live never so morally and uprightly, according to the sect or denomination to which they relate, yet, till Christ by his image is thus by a divine efficacy in them formed, it availeth nothing as to salvation; as it is written, "For in Christ Jesus, (i. e. now under the gospel) neither circumcision availeth any thing, nor uncircumcision, but a new creature, Gal. vi. 15; which new creature being his workmanship, is formed in us by nothing less than the exceeding greatness of his Almighty power or divine omnipotence, by which he raised Christ from the dead. Again,

Thirdly, the state and condition of fallen man, as to his recovery by grace, is set forth in scripture by opening the eyes of the blind. Corporal blindness in man is of two sorts; one is what happeneth to man by some accidental secondary cause, and this admits of difference and degrees; thus some are blinder and more hard to be cured than others, and some altogether incurable by medicine; and others there are who are born blind, which is the saddest and most miserable state of all: and this admits of no degrees; for take twenty or a hundred blind or deaf men together, who were so born, and one is not more blind nor deaf than another: and it is allowed by all, I think, that this kind of blindness is not, nor can possibly be cured except by the exceeding greatness of God's mighty power; much less can this spiritual blindness, which consisteth of two parts or degrees, as first one part is brought into the world with us, we being all by nature born blind and deaf, as to spiritual things; nor is one man or woman in this respect more or less blind and deaf than another: which blindness and deafness brought into the world with us, consist in a moral incapacity or inability to see and hearken, so as to make a true judgment of, and yield a spiritual obedience to God's revealed will. Which blindness lieth chiefly in the understanding or rational part of the soul, as hath been already declared; by which means the natural man cannot see, nor rightly judge of divine and spiritual things: though none more forward and fond of meddling with, and boldly determining concerning these things than such, notwithstanding the scripture calleth them but fools for their pains. "Where is the wise? Where is the scribe? Where is the disputer of this world? Hath not God made (i. e. declared) the wisdom of this world to be foolishness?" 1 Cor. i. 20, 21. forasmuch as by this, no man did ever yet, or possibly could attain to the true knowledge of God: and yet these, both among the Jews and Gentiles were, and are the only pretended *seers* of the day in which they did, or do now live; who with scorn and indignation, like their brethren to Christ reply, "Are we blind also?" John ix. 40. And now this spiritual blindness is received from Adam the first; as a just punishment of his endeavouring to be more wise and knowing than his Maker thought fit to make him; yea, as a just judgment for his aspiring to be like his Creator; by which means, and from which time, he grew more blind, dark, and ignorant; so that all the wise men and industrious students and philosophers that ever were, have with great pains and hard labour, but been gleaning up a few ears, or small pittance of that natural knowledge which Adam lost by eating the forbidden fruit: and more than a little natural knowledge they could never by nature, art, and industry obtain: for in the wisdom of God it was resolved that the world by all their arts, parts, scholarship, and wisdom, should never know God. He having hid the knowledge of himself in a mediator from the eyes of the wise and prudent.

This then is the case as to the first part of our blindness by nature; but this is not all, there is also a further degree of blindness and darkness contracted here, both by education, custom, prejudice, and prepossession: and so some are more blind in this respect than others, and, humanly speaking, more hardly and rarely cured, though to God nothing is too hard. And now it being more or less the sad condition of all mankind to be born blind, and afterwards to contract a greater degree of blindness through error and misapprehension; as well may the men born blind pretend to judge of the variety, beauty, and excellency of colours, or the deaf of the nature and sweetness of symphony and melody of voices or musical instruments, and their difference as to sound; as the natural man pretend, though big with arts and attainments, but more swelled with pride, to see, discern, and make true judgment of the things of the Spirit of God, unless the Spirit first vouchsafe to cure his blindness, and unveil and reveal the mysteries. Hence the first work of the gospel as in the hand of the Spirit was " to open the blind eyes, so as to turn them from darkness to light," Acts xxvi. 18; and that by a commanding and creating efficacy, after the same manner as light at first was given, as the apostle declareth; "But God, who commanded light to shine out of darkness, hath shined into our hearts, to give the light of the knowledge of God in the person of Christ," 2 Cor. iv. 6; which hearts before were not only dark, being darkened through the fall, but through error, superstition, and prejudice, they had received several degrees of further additional blindness and darkness: so as that the apostle expresseth the blindness of the Gentiles state, in the abstract instead of the superlative, according to the Hebrew idiom, saying, " For ye were sometimes darkness, but now ye are light in the Lord," Eph. v. 8. This then being the real state and condition of man both by nature and contracted error, nothing but the Divine Omnipotence can create and give the seeing eye, and hearing ear. Again,

Fourthly, the state and condition of fallen man, and the manner of his recovery out of the same, are in scripture represented to be like that of a prisoner chained fast, even hand and foot, in a deep pit or prison, and kept under a watchful eye and guard, which can only be freed and delivered by a foreign power, and not by the prisoner's force or skill. Hence one part of Christ's special work and office, both in his own personal ministry and that of the gospel, as it is continued in the world, was foretold by the prophet to be, to " proclaim liberty to the prisoners, and the opening of the prison doors to them that are bound," Iai. lxi. 1 ; as it is written, " I the Lord, have called thee in righteousness, and I will hold thine hand and will keep thee, and give thee for a covenant of the people, for a light of the Gentiles ; to open the blind eyes, to bring out the prisoners from the prison, and them that sit in darkness out of the prison-house," ch. xlii. 6, 7. Now it is well known that Christ did not deliver such out of the common gaols as were by authority committed thither ; it is therefore to be interpreted in a gospel sense, of Christ's delivering souls out the horrible pit of misery and thraldom, under the power of sin and Satan, as typified out by Israel's thraldom and captivity, both in Egypt and Babylon : and so it is written, "As for thee, (O Messias,) by the blood of the covenant, (says the Father,) I have sent forth thy prisoners out of the pit wherein is is no water," Zech. ix. 11. Thus David tells us that God brought him " out of an horrible pit, out of the miry clay; and set his feet upon a rock, and established his steps," Psal. xl. 2. If any condition may be compared to being catched and shut up in a pit, be sure that of a natural state may ; only with this difference, that sin and Satan's prisoners, before conviction, are greatly delighted with their state: this prison is to them a palace ; and the cords and chains of sin and darkness by which they are held fast, and retained in the devil's hold, are to them as so many ornaments; and the love of sin, and appetite, or lust he hath after iniquity, so far prevail, as that he loveth his chains and bondage, his master and service; the devil's works he will do. This then being his present case and carriage, his sin, guilt, and condemnation, are the more increased, as our Lord declares ; "This is the condemnation, that light is come into the world, and men love darkness rather than light, because their deeds are evil. For every one that doeth evil, hateth the light, neither cometh to it, lest his deeds should be reproved," John iii. 19, 20. And thus it is, Christ, by the gospel, proclaimeth liberty to captives and prisoners, but they love their thraldom more than true gospel-liberty; they care not for it, nor will they accept it at his hands, till he hath changed their minds, and of unwilling made them a willing people in the day of power: so that besides the proclaiming liberty to them, he must exert his mighty power, both to open the prison doors, and to break their bands, and also to pluck them thence: it is with sinners, before grace has made them spiritually free and willing, as it was with Lot and his wife, Gen. xix. 16, 26, who although they were warned of the danger, and bid to get out quickly from the city, that so they might not perish in the overthrow, yet they loitered and lingered: so as that the two angels were obliged to lay hold of them, and pull them out, as partly willing and partly unwilling; and thus the Lord being merciful to them, they brought them out, and set them clear of the city: and as it fared with Lot's wife, so it happeneth to many a one that setteth out, and runneth well for a while; she left her heart and idols behind, and so looking back, no doubt with a desire to return, she died under as severe a stroke as those who staid behind: thus some miserably perish, even after they are in part delivered: forasmuch as instead of hasting to their strong-hold, and fleeing for refuge to lay hold of the hope set before them, they turn aside or return back; as it is written, "They return, but not to the most High: they are like a deceitful (i. e. a warped) bow," Hosea, vii. 16; which, though the archer levels right, always casteth the arrow wide from the mark: and now, that any are drawn out of this horrible pit, so as to be set upon the rock, Christ, and preserved thereon, this is altogether of grace: forasmuch as in all these, God worketh first the will, and then the ability to do of his own good pleasure; and that by his Almighty power. But then,

Fifthly, there are some further representations made in the holy scriptures of man's impotency, and the necessity of an Almighty power on God's part to be exerted; and this is most excellently and fully set forth by our blessed Lord, by a three-fold parable or similitude, in the 15th of Luke, i. e. the lost piece of silver, the strayed sheep found and fetched home, and the prodigal son's coming to himself, and returning to his father. Now, no one of these can set forth the thing fully, but all three of them do most completely discover what there is of God, and what there is of man, as renewed, in his return to God by conversion and true saving faith. And now, as to the first, the small piece of money being lost first, and then sought for with so much care, pains, and diligence, doth most aptly declare and represent our being lost without any act of our own in the first Adam; and also our being found by another hand, we not contributing any thing thereunto, even as the lost piece could not in the least contribute towards its being found again. The gospel-moral, or doctrine of the parable, is this; the lost piece is an elect sinner; the woman whose it is, though lost, is Wisdom, as in Proverbs, or Messias; the house is the world; the light is the gospel-part of God's written word; the broom is the ministry or use of the law upon the natural conscience; and the sweeping the house may represent, first Christ's reforming both the Jewish church-state and the Pagan world; and, secondly, it may and doth represent his sending his Holy Spirit with the ministry of the word, as a Spirit of reproof and conviction, in and upon the hearts of his own elect, at the time of effectual calling, thereby to further and secure their return; in the first part of which, as hath already been declared, they are wholly passive, even as we all were in our being lost in the first Adam: and did not God first seek so as to find us effectually by his word and Spirit, we should never seek after him, such is our impotency through the fall: but then, forasmuch as the fallen creature, man, is guilty of an actual revolt and departure, in his going further off from God by transgression and rebellion; in that the more he calleth them, the further they go off, saying, we are lords over ourselves, we will come no more at thee; therefore this their actual straying and revolt, and the methods taken to secure their return, are set forth and declared to us in the second parable, i. e. the lost sheep; which, from a straggling principle, is ever prompt to go off and stray away from its shepherd, company, fold, and pasture: and there are three or four things to be gathered from this second parable, as the moral or doctrine thereof; as

1st, That fallen man from a vicious principle or instinct, like the sheep, is subject to stray and straggle out of the enclosure, and beyond the bounds set by the great Shepherd; as it is written, " All we like sheep have gone astray, we have turned every one to our own way: and the Lord hath laid upon him the iniquity of us all," Isai. liii. 6. There being in both sorts of sheep a like propensity to go off from the Shepherd, but not to return: and did not the good Shepherd go after it, and seek it till it is found, it would be for ever lost. We are here taught, secondly, in this parable, the office and care of the Shepherd who careth for his flock; he will not lose so much as one, though the least and worst of the whole flock; "he leaveth the ninety nine, and goeth after that which is lost until he find it;" that is, he sheweth such regard unto the lost sheep, as that he will leave all other business to go after that which is gone astray, nor will he give over till it is found: and when he hath found it, he then layeth it upon his own shoulders, and bringeth it home with joy; which, in the third place, teacheth that the sheep is a self-willed obstinate creature: and as it will never return of itself, so neither will it be driven home by itself, or being weak and faint, it tireth by the way, and therefore must be carried on the shepherd's back; so here, fallen man can do nothing but go astray, he refuseth to return, as it is written, "as they (i. e. the under-shepherds) called them, so they went from them; they refused to return," Hosea xi. 2, 5: so that neither calling, commanding, nor moral suasion will suffice nor prevail; but he that seeketh up and bringeth in the outcasts of Israel, must lay them upon his shoulder and bring them home by his own mighty power in this his day of efficacious grace; as it is written, "Other sheep I have, them I must bring home," John x. 16. But then to let us know that although man is passive, and first sought after by his God, the mediator, and that by reason of his weakness and wilfulness he must be brought home by an Almighty invincible power, yet, so as that being a reasonable creature, he is made willing in the day of power by the divine energy and persuasion; as it is written, " God shall persuade Japhet, and he shall dwell in the tents of Shem," Gen. ix. 27. Therefore, I say, to illustrate this, the third parable is put forth, which represents the sinner by the aforesaid means, brought to his right mind, upon which he maketh a voluntary return, and findeth mercy and acceptance, and a reception from his Father, far beyond what he asked, or could reasonably expect: and in the whole of the third parable we may learn these three or four things; as first, that no sooner is a sinner laid under convictions, as to his lost miserable perishing state, but he turneth aside to his own inventions, by seeking relief out of God's way; as it is written, " When Ephraim saw his sickness, and Judah saw his wound, then went Ephraim to the Assyrian, and sent to King Jareb; yet could he not heal you, nor cure you of your wound," Hosea v. 13. Thus, when the prodigal son, in the parable, was laid under the pressures of penury and pinching hunger, instead of returning by respentance to his Father, he essayeth to make provision for himself, thinking to support himself by his own labour and industry; but, alas! there is nothing but husks; the creature is empty, and either cannot be come at, as in the parable, or being come at affords no relief. Empty cisterns, in which is no water to be found. Thus the convinced soul is by degrees famished out of every thing short of the bread of life, and made to hunger and thirst after the true bread which the Father giveth to his children here. Hence, in the second place, the prodigal son in the parable, is said to come to himself, i. e. to his right mind: and so he not only bethinketh himself where help is, but being changed in his mind, he resolved upon a return: and now he being come to himself, thus reasoneth and resolveth; " How many hired servants of my Father's have bread enough, and to spare, and I perish with hunger! I will arise, and go to my Father, and will say unto him, Father, I have sinned against heaven, and before thee, and am no more worthy to be called thy son : make me as one of thy hired servants," Luke xv. 17, 18, 19. Now, thus it is in the conversion of a sinner, he is brought to his right mind; before which he is considered as a lunatic, and must be dealt with accordingly by the Physician of souls in the day of power: and when his heart is renewed, and his mind is changed, then he deliberates with himself rationally, and acteth freely: yet so as that it is faith that sets reason thus at work, both to meditate, resolve, and execute this return; which hath a most agreeable success and reception with the Father. And this is manifest in his meeting him at a distance, and entertaining him so cordially, and treating him with the best, as being most welcome to him; however others might grudge it, or be aggrieved thereat. The sum of this threefold evidence is, that though the sinner's return by saving faith and conversion is a free and deliberate act; yet it is the effect of that Almighty power and invincible grace, which by the Holy Spirit, as the efficient, worketh first conviction, then gives the heart or will, and after that the power thus to do; and all of his own good pleasure. And hence it is that we read of the gospel, that it is " the power of God unto salvation to every one who believeth, whether it be Jew or Gentile," Rom. i. 16: for this word in the Spirit's hand is quick and powerful, sharper than any two-edged sword: and the truly converted are said to be pricked to the heart; and to have their hearts opened by the Lord Christ, who hath the key of the elect sinners' heart in his own hand, and will not take their trifling answers or excuses for denials, so as to let all the success be determined by their unsanctified will. No, says he, " Other sheep I have, them I must bring home," i. e. into his gospel-church and fold, John x. 16. And that this is only the effect of Almighty power, the prophet more than suggests, when he saith; " Who hath believed our report? And to whom hath the arm of the Lord been revealed?" Isai. liii. 1. For indeed the gospel-message succeeds upon the soul according to that degree of power manifested by a divine efficiency upon the heart. And,

Thus having dispatched this fifth head, as a further argument by divers evidences of the necessity of an exceeding greatness of the Divine power, to be exerted in an invincible efficacious manner upon the heart of an elect sinner in conversion, I shall now pass on to the next head proposed.

CHAP. VII.

Shewing the peculiar Work of the Spirit, and the peculiar Epithets he bears with respect to Conversion under the New Testament, with the Use and Application of the whole.

THE sixth head was to shew you out of the holy scriptures, that the Spirit of God hath a peculiar work and office under the New Testament-administration, as given of the Father, and sent forth by Christ to accompany the word of the gospel in its public ministration in the world; and also that in respect of the church of Christ and its particular members, he has diverse peculiar epithets, and much work to do upon their souls, in beginning, carrying on, and completing the whole work of faith with power; thereby bringing them into a state of grace, and then preserving and fitting them for glory. In the prosecution of which I shall shew you more generally from the testimony of scripture-evidence, that the Holy Spirit hath a special office and trust committed to him under the New Testament, both with respect to common convictions and illumination, and also as to the calling and converting the elect, and bringing them to saving faith in the Lord Jesus: and then more particularly, shall set before you the special titles and epithets given him in the scripture, as expressive of the special work he hath to do, and office he sustains; as sent by the Father and Son, as the great efficient and guide of the church, his spouse and mystical body, the fulness of him who filleth all in all, in order to the growth, comfort, and perseverance of the whole body.

First of all, you are to take notice that the gospel, for special reasons, is called the " ministration of the Spirit," 2 Cor. iii. 8; first, as he is under that dispensation, and by its ministry more plentifully bestowed and sent forth, both into the world and church; and that in his gifts and operations, both ordinary and extraordinary: which as to the manner and plenty, he was not so manifestly given under the law, either as given at Sinai, or read daily in their synagogues; hence the apostle challengeth so much as a single instance from the Galatians: "This only would I know of you, received ye the Spirit by the works of the law, or by the hearing of faith? He therefore that ministereth to you the Spirit, and worketh miracles among you, doth he it by the works of the law, or by the hearing of faith?" Gal. iii. 2, 5.

But then, secondly, the gospel-ministry and state is the Spirit's ministry, for he thereby goeth forth into the world, and worketh common convictions upon mankind in general, wherever the gospel cometh: and so throweth down every high thing that standeth in its way, so far as way is to be made for common light, conviction and reformation in the Christian world. Thus, all the progress that the gospel ever made, either among the Jews or Gentiles, as to giving them a conviction of Christ being come in the flesh; and that Jesus of Nazareth is he, was from the more general work and the office of the Holy Spirit with the word of the gospel of an incarnate, crucified, risen, and ascended Jesus, as was by him foretold, saying; "If I go not away, the Comforter will not come unto you; but if I depart, I will send him unto you, and when he is come, he will reprove or convince the world of sin, and of righteousness, and of judgment," John xvi. 7, 8. And so all the more slight or common convictions, which either go off or end in despair, and also common illuminations, tastes and gifts, in such where the heart is never savingly reached and renewed, even these are all from the Holy Spirit, and are wrought by him only, by the gospel-ministration; and are peculiarly styled the " Gifts of the Holy Spirit," Heb. vi. 4, 5, and the powers of the present new Christian world, which the Jews always styled the world to come.

But then, thirdly, the gospel is called the ministration of the Spirit, in contradistinction from the law, which is styled " a dead letter," 2 Cor. iii. 6, 7; not only for that it is the ministration of death and condemnation, but for that it is a ministry that afforded no life nor spirit, to make it a quickening ministration to the worshippers under the law; whereas life and righteousness are ministered by the Spirit in the gospel; and so the words themselves, by a figure, are said to be spirit and life, because the quickening Spirit and power of God attended the same.

And, lastly, the gospel is the ministration of the Spirit, in that, by its ministry, the Spirit worketh all saving conviction and faith in the souls of God's chosen ones; and carrieth on and finisheth the the same by his own power; and that still by the gospel as the means: for as the gospel itself worketh not, nor effecteth any thing but by the Spirit, so the Spirit worketh not but by the word, both going together, by covenant-settlement and agreement, as it is written, "As for me (saith the Father to Messias,) this is my covenant with them, saith the Lord, my Spirit that is upon thee, and my words which I have put into thy mouth, shall not depart out of thy mouth, nor out of the mouth of thy seed, nor out of the mouth of thy seed's seed, from henceforth and for ever," Isai. lix. 21. Thus, Messias stands as everlasting Father at the head of his spiritual seed and offspring, and first receiveth the Spirit and word for himself, as in their nature; and as being the true prophet sent of God into the world, having God's Spirit resting or abiding on him, and God's word in his mouth and ministry; thus it was that the words he spake as the great prophet, and the works he wrought were not his own, but his who sent him, John xiv. 10; and having the Spirit not by measure, but in his infinite and unlimited power and Godhead, as proceeding from him and the Father, he could speak as never man spake, and say more than any others dare; as it is written, "And the words that I speak, they are SPIRIT, and they are LIFE," John vi. 63. And now from out of his fulness all his receive, who are sent of him to preach the word of life to a lost world: and as he was God's mouth, so his ministers are his mouth to the people: and as his word is in their mouths, so also is his Spirit as certainly given to attend the daily and constant ministration of the same, that so it may, by the elect, be received, not as the " word of man, but, as it is in truth, the word of God," 1 Thess. ii. 13; which inwardly and effectually worketh in them that believe.

The seed of Messias are believers; he hath no fleshly carnal seed, begot by natural generation, but only a spiritual seed, begotten by the word of truth and the Spirit of regeneration. His seed are not the natural offspring, but the successive generations of believers converted by the ministry, to whom his ministers are as spiritual parents; and thus, according to the Father's covenant-promise, the word and Spirit are to be continued in the church, the latter in order to make the ministry of the word successful and efficacious to the end of the world; as it is written, " His name shall endure for ever; his name shall be continued as long as the sun, and men shall be blessed in him: all nations shall call him blessed," Psal. lxxii. 17. And hence, all true gospel-ministers of Christ's choosing, calling, gifting, and sending forth into the work of the harvest, are styled ministers of the Spirit, i. e. the gospel, as it is opposed to the dead letter and ministry of the law: and also for that under their ministry, the Spirit was at first given to others, not only in its extraordinary gifts, but also in its grace and efficacious work upon the heart in effectual calling, conversion, and perseverance. Thus, as to the Spirit's office in general, as given to Christ, and by him sent forth into the church, both to convince the world, so as to bring it universally over to Christianity in God's own time; and also to convert and save the elect, and assist and comfort the church, and guide her safe through all storms and dangers.

Thus more generally. But to be particular; the works of the Spirit of God under the ministry of the gospel, as the great efficient, who works all in us and for us, shall be considered in this order:

First, He is the Spirit of the new birth. He works the new heart; it is his own peculiar work in the soul.

Secondly, He is the Spirit of grace, to give and implant all grace in the soul. He is in a peculiar manner styled the Spirit of grace, because grace comes only by him. It is his gift and his work.

Thirdly, He is the Spirit of Holiness under the gospel. Because all evangelical holiness flows from the indwelling of the Spirit in the hearts and souls of believers. And if you talk of holiness without the Spirit, and the quickening work of the Spirit of God in your souls, you talk of nothing but the whiting of a post, or daubing over an old wall. He is the very life and Spirit of all gospel-holiness; and without him no man can see God, neither can there be any true holiness in your life and conversation.

Fourthly, He is the Spirit of all gifts that are either for the ornament, or use, or profit of the church, or for particular persons. He is the disposer of them all.

Fifthly, He it is that carries on and finishes the work of God upon the soul. And shall we lose the Spirit, or give up to a ministry without the Spirit? Shall we look upon all this as nothing? Either these things are not so, or else the work of the Spirit, the person and office of the Spirit are more to be valued than every one is aware of, and earnestly to be contended for.

Now, whether these things are so or no, I shall leave to your judgments under the word and Spirit's guidance, and under the consideration of the scriptures hereafter named.

First, as to the new birth, which is the beginning of all religion. Tell me not how long thou hast been a professor, without it be as an introduction to shew how long thou hast been born again. Tell me how the work of God hath passed upon thy own soul. Canst thou answer to thyself and agreeable to the word, that puzzling question which posed Nicodemus a teacher in Israel? and that was the doctrine of the new birth, as it is a being born from above, a being born of water and the Spirit.

You have this doctrine laid down and enlarged upon by our Lord, in his discourse with Nicodemus, who was a ruler and a teacher; " Jesus answered and said unto him, Art thou a master of Israel, and knowest not these things ?" John iii. 10. A master was a teacher, one that had disciples under him. Art thou a leading man that pretends to expound the mind of God to others, and art thou ignorant of these things ? What poor preachers are they who are ignorant of the new birth! To this man Christ lays down this doctrine with as much certainty as can by words be expressed; " Verily, verily, I say unto thee, except a man be born again, he cannot see the kingdom of God," ver. 3. This is a notable truth, very great and worthy your notice and observation: it is the very beginning of Christianity; no man is a Christian, let his name be what it will, except he be born again. A second birth he must have, that is called a being born from above: for the word will admit of both significations, *again* and *above*. Nicodemus puts forth the ignorant man's question, mistaking what Christ said; " How can a man be born when he is old? Can he enter a second time into his mother's womb, and be born ?" You find he has no other notion of this second birth but as of the first, and looks upon it as a being born a second time as he was the first. You may find all natural men make blunders in divinity. When Jesus Christ comes to the woman of Samaria, and asks water of her, she wonders at his asking water of her; he answers and saith, "If thou knewest the gift of God, and who it is that saith unto thee, Give me to drink, thou wouldst have asked of him, and he would have given thee living water. Sir, saith she, whence hast thou that living water?" John iv. 10. Here her carnality appears. Woman, saith he, The water that I give, differs from that which is here. "Whosoever drinketh of the water that I shall give him, shall never thirst: but the water that I shall give him shall be in him a well of water, springing up into everlasting life. The woman saith unto him, Sir, give me this water, that I thirst not, neither come hither to draw," ver. 14, 15. Here is her ignorance, still she understands it of nothing but material water. Thus natural persons can think of nothing but that which is like themselves, merely natural.

Jesus saith to Nicodemus, "Except a man be born of water, and of the Spirit, he cannot enter into the kingdom of God," John iii. 5. Now Jesus begins to explain something of this heavenly doctrine; he tells him a man must be born of water and of the Spirit: our natural professors being destitute of the truth, and without the Spirit, have corrupted this text; and would have you understand it thus: except a person is born of water, is, except he be baptized: hence infant-baptism arose; from this corrupt notion the parents ignorantly imagining that their children could not go to heaven except they were born again, that is baptized, they were brought to be baptized. As from another mistake of that text, " except ye eat the flesh of the Son of Man, and drink his blood, ye have no life in you," chap. vi. 53; they gave their children the Lord's Supper, taking that text to mean the Supper. Now this is not the water of baptism that is spoken of in this text; for if it were, then all that were washed in this water would be saved, would see the kingdom of God, being born again. But the Christian world is a sufficient evidence against this, that the sacraments do not confer grace, but people remain as destitute of the Spirit of truth after the receiving them as they were before. Would you read the words thus, except a child is baptized he cannot go to heaven; the consequence will be, that as this baptism is the new birth, all that are baptized shall be saved; for there is a sufficient affirmation, that he that is born again, shall see the kingdom of God.

To be born of water then doth not intend baptism, but something else to go before it and make way for it. See the water spoken of in Ezekiel and in the New Testament; "Then will I sprinkle clean water upon you, and ye shall be clean; from all your filthiness, and from all your idols will I cleanse you," Ezek. xxxvi. 25. This alludes to the old way, under the law of sprinkling the unclean. When a man was unclean and came to be cleansed, there were first a sacrifice and then a sprinkling of water: the antitype of which you have, "For if the blood of bulls and of goats, and the ashes of an heifer sprinkling the unclean, sanctifieth to the purifying of the flesh, how much more shall the blood of Christ, who, through the eternal Spirit, offered himself without spot to God, purge your conscience from dead works to serve the living God;" Heb. ix. 13, 14. So that the blood of Christ is called water, because of its cleansing virtue. Christ calls it water by a figure, and by water it was typified under the law. When the leper was to be cleansed there were two birds, a lot was cast which was to die, that which was to die was killed over running water, and then the living bird was dipped in that blood and water, and the man was sprinkled, and had application of it made to him. This was the way of cleansing David alludes to: I am a leper in a mystical sense, and I must have the mystical blood and water, and the mystical hyssop; "Purge me with hyssop and I shall be clean; wash me, and I shall be whiter than snow," Psal. li. 7. This, then, is the water the blood of Jesus Christ. The Spirit is the next thing to be considered; the Spirit must go along with it. The blood and the water have no power but as in the Spirit's hand; and you find a man is said to be born more particularly of the Spirit, because the Spirit is the great efficient in it; therefore you read, "That which is born of the flesh is flesh, and that which is born of the Spirit, is spirit," John iii. 6. That is, as the natural birth is from the flesh, and the birth is agreeable to the parent, who is flesh and blood, so the new birth is the genuine offspring of the Holy Spirit, they are born of the Spirit. Hence, you will find, the new-born are said to be born of God; and God there may be put personally for the Spirit. "Whosoever is born of God, doth not commit sin: for this seed remaineth in him, and he cannot sin, because he is born of God," ver. 9. "For whatsoever is born of God, overcometh the world, and this is the victory that overcometh the world, even our faith," 1 John v. 4; "We know that whosoever is born of God sinneth not," ver. 18. Here you find, to be born of God refers to the new birth, to be born of the Spirit. The Spirit is the parent of it: it is of a divine nature, because it is immediately from God. It is styled the divine nature, because in it we are made partakers of that divine nature that is in Christ the head.

The principles we receive of our new birth are from above, as the naturalists own those of our first birth are from below. As to the distinction between *whatever* and *whoever* is born of God, there is only this, as I take it; the *whatever*, refers to the nature, and the *whoever*, to the person thus born; the *whatever*, refers to that holy thing, that new nature; this sinneth not, but is pure and undefiled, and therefore overcometh the world; it is like the house of David, while sin, in conjunction with the flesh, is as the house of Saul; for the house of Saul grew weaker and weaker, and the house of David grew stronger and stronger. This overcomes, because the old man dies. Grace will combat with the world, Satan and sin, and will overcome them all. Whoever is born of God, doth not sin, not that he doth not sin at all; for in this respect the just man may be said to fall seven times a-day; but he doth not sin from an unregenerate principle as others do. He doth not run into sin, as that which is his element, as others do. But the meaning here, and the whole that is intended in it, is, that whoever is born anew doth not sin the unpardonable sin. Thus, as to the first thing, that the Spirit of God hath a special work under the gospel-ministry in and upon the soul, and that is in the new birth.

Secondly, we shall consider the work of the Spirit of God, in which he is called the Spirit of grace.

This is an Old Testament-expression, but well comports with the work of the Spirit of God in the heart, under the New Testament-administration. It was a special promise that God would " pour out upon the house of David, and the inhabitants of Jerusalem, the Spirit of grace and supplication," Zech. xii. 10. Israel, in the Old Testament, is God's people in the New. Do you read of Jerusalem in the Old Testament? It is the church of God in the New. The Spirit is given as the Spirit of grace, because there is no grace without him. Where the Spirit of God is not, there is no grace in the heart. Where the Spirit of grace is, there is grace. And why is he called the Spirit of grace? But because he works grace in the soul, it is his special gift and workmanship: the ancient Jews in their cabalistical divinity, in which they had some glimmerings of the Trinity, which they called three glories, tell us, the third glory, which is the Holy Spirit, is the worker of faith. He is the worker of faith in the heart, and they had in this a right notion. It is he works all our works in us. If you compare a few texts together you will receive further light in this doctrine. You have a glorious prophecy of the Messiah's anointing for this great work, in Isaiah; " There shall come forth a rod out of the stem of Jesse, and a branch shall grow out of his roots. And the Spirit of the Lord shall rest upon him," Isai. xi. 1, 2, 3. We interpret it in the New Testament, " He upon whom you shall see the Spirit of God descending and remaining on him, the same is he which baptizeth with the Holy Ghost," John i. 33; that is, he is the true Messiah. 'The Spirit of the Lord shall rest upon him, the Spirit of wisdom and understanding, the Spirit of counsel and might, the Spirit of knowledge and of the fear of the Lord.' Here you find the Holy Spirit is given to Christ in his graces. For these are expressions of the graces of the Spirit: as the Spirit of wisdom, which is saving wisdom: and of understanding, by whom the understanding is enlightened, and so of the Spirit of counsel and the Spirit of power. We are strengthened with all might by the Spirit in our inner man; and this is set forth in these expressions, " the Spirit of knowledge and of the fear of the Lord." The fear of the Lord is put for all his work of renovation. The Spirit of knowledge and of the fear of the Lord comprehends the whole work; for what was given to the Messiah was given to him to give to others: it refers to the gift of the Spirit, to go along with the gospel, and accompany the ministry thereof. In the words before my text the apostle prays that he would give them the Spirit of wisdom and revelation, in the knowledge of him, that the eyes of their understanding being enlightened they might know what is the hope of his calling, &c. Eph. i. 17. So he is called the Spirit of truth, because he is to guide you into all truth. Thus he is called the Spirit of faith, " We having the same Spirit of faith," 2 Cor. iv. 13: that is, the Spirit is the worker of faith. Faith is his workmanship. It is the gift of God, and the work of God. It is the gift of the Father, the purchase of Christ, and the work of the Spirit, for he gives all graces, and works the new heart; all graces flow from him, and he that hath not the Spirit hath none of the Spirit's graces: and he that hath the Spirit of God, hath him as the Spirit of grace.

Thirdly, the Spirit of God hath a special work under the gospel in the hearts and souls of the people of God, as the Spirit of sanctification; there is a great noise in the world about holiness, and a mighty clatter some make of it, in pretending to preach it, and yet very rarely begin at the right end of it: they tell you, without holiness none can see God, and yet tell you of no other holiness but what you may go to hell with. To talk of holiness without the Spirit, is but a mere shadow of holiness. The gospel without the Spirit is but an empty sound. If it hath not the Spirit to accompany it, it is but a dead letter. If the Spirit doth not influence in all the parts of religion, it is but a dead religion. " He is called the Spirit of holiness," Rom. i 4, and he is so called because he is the very root and spring of it. It is he that must sanctify your heart. It is to me killing to hear men talk of holiness without the new birth. It is the Spirit's work first to renew the man, to give him an holy heart, and then there will be a holy life; there must be holiness within; what signifies it, if holiness was wrote upon the bells of your horses, if your hearts are like a sepulchre full of rottenness; you may have a great deal of outward holiness, and yet go to hell. The Pharisees had as much of it as any body, and yet they are gone to hell, to their father the devil, as Christ tells them. You must first have the Spirit of holiness to make you holy within, or you never will be holy, except in outward shew. You never shall know the work of the Spirit in sanctification, while you talk of promoting sanctification without the Spirit. Sanctification is a passive work wrought upon us; it is God the Spirit sanctifies. I pray God he may sanctify you wholly, says the apostle; " I pray God your whole spirit, soul, and body be preserved blameless," 1 Thess. v. 23. He doth not say, sanctify yourselves. He doth not build holiness in the life upon any other bottom than on a new heart and spirit. First, he supposes them to be saints by renovation, and then to be holy in conversation. The Spirit of holiness whereby he raised Christ from the dead, is that Spirit whereby he quickens a dead soul. Are you the temple of God? Why, that is holy. What makes it so? Had the materials any sanctity in them? No, but God had set it apart for himself. He was pleased to dwell there; so the saint is called the house of God, because the Spirit of God dwells in him. He sanctifies the heart wherever he comes. Thus the souls of believers, where the Spirit comes to inhabit, he makes holy. And as it is begun, so remember it is maintained by the indwelling of the Spirit of God there, that holiness may run through our lives and conversations.

This is the true spring of holiness; the Spirit's possessing the soul, dwelling in the hearts of the people of God, as a Holy Spirit, to consecrate the believer for the work and service of God; to renew his mind, to cleanse him, and make him a vessel fit for his master's use, a habitation of God through the Spirit.

This work of the Spirit would require a discourse by itself; but I would contract and not be too long upon a text. I could wish you were all acquainted with that one book called The Gospel-Mystery of Sanctification; a book wrote from the experience of a minister long labouring for sanctification without the Spirit: but I pass this to a

Fourth thing, in which the Spirit of God is in a special manner concerned in the New Testament-administration, and that is in giving gifts to men. All sorts of spiritual gifts. I will only instance in that for the work of the ministry: which is as little understood as most things are. The generality of the world think there is nothing required, but that if a man hath great natural parts, learned in the tongues, and is well read, it is enough. All these are good in themselves; but first let them have spiritual gifts for the ministry, and then let these serve as handmaids; for the work of the ministry is certainly something else. Gifts for the work of the ministry are gifts of the Spirit. I suppose you do not hear much of this abroad; but, let men think what they will, if they have not the gifts of the Spirit of God for the work of the ministry, they are none of Christ's ministers. The apostle is shewing something of the mystery of it, 1 Cor. xii. 1. " Now concerning Spiritual gifts, brethren, I would not have you ignorant." Certainly, we are got into an age that is very destitute of them, and ignorant: you know, saith he, that ye were Gentiles, carried away unto dumb idols, even as ye were led. Wherefore I give you to understand, that no man speaking by the Spirit of God, calleth Jesus accursed; and that no man can say, that Jesus is the Lord, but by the Holy Ghost. No man that hath the Spirit of God, can speak lightly of Jesus Christ. If you find a generation of preachers that make light of the person, divinity, and satisfaction of Christ; of his work as a mediator, or as prophet, priest, and king in the church, they have not the Spirit of God. Now, saith he, there are diversities of gifts, but the same Spirit; and there are differences of administrations, but the same Lord. Variety of gifts were given under the Old Testament, and variety of gifts are given under the New. Some had gifts for apostles, some evangelists, some prophets, and some pastors and teachers. Now, whence came all these? Why, saith he, I would have you know it is by the same Spirit. All the members of Christ, as the members of one body, are actuated by the same Spirit: there are particular gifts for every part of the body of Christ; and this is from one Spirit; as it is the same soul in the man that actuates all the organs and members of the body, that Spirit that quickens and influences the least member, quickens and influences the greatest. Thus in the mystical body; all the members of Christ partake of the same Spirit; though they all partake not of the same gifts. But the manifestation of the Spirit is given to every man to profit withal. How is this term, every man, abused by some persons that have a notion, that every man hath the Spirit of God, which is a grand mistake: some are enemies to the Spirit; they have him not. What is it then the apostle is speaking about? It is about the church and church-officers. To some Christ hath given apostles, to some evangelists, to some pastors and teachers; to all these there is a manifestation of the Spirit, because the Spirit appears in some, one way, and in others, another way. That is thus: to one is given by the Spirit the word of wisdom, to another the word of knowledge by the same Spirit, to another faith by the same Spirit, to another the working of miracles, to another prophecy, to another discerning of Spirits, to another divers kinds of tongues, &c. There are manifestations of the Spirit discovered, which are in some believers one way, and in others another way. All this is by one and the self same Spirit, dividing to every man severally as he will. The whole work of the church, the government of the church, and the influence of the church are all under the Spirit of God. Take away the Spirit and what will be left but a carcass? A shew of religion merely. The Spirit manages the church. The gifts for management of the church do not come by chance, industry, or edueation, but are the gift of the Spirit only. He will have the honour of this work. But one thing more.

Fifthly, the Spirit of God hath a finishing stroke upon the particular persons of the elect; the perfecting work is as much the work of the Spirit of God as the beginning of faith. The fitting you for glory, is the work of the Spirit of God. The author and finisher of faith is Christ, but he doth it all by the Spirit. It is he first forms faith; he strengthens and increases faith; he ripens it, and brings it on to perform its last acts. He ripens grace in the soul; concludes that grace here, which is to be concluded, and brings to its full bloom and glory, that which will hold to all eternity, and that is the grace of love. There are three notable graces which comprehend all others. Faith, Hope, and Love. These three graces are implanted in regeneration, and more and more improved by the Spirit of grace. Two are fitted for this world, and cease when death comes. The other is to last into eternity, there it is to be in its bloom and perfection. Faith is that whereby the soul ventures on the Lord Jesus Christ; it is that by which the soul closeth with Christ. Hope is the anchor of the soul, by which the soul always lays hold of the promise under all storms, temptations, and difficulties. The grace of faith is like the great sail that carries the ship to its haven. The grace of hope is like the anchor of the ship; this is of special use in time of need, in time of distress and afflictions, and in the time of Satan's buffetting of thee. When thou canst not go with a fresh gale towards heaven by the grace of faith, then lie at anchor, then thy soul lies as safe as if it was in a full gale. But, when the Spirit ripens the soul for glory, faith carries the soul to heaven. It is the last act of the soul when it is parting from the body, and passing to glory. When he goes through the territories of the prince of darkness he fears no ill; his sail is up, and he arrives at the desired haven; and when he is got there, he wants no more his anchor. Then comes on love; love in enjoyment. Love in fruition will grow more in one view of Christ than ever it grew since you were new born. It will grow to the greatest degree that a finite creature is capable of.

Thus, I have shewn you, in the doctrinal part of the text, somewhat of the exceeding greatness of God's power, put forth upon them which believe.

The seventh and last thing proposed, is what I call use and application, and this shall be divided into several parts. First, I shall draw some inferences from what hath already been spoken. Secondly, make a use of examination. Thirdly, give you some cautions, and Fourthly, some directions, and so close the whole.

First.—*Draw some Inferences.*

First, if there be such an exceeding greatness of power put forth upon the hearts and souls of God's elect in conversion, as the scriptures do abundantly manifest, and as hath been declared; then we infer hence, very justly, that conversion is no such easy thing, nor so common as most persons count it to be. Some persons, yea, many, as I shewed under the first head, mistake conversion and faith, and look upon reformation, and external holiness to be conversion; and that faith is no more, than an assent to this or the other doctrinal truth or proposition: whereas conversion-work, is an internal change; as hath been shewn. It begins in the heart, and ends in the life. There may be a reformation when there is no true, thorough conversion. There may be morality, a just, good, moral conversation between man and man; a religious conversation, a conscience made about performance of the duties of religion; and yet the heart unchanged. Who more zealous in religion than the Pharisees? Who more strict? Yea, some were in their conversations very exact. Saul for one, while in a state of unregeneracy, yea, as touching the righteousness of the law, as in the common notion of the Pharisee, blameless. He had as much to boast of and trust in, as to attainments in religion, as most men; yea, he ventures to say, I more than they; and yet (saith he) all this was short; he was but like a painted sepulchre. Conversion-work is not so easy and common as the generality of persons imagine; who think they want only to be told of their duties, and if they will attend, they may perform all that is told them; for this corrupt notion has got footing in the hearts of men, that God will require no more than they are able to perform; but I have shewn, that the law of God requires more than the creature is able to give; for otherwise righteousness would be by the law, and Christ would have died in vain. The law calls for a clean heart; "O Jerusalem, wash thine heart from wickedness," Jer. iv. 14. And by the prophet Ezekiel, the law calls upon the sinner and saith, "turn yourselves and live ye; make you a new spirit and a new heart," Ezek. xviii. 31. These scriptures, I have shewn, are the voice of God's law, discovering that the law calls for internal purity; and that external sanctity will not satisfy its demands. Now, though these demands are made upon the creature, the creature, being fallen, is unable for the performance of them. Therefore, there is a covenant of free grace made between the

Father and the Son on the behalf of the elect; in which God hath promised, he will give a pure, new, and clean heart; he will work a special saving change upon the soul; which promises would be useless and insignificant, if the creature could give himself this new heart; whatever thoughts men may have of their own power in a state of nature, they will find other things, if the Spirit of God comes to work effectually upon them. I have often compared the state of man by nature, with respect to his notion or ability, to a person in a fever, who thinks that he is stronger than other people: he tells them that he is well, and as strong as any body, &c. But alas! they that sit by him pity him; knowing that it all proceeds from the height of the distemper. Let but that be abated, and the man begins to feel a real weakness: he that was so strong that others could hardly hold him in his bed, cannot now so much as raise himself. When the Spirit of God comes to convince a sinner, he shews the soul its own weakness, and insufficiency. Now it is to be feared, there are but few among professors that have been made, from a felt experience of their own weakness, to cry out, "Turn me, and I shall be turned;" and but few to be found who are constant supplicants at the throne of grace, as David, saying, "create in me a clean heart, O God, and renew a right Spirit within me," Psal. li. 10. Professors are many. Many have the lamp, but few the oil. How few among the heap of professors have known the effectual work of God upon their souls. Conversion is a great work; and among the many professors, it is to be feared, the sound true converts are but few.

Secondly, If there be such an exceeding greatness of power, to be put forth upon the hearts of those who shall be converted, in order to turn them effectually; we may, without breach of charity, infer, that those who oppose and deny the power of the gospel are destitute of this work. Such men set themselves against the work of the Spirit; they cast contempt and reproach upon his person and office, and on the work of the Spirit of God upon the heart; being destitute of that Spirit, they blaspheme and reproach him. They who have seen an excellency in the person of Christ, and the need of him, as their alone Saviour, cannot speak slightly of him; and they who have also seen the need of a new heart and a new spirit, and that this is a special work of the Spirit of God in and upon the soul, cannot speak slightly of the Spirit and his operations. No person that ever knew what the new birth was, can ever speak slightly or reproachfully of the Holy Spirit, either with respect to his person, office, or operations; therefore it is an inference very just to say concerning these; they have a form of Godliness, but deny the power: they are destitute of the Spirit of God; they are like those Laodiceans, who conceited they were "rich, and full, and had need of nothing," Rev. iii. ver. 17; whereas, indeed, they were "wretched, and miserable, and poor, and blind, and naked." The worst was, they knew it not, neither would they believe it.

Thirdly, if there be such an exceeding greatness of power put forth upon the hearts and souls of those who believe, then the Spirit of God, in his work and office, ought to be greatly prized and valued by those who have felt any thing of his power and operations upon their souls. They ought also to have a high esteem for that ministry, for that gospel, and for that Spirit's work and office, which others speak so slightly and reproachfully of. Those who never saw a beauty in, and need of Jesus, may speak slightly of him; but can those who have seen the need of a Saviour, and have had him discovered to them so opportunely, as one full of grace and truth; can they, I say, disesteem him? Surely no. To you who believe, he is precious, while to others he is a stone of stumbling. So those who are ignorant of the Spirit's work, may stigmatize him; but those who have felt his work upon their hearts, can they speak slightingly of the

Spirit? can they hear him reproached? No, surely. They love him, and value him above all. Those who have come under the Spirit's work, it is their duty, in point of gratitude, to love and value him; to esteem his person and office, and all his operations and undertakings. But,

Fourthly, if there is such an exceeding greatness of power put forth upon the souls of those who believe; then we may infer hence, the need of the Spirit of God, to accompany the ministry of the word. There is a generation of professors, who tell us in so many words; that God hath made known his mind so plainly and clearly in the holy scriptures, as that any man who will attend to them, may read it, and know it; there needs no more than a close application on our part; and this they do to decry the teachings of the Spirit: it is done to advance nature, and nature's abilities, and to reproach them who profess to be under the Spirit's teachings. Indeed, if there was no work of God put forth in conversion, then the word without the Spirit might do: but forasmuch as there must be a mighty power put forth upon them who believe, there must be the Holy Spirit. The Spirit and the word together make the gospel the power of God to salvation. There is a need of the Spirit, that so the Spirit and the word may go together; that wherever the gospel is received by any, it may be received not in word only; "For our gospel came not unto you in word only, but also in power, and in the Holy Ghost, and in much assurance," 1 Thess. i. 5. Assurance here I do not take to be that which is personal.; though that comes in the gospel and by the Holy Ghost: but that evidence and demonstration of the truths delivered; that they came with such power and authority, being backed by the Holy Spirit, upon the hearts of those who heard them, that they were assured these were the truths of God; that it was not enthusiasm; but that there was a reality in those truths, and they were agreeable to the mind of God. But what I would particularly take notice of is, that they received it not in word only: it is a sad thing to be left to a gospel only of words, though they are never so well put together; it will have no success; it may please the ear, but it will never reach the heart. "When ye received the word of God which ye heard of us, ye received it not as the word of man, but, as it is in truth, the word of God, which effectually worketh also in you that believe," 1 Thess. ii. ver. 13. Here is the internal power which the Spirit of God, with the word, hath upon the soul. The word of man only reaches the ear. The word of man always supposes a power in the subject to perform what is called for, but the word of God doth not. God said, "Let there be light, and it was so;" but it could not be supposed that the creature could make itself; man cannot make the new creature; man can only use words, and recommend what he hath to say with close argument; but it must drop if a power do not accompany it. But the word of God is made effectual to conversion when the Spirit of God works with it. Thus as to the first thing. I come now,

Secondly,—To a Use of Examination.

Is there an exceeding greatness of power put forth upon the hearts and souls of those that are truly converted? Then the first grand question now to be put to your souls is, What of this have you experienced? Some have been hearers a long time, others, perhaps, but lately; What of the power of God have you felt upon your souls? What change hath it wrought in you? With what efficacy hath the word of God come upon your hearts? Hath it come as the word of man only, or as the word of God? If it come as the word of man only, you are like the son in the parable, who said, "Sir, I go, but went not." It hath then been much like that message which Ezekiel delivered to his auditory, they were pleased with it. They hear the word, but they do it not. Man's ministry is ineffectual; yea, the ministry of the gospel is so, till the power of the gospel hath reached thy soul. What canst thou say to God's question? Is not my word as a hammer, saith the Lord, and as the fire? Hast thou felt the power of the word breaking thy rocky heart? Melting thy hard heart? Hast thou been truly humbled for thy sinful transgressions and disobedience? If the word of God hath come to thee with power, it hath reached thy heart, it hath pricked thee to the heart: prick thy conscience it may, it may make wounds skin deep; but if it hath reached thy heart, it hath killed thee: common convictions are but slight wounds in the flesh, they may bleed for some time, and smart for some time, but they are healed: and the person is just where he was, when they are over: how many persons have come under mighty anguish of conscience? Conscience hath smote them, they have received deep wounds there, that some that have conversed with them have thought them to have been effectual; and yet they have all gone off again, and the person hath returned to his old ways; this discovers the work of God is not wrought upon the soul; but when it reaches the heart effectually, it is a work of exceeding great power. You have it most excellently set forth in the Hebrews; "For the word of God is quick and powerful, and sharper than any two-edged sword; piercing even to the dividing asunder of the soul and spirit, and of the joints and marrow: and is a discerner of the thoughts and intents of the heart," Heb. iv. ver. 12. Here is the great word, the eternal word, couched under these expressions; but it is the word of the gospel of salvation, the ministerial word, that the apostle hath in his eye. The word preached when the Spirit sets it home upon the heart, is " quick and powerful, sharper than any two-edged sword," &c. As a sharp two-edged sword, thrust by an able hand into the naked breast, will let out the heart's blood, and kill the man; as a sharp two-edged sword will rip up and discover the inside of the man; so the word of the gospel of salvation rips up the heart of the sinner; stabs him to the heart; lets him see the plague of his own heart, the pollution of his own nature, and kills him downright; slays him in his own apprehensions, as to any ability of himself to perform any thing, but must now be saved only by grace; now he is really lost and undone; now for a Saviour; now is a Jesus precious to such a soul. All the while the wound was skin deep he could be his own surgeon; but now he is mortally wounded, when he is led to see his nature, how he was conceived in sin, and shapen in iniquity: he is now humbled; he is slain as to any merit, power, or ability he hath in himself; he must be saved alone by grace, or he sees he is eternally lost and undone. This I take to be one thing the apostle had in his eye, where he saith, "I was alive without the law once, but when the commandment came, sin revived, and I died." Here is the straight rule of the law laid to our crooked nature. When the soul sees the law calls for internal purity, then it is he finds the word of the Lord is as a hammer to break the rock, and as fire to melt and dissolve him, and brings him to be saved as a poor lost perishing sinner in himself. Peter did not cry out more earnestly, " Save, Lord, or I perish," than the poor sinner cries out in his heart, as well as with his tongue, " Turn me and I shall be turned; create in me a clean heart, O Lord, and renew a right spirit within me." This is the first question, What of this exceeding greatness of power hast thou felt upon thy soul? Hast thou received the word only as the word of man; or as it is, indeed, the word of God?

Secondly, What fruits, what effects hath this word had upon thy soul? Doth not my word do good, saith God, to them that walk uprightly? What are the fruits of it? Are the fruits manifested in thy life and conversation? Doth it bring forth fruit Godward? May it be said of thee since thou camest under this power, as it was of Saul? " Behold he prays." Hath it brought thee to be a daily and constant supplicant at the throne of grace? Not out of compliment, form, custom, or education, to quiet conscience, to make all easy within, but as one that depends upon God for all grace and all good; and can no more live without going to his throne of grace, than a poor creature can live wholly upon charity, without going to such as are the donors thereof. Saul had said his prayers before, but there was no notice taken of that; but now he breathed out his soul in prayer before God; and therefore now it is said, "Behold he prays." If thou art a converted person, then certainly thou art a praying person; not in form or custom, but from the very heart, under the sense of soul-want and a daily need. Yea,

Thirdly, What effect hath it had upon thee in thy life? Art thou brought to a loathing of thyself in all thy false ways? Hath it brought thee to set a watch upon thy tongue? Hath it brought thee to leave thy evil company, and thy vain ways? Hath it brought thee to turn thy back upon these, and say, as Ephraim of his idols, Get ye hence; I have seen him, I have heard and learned of him? The true work of God brings the soul to a hating of that which before was its love and delight, and to love that which before it had an aversion to. The Grace of God where it reaches the soul in power, teaches the denying ungodliness and worldly lusts, and that we should have our conversation soberly and righteously in this world. But I shall now proceed,

Thirdly, to give you some cautions.

First, to such souls who have in some measure

found and experienced a power attending the ministry of the gospel, reaching their hearts. Have a care of those ways, those practices, those customs and companions, that may have a tendency to harden thee again. Avoid the ways of sin and vice. Take care not to grieve that Spirit which hath begun thus to work; quench it not, grieve it not, and resist it not; these are cautions given by the Holy Ghost, and they are not needless. They are suited to such as are under the begun work of the Spirit; that they do not turn their backs upon him that speaketh thus in a peculiar manner to your soul; and saith to you in particular, To you is this gospel sent: let the language of your soul be, "I will hear what God the Lord will say unto me. He will speak peace to his people, but let them not turn again unto folly. Sin is of a hardening nature; and one sinner hath destroyed much good. Though many have begun well, and have given some good hopes to others, that the work of God was begun in their souls; yet in a little time, by giving way to vicious company, they have been swallowed up in sin; they have quite lost their profession; I still believe " the foundation of the Lord stands sure," he will bring them back again; but it will be with broken bones. I speak this, with concern, to young ones. Since I have been here, I have seen some begin well, who have had sad ends. Therefore have a care of bad companions. Be not as " the horse that hath no understanding, whose mouth must be held in with bit and bridle." Turn not again unto folly; have a care of that

Secondly, more generally to all professors; take care who and what you hear; corrupt doctrine is like leaven, it will sour the man. You have a generation of men that will tell you, it is no matter what you believe; so you walk morally, all is well enough; therefore you ought to take heed what you hear. There are some whose words will eat, as doth a gangrene: when a gangrene is in the flesh, what work doth it make wherever it goes? And are there not such doctrines that eat as a gangrene? They are as destructive to the soul as a gangrene is to the body. And must not persons then take care what they hear? Certainly they ought to be more cautious. Let me give you what I have farther to say only in scripture-language. Take that as a caution worthy your reception, which you have, 2 Tim. iii. 5, "Having the form of godliness, but denying the power thereof; from such turn away." Those that have got the form, and deny the power, may please thy ear; but their words will eat as a canker; and thou dost not know but they may catch thee. They deny the power: experimental religion they laugh at, and deny; therefore saith the Holy Spirit, "From such turn away. My Son, consent thou not." Let me give you one word more, which you will find in the second Epistle of St. John: I will read several verses of that little epistle: "For many deceivers are entered into the world, who confess not that Jesus Christ is come in the flesh. This is a deceiver and an antichrist," 2 Ep. St. John, ver. 7. The deceivers that then pestered the church were such, as would not own that Jesus Christ was come in the flesh. Now what was said to them is applicable to all deceivers, they are all antichrists; "Look to yourselves, that we lose not these things which we have wrought," ver. 8. Have a care ye be not corrupted: What! in your morals? No, but in your judgments; in your notions about the doctrine of Christ, and of the Spirit! Have a care you do not lose those truths you have received, that somebody doth not give you falsehood for truth. "Whoever transgresseth and abideth not in the doctrine of Christ hath not God: he that abideth in the doctrine of Christ, he hath both the Father and the Son," ver. 9. "If there come any unto you and bring not this doctrine, receive him not into your house, neither bid him God speed," ver. 10. The meaning of which, is, give him no countenance, either by making him your companion, or by hearing him; "For he that biddeth him God speed, is partaker of his evil deeds," 2 Ep. St. John, 11. They are sharers with him in his sins, and must expect to share with him in his punishment. I come now,

Fourthly, to give you some direction and exhortation:

First, beg for much of the Spirit of God upon your own souls; much of the Spirit's teaching in your own hearts; let others say what they will of it. Lie as a constant supplicant at the throne of grace abasing your own wisdom, and crying out, 'That which I know not, teach thou me.'

Beg the Spirit of Revelation in the knowledge of Christ, that "the eyes of your understanding may be enlightened, and that you may know what is the hope of his calling, and what the riches of the glory of his inheritance in the saints: and what is the exceeding greatness of his power to us-ward who believe," Ephes. i. 18.

Secondly, beg a gospel-ministry; that God would maintain a gospel-ministry, and his presence with us. It is only a gospel-ministry that is effectual for the conversion of poor sinners. It is not enough that you have a ministry, but you must have a gospel-ministry; if ever you expect profit to yourselves, or conversion for others, know, it must be by a gospel-ministry, attended by the Holy Spirit. Therefore, beg your ministers may come full of the Holy Spirit.

Thirdly, have you good hope, you have received this word of faith in your souls? Lie low in your own minds; give God the thanks; have a care of pride. "What hast thou, O man, that thou hast not received?" Take a daily view of thine own ignorance and short-comings: there is enough to keep thee humble with God; as one that depends upon him; as one that receives much, yet comest short in thy duties. Have a care of being proud, because thou knowest much, lest from thence thou art brought to despise and contemn the Holy Spirit.

FINIS.

Printed by T. Bensley,
Bolt Court, Fleet Street, London.

THE BAPTIST STANDARD BEARER, INC.
A non-profit, tax-exempt corporation
committed to the Publication & Preservation
of The Baptist Heritage.

SAMPLE TITLES FOR PUBLICATIONS AVAILABLE IN OUR VARIOUS SERIES:

THE BAPTIST *COMMENTARY* SERIES
Sample of authors/works in stock or in production:
 John Gill - *Exposition of the Old & New Testaments (9 Vol. Set)*
 John Gill - *Exposition of Solomon's Song*

THE BAPTIST *FAITH* SERIES:
Sample of authors/works in stock or in production:
 Abraham Booth - *The Reign of Grace*
 John Fawcett - *Christ Precious to Those That Believe*
 John Gill - *A Complete Body of Doctrinal & Practical Divinity (2 Vols.)*

THE BAPTIST *HISTORY* SERIES:
Sample of authors/works in stock or in production:
 Thomas Armitage - *A History of the Baptists (2 Vols.)*
 Isaac Backus - *History of the New England Baptists (2 Vols.)*
 William Cathcart - *The Baptist Encyclopaedia (3 Vols.)*
 J. M. Cramp - *Baptist History*

THE BAPTIST *DISTINCTIVES* SERIES:
Sample of authors/works in stock or in production:
 Abraham Booth - *Paedobaptism Examined (3 Vols.)*
 Alexander Carson - *Ecclesiastical Polity of the New Testament Churches*
 E. C. Dargan - *Ecclesiology: A Study of the Churches*
 J. M. Frost - *Pedobaptism: Is It From Heaven?*
 R. B. C. Howell - *The Evils of Infant Baptism*

THE *DISSENT & NONCONFORMITY* SERIES:
Sample of authors/works in stock or in production:
 Champlin Burrage - *The Early English Dissenters (2 Vols.)*
 Albert H. Newman - *History of Anti-Pedobaptism*
 Walter Wilson - *The History & Antiquities of the Dissenting Churches (4 Vols.)*

For a complete list of current authors/titles, visit our internet site at
www.standardbearer.org or write us at:

The Baptist Standard Bearer, Inc.
No. 1 Iron Oaks Drive • Paris, Arkansas 72855

Telephone: (479) 963-3831   Fax: (479) 963-8083
E-mail: baptist@arkansas.net
Internet: http://www.standardbearer.org

www.ingramcontent.com/pod-product-compliance
Lightning Source LLC
Chambersburg PA
CBHW021135230426
43667CB00005B/122